Anyone who sees – however dimly – that social media could help market their business will benefit from this hands-on workbook.

How Does This Workbook Work?

This workbook starts first with an overview to **social media *marketing***. Beyond the positive "can do" attitude that you already have (if you've read this far, or purchased this book), the next most important asset is a "mental model" of what social media is, and how it can be used to market to your customers. It's simple. If social media is a **party**, then **using social media** is akin to just *showing up*. **Marketing** on social media, in contrast, isn't about showing up. It's about ***throwing*** the party!

Understanding that distinction between "attending" the social media party and "throwing" the social media party is the subject of **Chapter One.**

Chapters Two through **Eight** are deep dives into social media marketing, one medium at a time. We'll start, for example, with **Facebook**. First, we'll provide an overview to how Facebook works, explain everything from profiles to pages, likes to comments to shares, Edgerank to posting rhythm. It will all become much clearer, as we work through Facebook in plain English, written for "mere mortals." Along the way, I'll provide **worksheets** that will act as "Jason as therapist," so you can fill them out and begin to outline your own unique Facebook marketing plan. My goal is for you to not only *understand* Facebook marketing but actually to begin to *do* marketing on Facebook. Ditto for LinkedIn, Twitter, and the rest of the gang.

Table of Contents

6. **Pinterest** – the most effective social media for eCommerce stores and retailers, do-it-yourselfers, and those serving the female shopping demographic such as wedding photographers. Pg. 196
7. **Yelp & Google Local** – how the "Review Revolution" is impacting local businesses, and how to use Yelp, Google local (formerly Google+), and other local review sites to promote your business via reviews. Pg. 222
8. **Epilogue** – the "new" new kids on the block: Snapchat, Tumblr, Periscope, Amazon, and new ways to go social and go marketing. Pg. 268

Use the Internet to Master the Internet

Finally, this workbook is meant to leverage the power of the Internet. Register your copy online to get a PDF copy of this book (with clickable links to make it easy to access online resources), and a complimentary copy of my *Social Media Toolbook*, a compilation of hundreds of social media tools not just for Facebook, LinkedIn, Twitter, etc., but for all the major platforms as well as pointers to learning resources for even more fun in the world of social media. You'll also get free access to my *Social Media Dashboard*, my absolute favorite free tools all set out for you to use in easy click-to-go format.

Here's how to **register** your copy of this workbook:

1. Go to https://jm-seo.org/workbooks
2. Click on *Social Media Workbook 2016*.
3. Use this password: **smm2016**
4. You're in. Simply click on the link for a PDF copy of the *Social Media Toolbook* as well as access to the worksheets referenced herein.

OK, now that we know what this workbook is about, who it is for, and our plan of action...

Let's get started!

▶ MEET THE AUTHOR

My name is Jason McDonald, and I have been active on the Internet since 1994 (*having invented the Internet along with Al Gore*) and taught SEO, AdWords, and Social Media

SOCIAL MEDIA MARKETING WORKBOOK:

HOW TO USE SOCIAL MEDIA FOR BUSINESS

2016 EDITION – JULY, UPDATE

BY JASON MCDONALD, PH.D.

© 2016, JM INTERNET GROUP

https://www.jm-seo.org/

Tel. 800-298-4065

0

INTRODUCTION

Welcome to the *Social Media Marketing Workbook, 2016 edition!* With a new update as of July, 2016, get ready to:

- Have some **fun**.
- **Learn how Social Media works.**
- Understand how to use **Social Media** to **market your business**.
- Create a step-by-step **Social Media Marketing plan**.

Fully revised and updated as of July, 2016, this workbook not only explains how to market on social media (from Facebook to LinkedIn, YouTube to Pinterest, Twitter to Yelp and back again) but also provides access to **free social media marketing tools**. It provides overviews, step-by-step instructions, tips and secrets, resource tips and free tools for social media marketing, and access to step-by-step **worksheets** that will help you market your product, service, or business on social media.

Free Tools

Even better, if you register your copy, you also get access to my complete *Social Media Toolbook* and *Dashboard*, with literally hundreds of **free social media marketing tools** to turbocharge your social media marketing not just on Facebook but also on LinkedIn, Twitter, YouTube, Google+, Instagram and other major social media platforms.

> *It slices, it dices. It explains how social media works. It gives you free tools. And it helps you make a social media marketing plan.*

Why Market via Social Media?

If you own a business or work as a marketing manager at a business, you're probably intrigued by **social media** as a **marketing platform**. Hardly a day goes by that the "traditional" news media doesn't talk about Twitter, Facebook, or YouTube, often in the context of some new way to reach customers and build buzz. Between TV shows like *Ellen* or radio shows like *Marketplace* encouraging you to "like" them on Facebook, or your next door neighbor or perhaps a business competitor bragging about their latest tweet, it seems like everyone is promoting their Facebook Page, their YouTube channel, their reviews on Yelp, or encouraging you to check them out on Snapchat. What do they understand that you don't get? Or, even if you get a lot, what are secret tips and tricks that can improve your marketing even further? Social media is everywhere, and yet it can seem very confusing to the uninitiated. What is this *magical marketing* being conducted on *social media*, and how does it work?

Let's Talk about You

Let's talk about you for a moment. Perhaps you own a small business, perhaps you're the marketing manager at a mid-size company producing ball bearings, or perhaps you are an ad agency guru charged with setting up a Facebook plan for a local non-profit. It's easy to be overwhelmed, and natural to feel like you're not sure how to market on social media. Perhaps you're just starting out with a **Facebook Page** for your **business**, or perhaps you've seen your teenager spend hours on **Instagram** or **YouTube**, or you realize that the female, shopping demographic is "on" **Pinterest**. Perhaps the hip coworker dressed in black or one of his friends has looked down on you, condescendingly, when you don't understand the difference between a *hashtag* or a *retweet*. Or you've painfully learned that **Yelp** or **Google** reviews can make (or break) your business, only after an unhappy customer has trashed you online. Social media, after all, is all around us in today's 24/7 desktop, tablet, and mobile phone environment, and it does not seem to be simple!

Maybe you have already attempted a Facebook Page, a YouTube Channel, or a Pinterest board, but it hasn't really worked out. "How does social media really work?," you wonder. "What's all the fuss about, and can it really bring in customers and make sales?"

Don't worry. Enter the Social Media Marketing Workbook to the rescue, with step-by-step instructions on how to market on each social media network plus a conceptual framework so you actually understand the nature of marketing itself.

This book will explain the "how" – a step by step, systematic method to effective social media marketing. But before we dive in to the "how," let's step back for a minute and ask the "why":

Why market on social media?

Here are some reasons why **social media marketing** is valuable:

- **Social media is big.** Facebook, the largest social media platform, has over one billion users worldwide and climbing; LinkedIn with over 350 million members is "the" network for B2B marketers. Every minute 300 hours of video are uploaded to YouTube, and nearly everyone goes to Yelp or Google+ to check out reviews on local businesses.
- **Your customers are on social media.** Nearly everyone uses Facebook – from teenagers to grandmas, business executives to flight attendants. Most professionals have at least a LinkedIn profile. Everyone reads reviews online, many post pictures to Instagram, etc. *Fish where the fish are.* By participating in social media, you can reach your customers where they "hang out."
- **Social media is free**. Facebook, Yelp, Google+, YouTube, Instagram, Pinterest... are, of course, free to use. Users love them because "for free" they get access to their friends and family, plus information on brands that they love. And in terms of marketing there is a lot you can do, for free, to build your brand, spread eWOM (electronic word of mouth), help you stay top-of-mind with your customers, and even "get shares" or "go viral." (*Free, as we will learn, does not mean easy or no hard work involved – more on that later!*)
- **Social Media can reach not only existing but also new customers.** Between organic ("free") and paid reach on sites like Facebook or Twitter, you can not only stay in touch with your existing customers, you can also be discovered by new customers. Unlike on search engines like Google (where customers must pro-actively look for you), on social media you can be discovered as customer No. 1 shares information with customer No 2. You can also be discovered not when a customer is pro-actively searching for you but when he

just happens to be checking his Facebook news feed, or browsing photos on Instagram.

Social Media (Seems) Complicated

Social media, however, is also **complicated**. First of all, *using* social media is one thing, and *marketing* on social media is another. That snappy teenager might understand how to *use* Snapchat, but this doesn't mean she knows how to *market* on it. Even many experienced marketers are befuddled, as their knowledge of traditional marketing channels does not translate easily to social media networks like Instagram or Twitter. Indeed, many businesses simply fail at social media marketing, either doing nothing or spinning their wheels with endless busy work. They don't understand how social media works, and they fail to see the incredible marketing opportunities beneath the surface of this huge but messy brave new world of marketing. Quite simply, you have to invest some time to learn "how" to market on social media

Fortunately, you hold in your hand (or at least hold it virtually in your Kindle or PC), the *Social Media Marketing Workbook*, a workbook that helps you understand the "how" of marketing your business on social media. You've joined that elite group of people who have taken the most important step: proactively seeking to educate themselves on how to market via this new world order.

Who is This Workbook For?

This workbook is aimed primarily at **small business owners** and **marketing managers**. **Non-profits** will also find it useful. If you want to build buzz around your company or brand, increase your sales or sales leads, or expand your reach from your most loyal customers to their friends and family, and to the friends and family of those friends and family, this workbook is for you.

If you are a person whose job involves advertising, marketing, and/or branding, this workbook is for you. If you are a small business that sees a marketing opportunity in social media of any type, this workbook is for you. And if your job is to market a business or organization online in today's Internet economy, this book is for you. Anyone who wants to look behind the curtain and understand the mechanics of how to market on social media (from Facebook to LinkedIn, Twitter to Yelp, Pinterest to YouTube and beyond) will benefit from this book.

since 2009 – online, at Stanford University Continuing Studies, at both AcademyX and the Bay Area Video Coalition in San Francisco, at workshops, and in corporate trainings across these United States. I love figuring out how things work, and I love teaching others! Social media marketing is an endeavor that I understand, and I want to empower you to understand it as well.

Learn more about me at https://www.jasonmcdonald.org/ or at my corporate website https://www.jm-seo.org/. Or just call 800-298-4065, say something flattering, and I my secretary will put you through. *(Like I have a secretary! Just call if you have something to ask or say)*. Visit the websites above to follow me on Twitter, connect with me on LinkedIn, or like me on Facebook. *Sorry my Snapchat feed is so crazy it's for friends and family, only.*

⏩ SPREAD THE WORD: WRITE A REVIEW & GET A FREE eBOOK!

If you like this workbook, please take a moment to write an **honest review** on Amazon.com. Here are three reasons why you should write a review. First, the more reviews I get on Amazon, the better the book ranks, and the more people will learn how to market effectively on social media marketing. I will also earn enough money to stop having to eat Mac N Cheese as I send my older daughter to college, and prepare to send my younger daughter to the college of her own choice. *You'll be literally helping to send kids to college*, ha ha. Second, I actually read the reviews, and gain insights into how my books are working (or not). I relish your feedback – good, bad, ugly, as long as its honest – and feel free to email me, or even call. And third, if you write a review, I'll be happy to send you a free copy of one of my other books, the *SEO Fitness Workbook*, the *Job Search & Career-building Workbook*, or *AdWords Gotchas*.

Here's how –

1. Write your **honest review** on Amazon.com.
2. **Contact** me via https://www.jm-seo.org/contact, email me at j.mcdonald@jm-seo.net, or call 800-298-4065, and let me know your review is up.
3. I will send you a **free** copy of one of my other eBooks which cover AdWords, SEO, and Internet job search / personal branding – just indicate which one.

This offer is limited to the first 100 reviewers, and only for reviewers who have purchased a paid copy of the book. You may be required to show proof of purchase and the birth certificate of your first born child, cat, or goldfish. If you don't have a child, cat, or goldfish, you may be required to prove telepathically that you bought the book.

» QUESTIONS AND MORE INFORMATION

I **encourage** my students to ask questions! If you have questions, submit them via https://www.jm-seo.org/contact/. There are two sorts of questions: ones that I know instantly, for which I'll zip you an email answer right away, and ones I do not know instantly, in which case I will investigate and we'll figure out the answer together.

As a teacher, I learn most from my students. So please don't be shy!

» COPYRIGHT AND DISCLAIMER

I knew you just couldn't wait for the legal stuff. Calm yourself down, and get ready for some truly fun reading.

This is a completely **unofficial** workbook to social media marketing. No one at Facebook, LinkedIn, Twitter, YouTube, Instagram, Pinterest, Yelp, Google, Instagram, Snapchat or any other social media company has <u>endorsed this workbook</u>, nor has anyone affiliated with any of those companies been involved in the production of this workbook.

That's a *good thing*. This workbook is **independent**. My aim is to "tell it as I see it," giving you no-nonsense information on how to succeed at social media marketing.

In addition, please note the following:

- All trademarks are the property of their respective owners. I have no relationship with nor endorsement from the mark holders. Any use of their marks is so I can provide information to you. Don't confuse them for me, or me for them. I'm just a poor intellectual living in California, and they are big, rich powerful corporations with teams of money-grubbing lawyers.

- Any reference to or citation of third party products or services whether for Facebook, LinkedIn, Twitter, Yelp, Google / Google+, Yahoo, Bing, Pinterest,

YouTube, or other businesses, search engines, or social media platforms, should not be construed as an endorsement of those products or services tools, nor as a warranty as to their effectiveness or compliance with the terms of service with any search engine or social media platform.

The information used in this workbook was derived in June, 2016. However, social media marketing changes rapidly, so please be aware that scenarios, facts, and conclusions are subject to change without notice.

Additional Disclaimer. Internet marketing is an art, and not a science. Any changes to your Internet marketing strategy, including SEO, Social Media Marketing, and AdWords, is at your own risk. Neither Jason McDonald, Excerpti Communications, Inc., nor the JM Internet Group assumes any responsibility for the effect of any changes you may, or may not, make to your website or AdWords advertising based on the information in this workbook.

Additional Additional Disclaimer. Please keep your arms and legs in the vehicle at all times, be kind to one another, and do not cut other people off while driving.

▶▶ ACKNOWLEDGEMENTS

No man is an island. I would like to thank my beloved wife, Noelle Decambra, for helping me hand-in-hand as the world's best moderator for our online classes, and as my personal cheerleader in the book industry. Gloria McNabb has done her usual tireless job as first assistant, including updating this edition as well the *Social Media Marketing* toolbook. I would also like to thank my black Labrador retriever, Buddy, for countless walks and games of fetch, during which I refined my ideas about marketing and about life.

And, again, a huge thank you to my students – online, in San Francisco, and at Stanford Continuing Studies. You challenge me, you inspire me, and you motivate me!

1
PARTY ON

Most books on **social media marketing** (or **SMM** for short) either focus on the high, high level of over-the-top hype or focus on the in-the-weeds level of micro technical details. It's either Malcolm Gladwell's *Blink*, Seth Godin's *Purple Cow*, David Meerman Scott's *The New Rules of Marketing and PR* – or it's *Social Media for Dummies*, *LinkedIn for Dummies*, or *Teach Yourself Facebook in Ten Minutes*.

You're either up in the sky, or lost in the weeds.

This book is different: it focuses on the middle, productive ground – part **theory**, and part **practice**. It gives you a framework for how to "think" about social media marketing as well as concrete advice on how to "do" social media marketing on each particular network.

Throughout, it provides worksheets, videos, **TODOS** and deliverables, to help you create a step-by-step **social media marketing plan** as well as a step-by-step LinkedIn marketing plan, Twitter marketing plan, etc. Used in combination with the *Social Media Toolbook* and *dashboard*, which identify hundreds of **free** tools for social media marketing all in one convenient place, small business owners and marketers finally have a practical, hands-on method for social media marketing.

This first chapter is about *how to think about social media marketing*. What is social media marketing? Why are you doing it? What should you do, step-by-step, to succeed?

Let's get started!

TODO LIST:

>> Understand that Social Media Marketing is Like Throwing a Party

>> Recognize the Social Media Marketing Illusion

>> Identify Relevant Discovery Paths

>> Establish Goals and KPIs

>> Create a Content Marketing System

>> Sharing is Caring: Blogging for Social Media Marketing

>> Remember the Big Picture

>> >> Deliverable: a "Big Picture" Social Media Marketing Plan

>> Appendix: Top Content Marketing Tools and Resources

>> UNDERSTAND THAT SOCIAL MEDIA MARKETING IS LIKE THROWING A PARTY

Have you ever **attended** a party? You know, received an invitation, showed up, said hello and various meets and greets to other guests, ate the *yummy yummy* food, drank the liquor (or the diet soda), hobnobbed with other guests, ate some more food, danced the night away, thanked the hosts, and left?

> *Attending* a party is all about *showing up, enjoying* the entertainment and food, and *leaving*.

Have you ever **used** Twitter? Facebook? Instagram? You know, logged in, checked out some funny accounts, read some posts, posted back and forth with friends and family, checked your updates, and then logged out?

That's *attending* a party. That's *using* social media.

> *Using* social media is all about *logging in, enjoying* what's new and exciting, and *logging out*.

Throwing a party, however, is something entirely different from **attending** a party. Similarly, **marketing** via social media is something entirely different from **using** social media.

This chapter explores the basics of social media *marketing*: of **throwing** the "social media party" vs. just **showing up**. That word *marketing* is very important: we're exploring how to use social media to enhance our brand, grow the visibility of our company, product or service, or even (gasp!) use social media to sell more stuff.

PARTY ON: BECOME A
GREAT PARTY-THROWER

Social media marketing is the art and science of throwing "great parties" on Twitter, Facebook, LinkedIn, Pinterest and the like in such a way that people not only show up to enjoy the party but also are primed to buy your product or service.

Let's explore this analogy further: how is social media *marketing* like *throwing a party*?

Here are three ways:

Invitations = Promotion. A great party needs great guests, and the first step to getting guests is to identify an attendee list, and send out invitations. Who will be invited? How will we invite them – will it be by phone call, email, postal mail, etc.? For your social media marketing, you'll need to identify your target audience(s) and brainstorm how to get them to "show up" on your social media page via tactics like sending out emails, cross-posting your Facebook to your Twitter, or your LinkedIn to your blog, advertising, or even using "real world" face-to-face invitations like "Hey, follow us on Twitter to get coupons and insider deals."

Social media marketing requires having a promotion strategy.

Entertainment = Content. Will your party have a band, a magician, a comedian, or just music? What is your entertainment strategy? What kind of food will you serve: Mexican, Chinese, Tapas, or something else? Similarly for your social media marketing: why will people "hang out" on your Facebook page or YouTube channel? Will it be to learn something? Will it be because it's fun or funny?

Social media marketing requires having a content marketing strategy, a way to systematically produce yummy yummy content (blog posts, infographics, images, videos) that people will enjoy enough to "hang out" on your social media page or channel.

Hosting =- On-going Management. As the host of your party, you'll "hang out" at the party, but while the guests are busy enjoying themselves, you'll be busy, meeting and greeting, making sure everything is running smoothly, and doing other behind-the-scenes tasks. Similarly, in your social media marketing, you'll be busy coordinating content, interacting with guests and even policing the party to "kick out" rude or obnoxious guests.

Social media marketing requires behind-the-scenes on-going management, often on a day-to-day basis, to ensure that everything is running smoothly up to and including dealing with "rude" guests.

SOCIAL MEDIA MARKETING IS THROWING A PARTY

In addition, you want to think like a "party detective." Let's assume, for example, you're going to throw your spouse an amazing 40th birthday party. Before that party, you'll probably start attending other parties with a critical eye – noting what you like, and what you don't like, what you want to imitate, and even reaching out to the magicians, bands, and bartenders to find out what they cost and possibly hire them for your own party.

Inventory Other Parties

You'll "inventory" other parties and make a list of likes and dislikes, ideas and do-not-dos, and use that information to systematically plan your own party.

As a social media marketer, therefore, you should "attend" the parties of other brands online. Identify brands you like (REI, Whole Foods, Bishop Robert Barron), "follow" or "like" them, and keep a critical eye on what they're doing. **Inventory** your likes and dislikes, and **reverse engineer** what other marketers are up to. And in your industry, do the same: follow companies in your own industry, again with the goal of "reverse engineering" their social media marketing strategy, successes, and failures.

For your first **TODO**, identify some brands you admire and "follow" them on Twitter, LinkedIn, Facebook, Pinterest etc. Start making a list of what you like, or dislike, based on reverse engineering their online marketing strategy. Become a good user of social media, but with an eye to the marketing strategy "behind the scenes." Here are the steps:

1. **Log in** to your **social media account** (e.g., Twitter or Facebook).
2. Using the search function, **search for keywords** that are relevant to your business. If you are a wedding planner, for example, search for keywords such as 'wedding planning' or 'weddings' or 'party planners.'
   a. You can use a special Google search of site:network as in *site:facebook.com* "accounting firms" to use Google to rapidly find interesting items on any social media site. Note: there is NO SPACE between the : and the network. Visit http://jmlinks.com/12v to see this in action.
3. Write down or **bookmark accounts that you find**. If you search for "hamburgers," and you find the Facebook page of the Palo Alto restaurant, "The Counter," then "like" that Page on Facebook and/or bookmark it. You'll need a list of five to ten companies that are like yours and/or that you can see are doing a good job on the platform.
4. Begin to **inventory** what you **like** and **dislike** about how they are running their social media effort. For Facebook, do you like their cover photo? Why or why not? Do you like their profile pictures? What about what they post, and how frequently? Imagine you are attending their party not "to have fun," but to "reverse engineer" how they are putting it on. Write this down on a spreadsheet or document.

For example, I love the brand REI, which is a sporting goods company. I love it not so much because I am a big outdoors person (I'm not), but because they do an awesome job on social media. Here's a screenshot of their Facebook page, with the arrow indicating where you click to "like" their Page:

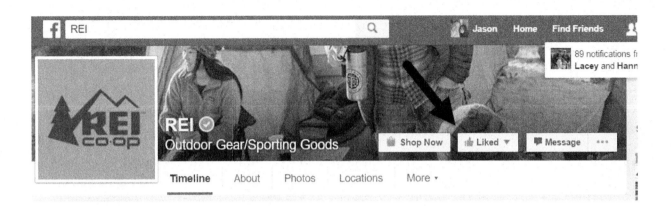

Your task is to go on Twitter, Facebook, Instagram, LinkedIn, and identify companies that intrigue you. "Like" or "follow" them and start to think about their social media marketing "as if" you were attending their "party." And, in addition, you have an ulterior motive: to "reverse engineer" how they are throwing such great parties, and how you can use that knowledge to improve your own.

▶ RECOGNIZE THE SOCIAL MEDIA MARKETING ILLUSION

As you begin to identify and monitor brands that you like on a given social media platform, you may be tempted to conclude that it's either really easy or they are just geniuses. Successful social media is based on **illusion**, just like successful parties are based on illusion.

How so?

Let's think for a second about an amazing party. Think back to a holiday party you attended, a great birthday or graduation party, or even a corporate event. Was it fun? Did it seem magical? It probably did.

Now, if you've ever had the (mis)fortune of planning such an event – what was that like? Was it fun? Was it magical? Yes and no, but it was also probably a lot of work, "in the background," to make sure that the party ran smoothly.

The Party Illusion

Great parties have an element of **illusion** in them: they *seem* effortless, while *in reality* (behind the scenes) an incredible amount of strategy, planning, and hard work goes on. Similarly, great social media marketing efforts (*think Katy Perry or Lady Gaga on YouTube, think Whole Foods on Facebook or blogging, or REI, Zappos, Burt's Bees, or even Nutella on Twitter*), create an illusion. They (only) "seem" spontaneous, they (only) "seem" effortless. But in the background a ton of work is going on to promote, manage, and grow these "social media parties."

ILLUSION IS COMMON TO GREAT PARTIES AND GREAT SOCIAL MEDIA MARKETING

With respect to social media marketing, this **illusion phenomenon** often creates a weird problem for you vis-a-vis upper management or the boss. Upper management or your boss might mistakenly believe that "social media is easy," and/or "social media is free." You, as the marketer, might have to educate your boss that it only "looks" easy, or "seems" free. Social media marketing requires a ton of strategy, hard work, and (gasp!) even money or sweat equity to make it happen. Among your early tasks at social media marketing may be to explain the "social media marketing" illusion to your boss.

It only seems easy. It only seems free.

For your second **TODO**, organize a meeting with your boss and/or marketing team. Discuss all the things that have to get done to be successful at social media marketing, ranging from conducting an **inventory** of competitor efforts, to **setting up basic accounts** on Twitter, Facebook, LinkedIn, etc., to **creating content** to share on social media (images, photos, blog posts, infographics, videos), to **monitoring** social media channels on an on-going basis, and finally to **measuring** your successes. Educate the team that although it might not take a lot of money, social media marketing does take a significant amount of work!

We're planning an awesome party here, people. It's going to take a ton of work, it's going to be a ton of fun, and it's going to be incredibly successful!

Now, don't get discouraged. *Please don't get discouraged or overwhelmed.* It seems hard, and it seems like a ton of work, but once you know what to do, and you become systematic at doing it, you can do amazing social media marketing in just a few hours each week. Like preparing to run a marathon, you'll need to commit to regular activities. But, like running a marathon, thousands of people do it, and do it well. It takes discipline, but YOU CAN DO IT!

Imagine me in Richard Simmons-looking hot pants, jumping up and down and leading you and your marketing team (plus the boss) in a chant: WE CAN DO THIS WE CAN DO THIS.

Now, stop imaging me as Richard Simmons. It's getting weird.

And here's a screenshot of Richard Simmon's Facebook Page:

You'll noticed that I've "liked" his Page. You should, too. (Or find other Pages that amaze you with their marketing prowess). Richard Simmons has more than 300,000 fans on Facebook!

Be Positive

There is nothing as powerful as the power of positive thinking. As marketers, we are so fortunate to live in an amazing time with incredible new opportunities to reach our target customers. Can you imagine being a marketer in the sad decades of the 1970s or 1980s, when all they had was the Yellow Pages, trade shows, cold calling, and direct mail pieces? I mean, "Let your fingers do the walking," how pathetic was that? Feel sorry for those people in the past, as you and I are lucky to live during an **amazing marketing revolution**. We live in amazing times – Twitter, Facebook, Snapchat, Instagram, and even Google are just a few years or a few decades old (if that). It's like 1776 in the USA, 1917 in Russia, or 1789 in Paris!

Be **positive** about the present and the future. You are not only lucky enough to live during the *social media marketing revolution*. You are taking positive steps to become an expert at it!

Know the Question and Find the Answer

Once you start to view social media marketing as a systematic process, a great thing will happen: you'll formulate concrete, *specific* questions. You'll formulate concrete *specific* tasks, such as "how do I create an infographic?" or "what are the dimensions of a Facebook cover photo?," and "how do I automate my posting to Twitter?"

> *Once you know a question you can find the answer.*

I am going to share with you one of my best kept, secret websites. It's an amazing, powerful website that can literally answer almost any question. It's called, **Google**, and you can find it at https://www.google.com/. Bookmark this site. It's very useful.

Here's a screenshot:

Google

Once you formulate a specific question, such as "What is the character limit of a tweet?," you can Google it, to find the answer.

IF YOU KNOW THE QUESTION, YOU CAN GOOGLE THE ANSWER

Similarly, once you realize, for example, that Facebook allows cover photos, and that smart Facebook marketers swap theirs out from time to time, you can create the "questions" of "How do you create a cover photo for Facebook?," "What are the dimensions of a Facebook cover photo,?" etc. You can then type them into Google to find the answers; Google will point you to the official Facebook help files as well as other helpful blog posts or answer sites on the Web. Indeed, people often make amazing "how to" videos on YouTube, and once you know a question, you'll almost always find someone who has made a YouTube of the answer. (YouTube is my second favorite top secret site to find answers; check it out at https://www.youtube.com/).

Yes, I know I'm being tongue in cheek, but you'd be amazed at how few people actually realize that they can Google their marketing questions about social media!

≫ IDENTIFY RELEVANT DISCOVERY PATHS

Before we plunge into Facebook, LinkedIn, Twitter, and social media networks on a step-by-step basis, it's worthwhile to sit back and ponder the big questions of marketing.

What do you sell?

Who wants it and why?

And, very directly: how do customers find you?

This last one might seem like a simple question, but a great social marketer has a very specific understanding of the paths by which customers find her product, service, or company. This understanding then guides -

> *How much should you focus on SEO (Search Engine Optimization)? How much should you focus on AdWords? How much on Facebook? Or Twitter? Should you buy ads on Television, or (gasp!) send out unsolicited email (spam)? Is Pinterest worth the effort?*

It makes sense if you think like a fisherman, and you think of your customers like fish. If your "fish" tend to be on Facebook, then you need to prioritize Facebook in your marketing strategy; if your "fish" tend to be using LinkedIn, then you need to prioritize LinkedIn; and if your "fish" tend to read reviews on Yelp, you need to priorize Yelp.

In marketing speak, these are called **"discovery paths,"** and there are five – and only five – discovery paths that really matter in terms of social media marketing.

How do customers find you? Let us count the ways.

> **SEARCH.** The search path occurs when the customer is "searching" for a company, product, or service. For example, a customer is hungry. He types into Google or Yelp, "pizza." He browses available restaurants, chooses one, and shows up to get pizza. *He searched for pizza. He found pizza. He made a decision.* The search path is the province of SEO (Search Engine Optimization), largely on Google but also on sites such as Yelp or Amazon that work via "keywords" to help customers find stuff that they want. AdWords advertising is also helpful in this path.

> **REVIEW / RECOMMEND / TRUST.** The review / recommend /trust path is based on "trust indicators." In it, the customer already has created a list of vendors he or she might use, but he is researching "whom to trust." In this path, he might use the "reviews" and/or "stars" on Yelp or Google as "trust indicators" to predict

which pizza restaurant is good (or bad). Reviews and stars are the most common trust indicators in social media marketing, but having a robust Facebook page, with many followers and interesting posts can also be a "trust indicator." Having an expert-looking profile on LinkedIn can be a "trust indicator" for a CPA or an architect. A recommendation from a friend or colleague also plays into reviews and trust.

EWOM / SHARE / VIRAL. *Wow! That pizza was great! Let me take a selfie of me chowing down on the pizza, and post it to Instagram. Or, wow, here is a cat video of cats at the pizza restaurant puzzled by the self-serve soda fountain. It's "gone viral" on YouTube and has sixteen million views!* The **share path** occurs when a customer loves the product, service, or experience enough to "share" it on social media – be that via electronic word of mouth, a share on his or her Facebook page, a "selfie" on Instagram, or a viral video on YouTube.

INTERRUPT. The interrupt path is the bad boy of online marketing. Interrupt marketing occurs when you want to watch a YouTube video but before you can watch it, you have to view an annoying ad. Or, when you get a cold call from a recruiter who's viewed your Profile on LinkedIn, or when you get a spam email on "amazing Viagra." *Interrupt* is largely used in advertising, and largely used to "push" products that people aren't proactively looking for.

BROWSE. The browse path is all about getting your message *adjacent* to what a person is reading or viewing on the Internet. In it, you're looking for something, reading something, or watching something, and alongside comes something else. For example, you go to YouTube to look up "how to tie a tie," and in the suggested videos at the end is a video for Dollar Shave Club. Or you see Dollar Shave Club videos suggested at the right of the screen. You're not proactively looking for Dollar Shave Club, but you see their information as you "browse" for related content on sites like YouTube, Facebook, or blogs.

All of these paths can come into play in an effective social media marketing strategy. Your job is to identify your customers, figure out where they hang out on social media, and position your message in front of their "eyeballs," to use the industry slang for getting *what you sell* in front of *how they see*.

Outline Your Marketing "Big Picture"

For your third **TODO**, download the **Big Picture Marketing worksheet**. For the worksheet, go to https://www.jm-seo.org/workbooks (click on Social Media Workbook, enter the code 'smm2016' to register if you have not already done so), and click on the link to the "Big Picture Marketing."

In this worksheet, you'll write a "business value proposition" explaining what you sell, and who are the target customers. You'll also identify the most relevant "discovery paths" by which potential customers find your products. You will begin to realize that there is a "method" to the "madness," as you identify where your customers are and how best to reach them.

» ESTABLISH GOALS AND KPIS (KEY PERFORMANCE INDICATORS)

Marketing is about measurement. Are we helping our brand image? Are we encouraging sales? How do we know where we are succeeding, and where there is more work to be done? Why are we spending all this blood, sweat, and tears on social media marketing anyway? Is it paying off?

In today's overhyped social media environment, many marketers feel like they "must" be on Twitter, or they "must" have a presence on Pinterest, etc. All of the social media companies – Facebook, Twitter, Pinterest, Yelp – have a vested interest in overhyping the importance of their platform, and using fear to compel marketers to "not miss out" by massively jumping on the latest and greatest social platform. **Social media guilt**, however, is to be avoided: if you define a clear business value proposition, know where your customers are, and establish clear goals and KPIs (Key Performance Indicators), you'll be able to focus on those social platforms that really help you and ignore the ones that are just hype.

AVOID SOCIAL MEDIA GUILT: YOU CAN'T (AND SHOULDN'T) USE EVERY NETWORK

Let's identify some common **goals** for effective social media marketing. The boss might have an ultimate "hard" goal of getting sales leads or selling stuff online. Those are definitely important, but as marketers, we might look to intermediary or "soft goals" such as nurturing a positive brand image online or growing our online reviews.

Generally speaking, social media excels at the "soft goals" of growing brand awareness, nurturing customer conversations, encouraging reviews and the like and is not so good at immediate, direct goals like lead captures or sales.

In any case, having high-level yet soft goals is essential to being able to create a systematic, social media marketing strategy as well as a "drilldown" strategy for an individual social medium, whether that be Twitter or LinkedIn, Instagram or YouTube.

Here are common goals for social media marketing:

eWOM (electronic Word of Mouth). Every brand wants people to talk about it in a positive way, and today a lot of that conversation occurs on social media. If you are a local pizza restaurant, you want people "talking" about you and your pizza on Yelp, on Facebook, on Twitter as a great place to get pizza, eat Italian food, cater a wedding, or host a birthday party for little Jimmy. As marketers, a common goal for social media is to grow and nurture positive eWOM, which might be positive conversations on Facebook, positive reviews on Yelp or Google+ local, relationships between us and customers and among customers, and the sharing of our brand across media.

Customer Continuum. *A prospect becomes a customer, a customer becomes a fan, and a fan becomes an evangelist.* For example, I'm hungry. I search for "great pizza" in Palo Alto, California, and I find your pizza restaurant. I try your pizza, thereby becoming a customer. It's good, and I'm a fan: if someone asks me, I'll recommend *Jason's Palo Alto Pizza*. And finally, I love your pizza so much, I wrote a positive review on Yelp, I created a YouTube video of me eating your pizza, and I have a new blog on Tumblr about your pizza. As marketers, we want to encourage customers to move to the right on the customer continuum: *from prospect to customer, customer to fan, and fan to evangelist.*

Customer from Hell. You also need to be aware of (and seek to mitigate) the "customer from hell" who can hate a brand so much that she writes a negative review on Yelp, posts negative comments on Facebook, or creates a viral YouTube video about your terrible pizza (**reputation management**). Social media marketing is also about reputation management, and especially mitigating "customers from Hell."

Trust Indicators. Customers want pizza. Customers read reviews. Customers use reviews to decide which pizza restaurant is probably good. Similarly, when customers want to go to a theme park, they might check out the Facebook page. They like theme parks that have lively Facebook pages over those that having boring Facebook pages. **Trust indicators** are all about mental "short cuts" that customers make to identify possible vendors, services, or products. A common goal of social media marketing, therefore, is to nurture positive trust indicators about our brand online: reviews, especially but not only.

Here's a screenshot of "Sushi" from Yelp. Ask yourself, which restaurant is probably better – the one with 169 reviews, or the one with 88?

One Touch to Many. You visit the pizza restaurant, one time. As a marketer, I want to convert that "one touch" to "many." I want you to follow us on Twitter, so I can Tweet special deals, promotions, what's cooking, and stay "top of mind," so that when you're hungry again, you think, *Jason's Palo Alto Pizza.* Using social media to convert one touch to many and stay top of mind is an excellent goal.

Promotion, promotion, promotion. Social sharing – getting customers to market your brand to their friends, family, and colleagues – is probably the most common social media goal. You want your customers to Instagram their happy kids having a great pizza party at your pizza restaurant! You want your customers to share tweets about their amazing corporate catering event with their Facebook friends. And you want your customers to share your informative industry blog post on cybersecurity with their contacts on LinkedIn. *Encouraging social promotion is a huge, huge goal for SMM.*

Your **TODO** here begins by simply taking out a piece of paper, or opening up a Word document, and jotting down "soft" and "hard" goals for your social media marketing efforts. For extra credit, start to hypothesize which goals might be best accomplished on which social media network.

The Virtuous Circle

When you sum all of the goals listed above, and probably some you may have identified that I've missed, you get to the **virtuous circle** of social media marketing. When your social media marketing efforts are really working well, you can create a positive feedback loop.

> *The more positive reviews you have on Yelp, the most customers you get, the most customers you get, the more positive reviews. The more followers on Twitter you get, the more chances you have to get them to share your discounts, the more discounts they share, the more followers you get. The more people who like / share / comment on your Facebook page, the better your Edgerank (a measurement of how engaging one's content is), the better your Edgerank, the more people see your content, the more people see your content, the more shares you get on Facebook, the better your Edgerank....*

NURTURE A VIRTUOUS CIRCLE

Nurturing a virtuous circle is a major, major goal of an effective social media marketing system. And finally, don't forget, that in most cases you want all of these "soft goals" to turn into "hard goals": a positive brand image to lead to more sales, and a stronger bottom line. All of this can be measured.

For your next **TODO**, download the **Marketing Goals Worksheet**. For the worksheet, go to https://www.jm-seo.org/workbooks (click on Social Media Workbook, enter the code 'smm2016' to register if you have not already done so), and click on the link to the "Marketing Goals Marketing."

In this worksheet, you'll identify your "hard" goals, whether you have something "free" to offer, and your "soft" goals on social media. Ultimately, these big picture goals will be translated into much more specific goals, germane to a social medium such as YouTube, Twitter, or Facebook. Don't forget to conceptualize what a *virtuous marketing circle* would look like for your company. Visualize social media marketing success; you'll get there step-by-step.

» CREATE A CONTENT MARKETING SYSTEM

Bring on the chips! Carry out the diet coke! Turn on the band! A great party needs great food and great entertainment. These are the "fuel" of the successful party. Similarly, great social media marketing needs the "fuel" of content: interesting (funny, shocking, outrageous, sentimental) blog posts, images, photographs, infographics and instructographics, memes and even videos that will make it worthwhile to "subscribe" to your social channel (like / follow / circle) and keep coming back for more.

To succeed at social media marketing you must succeed at **content marketing**. You **MUST** create a system for identifying and creating interesting content to share via your social networks. Without *content*, your social media marketing efforts will wither like a frat party without *beer*, or a corporate networking event without expensive *Sauvignon Blanc*.

What kind of content do people generally want? What kind of content gets shared? Among the most popular and commonly shared items on social media are the following:

> **Images**. Photographs and images are the bread-and-butter of Facebook, Instagram, and even Twitter.
>
> **Memes**. From grumpy cat to success kid, memes make the funny and memorable, sticky and shareable on social media. I love memes; here's a screenshot of one on "Social Media Marketing:"

Infographics and Instructographics. From how to tie a tie to sixteen ways you can help stop global warming, people love to read and share pictures that tell a story, hopefully with facts.

Blog Posts. An oldie but goodie: an informative, witty, funny, informational, or fact-filled post about a topic that matters to your customers.

Short Text Posts. Funny, important, moving, informative quotations. Cute and clever quips on industry events. Even within the 140 character limit of Twitter, you can share ideas that are short, sweet, and powerful. Here's a funny meme on that topic:

Slide Shows. From Slideshare to just posting your PowerPoints online, a hybrid visual and textual cornucopia of social sharing fun.

Videos. If a picture tells a thousand words, a video can tell ten thousand. YouTube is a social medium in its own right, but the videos themselves are content that can be enjoyed and shared.

Build a Content Marketing System

In summary, you'll need fuel to power your social media marketing. You need **content**, and you need to be very **efficient** and **systematic** at producing content. Just as a successful party host has "planned out" how many tacos she needs for her Mexican taco buffet, and just as she "keeps the tacos coming" as the hungry guests devour them, so you'll need to plan out the yummy yummy content you'll need, and you'll need to keep producing it so that visitors to your Facebook, Twitter, YouTube, etc., find a continuous stream of interesting, informative content that makes them want to stay, makes them want to share, and makes them want to keep coming back.

You do not want to run out of food at a party, and you do not want to run out of content for your social media marketing. So plan ahead!

Effective content for social media comes in two main varieties: **other people's content**, and **your own content**. For example, you can write your own blog post on "Seven Tips to a More Effective Business Meeting," or you can share a blog post written by a famous guru on "Seven Tips to a More Effective Business Meeting." This is just the same as you can buy pre-made tacos from a local taco joint (or from Safeway's refrigerated case) to use "other people's" tacos or you can make your own tacos from scratch for your guests. It's either you do-it-yourself or you leverage items that have been made by others.

Advantages and Disadvantages

The advantage of other people's tacos is that they take less effort on your own part. The advantage of your own tacos is that they taste better. Similarly, the advantage of other people's content is that it is easy to get, while the advantage of your own content is that because it's yours, you can customize it to your desired message. The disadvantage of other people's content is that you do not control the message (and it thereby promotes them to some extent), while the disadvantage of your own content is that its takes time and effort to produce.

TWO TYPES OF CONTENT

Your goal is to position yourself (your company, your CEO, your brand) as a "useful expert," the "goto" person or brand that people come to to find interesting and useful stuff in your market ecosystem. You need a lot of content to do this, and you're going to systematically need both your own content and other people's content to create your **content marketing machine**.

Going back to review the "types" of content you may want for your social media marketing content machine, you'll see that you have –

Your own blog post vs. the blog post of an industry guru

Your own photograph vs. the photograph of a great photographer

Your own quote vs. a famous quote by somebody else

Your own webinar vs. the webinar being put on by industry luminaries.

Go back and review some companies that are doing social media well (e.g., Whole Foods, REI, HP, Bishop Robert Barron, Seth Godin), and you'll see that many of them mix and match "their own content" and "other people's content" plus sometimes they commentate on the content of others (a "hybrid" model).

Let's drill down.

Other People's Content

You want to start systematically identifying great content in your industry, and queuing this up to be shared on your social networks. Your goal is to be a "helpful expert," the person who tells others, "Hey! Did you know that so-and-so is having an amazing free webinar on Thursday?," or "Hey! Did you see that our industry journal just published an in-depth study on such-and-such topic?" Other People's Content or OPC is easy to find, easy to share, and helps to position you as the person or company that really has their ear to the industry pulse.

How do you find quality content produced by other people? How do you do this in an easy and systematic way?

Fortunately, there are tools to help you systematically identify and share other people's content. (All are listed in the *Social Media Toolbook*, content marketing section and on the *Dashboard*). Here are some of my favorites:

Buzzsumo (http://buzzsumo.com) - Buzzsumo is a 'buzz' monitoring tool for social media. Input a keyword, select a date range like "last week," and this tool will show you what is being most shared across Facebook, Twitter, LinkedIn, etc. You can also input a domain such as *nytimes.com* or one of your industry blogs and also see what is being most shared from that domain.

Google Alerts (https://www.google.com/alert). Use Google to input keywords and send you daily or weekly alerts of new items that the Google search engine finds on those keywords.

Feedly (http://feedly.com) - Feedly is a newsreader integrated with Google+ or Facebook. It's useful for social media because you can follow important blogs or other content and share it with your followers. It can also spur great blog ideas.

Easely (http://easel.ly) - Use thousands of templates and design objects to easily create infographics for your blog. A competitor is Piktochart (http://piktochart.com).

Meme Generator (http://memegenerator.net) - Memes are shareable photos, usually with text. Memegenerator.net makes it easy to find, and create, memes of your very own to share.

Bookmark / Read Industry Blogs. Identify the top industry blogs in your industry, bookmark them (and/or input them to Feedly), plus follow them on social media as on Facebook, LinkedIn, Twitter. You can share their content to your followers, plus commentate on content that they're producing. To find blogs in the first place, go to Google and type in a keyword relevant to your company's industry and the word blog. For example, visit http://jmlinks.com/12w which is a sample search for blogs on proteomics. Here's a screenshot:

Google   proteomic blog

All   Images   News   Videos   Shopping   Mo

About 189,000 results (0.25 seconds)

News in Proteomics Research - Blogger
proteomicsnews.blogspot.com/ ▾
Genome Alley is finally realizing the power of **Proteomics** and politically neutral I think, but I still personally find that App ...

By identifying relevant keyword themes that interest your target customers and by using the tools above, you can systematically generate a list of content to share on a daily, weekly, and monthly basis. Just a few hours spent each week will give you an abundance of informative, cool content that will make you be the "helpful expert" with your finger on the industry pulse. (And, as part of the social media illusion, you don't have to share the amazing tools above with your customers. They'll just think you are gung-ho awesome).

Finally, once you start building a list of content to share, you can use free tools to schedule and control what posts when, where, and how across social media networks. My favorite scheduling tool is Hootsuite (https://www.hootsuite.com/), which is a cloud-based software that allows for team input. You can manage three networks for free, and for about $20 or less per month, you can manage many more.

Other People's Content: an Example

In terms of other people's content, you want to first identify the "themes" or "keywords" of social media that interest your customers and connect to your own marketing messages. An expert in tax issues, for example, might monitor California tax law, small business, and individual tax shelter issues. He can then systematically monitor them via a tool such as Feedly, and use Hootsuite to easily share other people's content across his social networks. A Palo Alto California cuisine restaurant might monitor content on the San Francisco Bay Area as well as healthy food, vegan food, and French cuisine, as well as ideas for wedding catering and birthday parties. By being a "helpful sharer" of this information, the restaurant can stay "top of mind" by providing useful content to people planning corporate events, weddings, and birthday parties as well as looking for fun things to do in the Bay Area.

Your Own Content

The process for your own content is not dissimilar, just more work. The steps are to *first* brainstorm a useful content idea (e.g., an infographic on common ways for small business owners to save on taxes, or sixteen ways weddings can go terribly wrong), *second* to create it in whatever format you want (image, infographic, blog post, video), and *third* to share it across your relevant social networks.

To really be good at sharing, you must have a company blog. **A blog is an absolute must to be successful at social media marketing**, for two reasons:

1. A blog allows you to create custom blog posts, and blog posts are among the most common content consumed and shared across most social media platforms (e.g., LinkedIn, Twitter, Google+).

2. A blog gives you a place on the web to host other types of content, such as embedded YouTube videos, infographics or instructographics, downloadable PDF eBooks, or even images with captions.

If your company website doesn't already have a blog, insist that your web developer set one up immediately if not sooner. If possible, use the WordPress software to manage your blog, as it is by far the easiest CMS (Content Management System). Alternatively, if you are just getting started you can use a free blogging platform such as Blogger or WordPress.com to host your blog.

If you are creating images, a Flickr account or a Google+ photo sharing account makes it easy to store, and share photos. If you are creating videos, having a YouTube channel is a no brainer. But blogs are the foundation, and you must create a blog.

>> SHARING IS CARING: BLOGGING FOR SOCIAL MEDIA

Blogs are so important for social media content, that I want to spend some time on blogging. I'm assuming you have set up a company blog, so structurally you're ready to write your first post. (If you've already written a few posts, you can also revisit and reoptimize them as indicated below).

Your blog and the blog posts on it can serve any or all of three purposes.

1. as a **trust indicator** to substantiate your company as a "helpful expert)
2. as an **SEO asset**, that is - as a way to get to the top of relevant Google, Yahoo, and Bing searches via basic SEO) (*This is covered in-depth in my SEO Fitness Workbook, so we will not cover it here*).
3. as **content** for posting and **sharing** to your social media networks.

Each of these, conceptually, are different things, but one blog post can be oriented towards one, or all, of them. For example, a blog post on "Seven Tax Tips for Expatriates Living in the USA," can be a *trust indicator* substantiating your CPA firm as experts in international tax issues, it can be an *SEO asset* helping get your company to the top of relevant Google searches, and it can be *content* that you can share on social media networks like LinkedIn to stay top of mind among potential customers and encourage social sharing.

Identifying Keyword Themes for Your Blog

What should you blog about? What type of content should you create? The answer is to identify **keyword themes** that touch on what your target customers want to know about. Clients seeking international tax advice, for example, would be interested in reading blog posts on ways to minimize double taxation, or what types of behavior is most likely to provoke an IRS audit. Persons planning a wedding might be interested in comparing the merits of a "destination wedding" in Mexico, with an "at home" wedding in Los Angeles. And persons interested in cybersecurity for their corporations might be interested in a blog post with infographic on the twelve most common security holes in a typical corporate network.

A Strong Blog Touches on Keyword Themes that People Care About

A best practice is to do **keyword research**, and build out a **keyword worksheet** for your social media marketing efforts. The keyword worksheet will identify the **themes** that you and your blog (or other content sources such as images or videos) will touch on again and again. Short of mentally brainstorming your keywords, are there tools that can assist you in identifying popular topics among your target customers?

Of course there are!

First, let's turn to **Google tools**. As the world's most popular search engine, Google has the best tools that identify what people search on, and accordingly, what interests them. Visit the Google tools listed below to research which keywords have search volume on Google. Let's continue with this example of an accounting firm specializing in international taxation. Are people Googling "international tax," "FBAR," "Foreign Bank Account Report," or even "international tax compliance" or "what to do in case of an IRS audit?" If so, the keywords that people search for will also likely be strong magnets for creating social-media-friendly content.

Here are three handy Google tools to help you brainstorm your most desirable keywords:

Google Autocomplete. Simply go to Google, and start typing in a keyword that hits on one of your keywords. For example, brainstorm "international tax" and just type "international tax" into Google. Then hit your "A," key, your "F" key, etc., and pay attention to the suggestions Google gives you. These autocomplete suggestions make for great ideas to write interesting blog posts that touch on what real people actually want.

Google Related Searches. Type in a full search such as "international tax for expatriates" Scroll to the bottom of the page and look at the "related searches."

AdWords Keyword Planner. Sign up for a Google AdWords account, and use the official Google AdWords keyword planner. Watch a video explaining how to use this tool at http://jmlinks.com/9s. (*Note: you'll need to sign up for an AdWords account in order to use this tool including a credit card, but you do not actually have to spend any money.*)

Your **TODO**, therefore, is to build a short but focused **keyword worksheet** or list of keywords, that reflect what your customers or potential customers are searching for on Google. These search queries easily translate into themes or topics that can become the focus of your blog posts for social media!

Content Being Shared vs. Being Searched For

Google tools are based on "search," on what people are searching for. What about what people are "sharing?" A lot of the action on social media, after all, is the sharing of trending content. Are there tools that identify content being shared?

Of course they are, and we've already touched on them.

Buzzsumo (http://buzzsumo.com) and Feedly (http://feedly.com/), for example, can be used to keep an eye on industry trends. Once you know what's trending, you can not only share that content ("other people's content") but you can brainstorm similar content, or content that builds upon trends. If, for example, a discussion of a famous movie star's latest wedding is trending on Facebook, you can build on that to write a blog post with your commentary on what she did right, and what she did wrong, but choosing that particular destination. Your goals is to become and be seen as an "authoritative commentator" on these trends, and a trend-setter in your own right.

In addition, be sure to follow people or companies who are seen as authoritative in your industry as well as competitors: pay attention to what they write on their blogs, and reverse engineer the content that they are sharing on their Twitter, LinkedIn, Facebook, etc., which is getting a lot of likes, comments, and shares.

Emotion, Emotion, Emotion (and Some Utility)

Nothing succeeds like success, and nothing tells you what is most likely to be popular and shared on social media, like what is *already popular and being shared* on social media. In general, things that are shared will hit emotional theme such as usefulness, being counterintuitive or counterfactual, being shocking, provoking fear or outrage, or being funny. It's really all about utility or emotion; outside of LinkedIn (which is the most serious network), emotional triggers are by far the most common content.

Accordingly, if there is an "emotional" angle to your blog post, be sure to touch on it, and be sure to include it in your headline.

Once you have the keyword target, the next step is to write a catchy headline and write a catchy blog post that hits on either emotion or usefulness.

Sticking with our example of international tax issues, we might take the topic of "FBAR compliance," and spin out blog headlines such as:

Why FBAR Matters to Your Clients (Even If They Don't Know It Yet) ("utility").

Why What You as a CPA Don't Know About FBAR Is Going to Cost You ("fear").

The FBAR: An Outrageous Intervention of the Government in our Lives ("shocking")

An FBAR Tragedy: A Small Businessperson Forced into Bankruptcy ("Outrage or sentimentality")

Fun tools that will help you "spin" blog topics and titles for social media are the Portent Idea Generator (http://jmlinks.com/9u) and Hubspot's topic generator (http://jmlinks.com/9w).

Finally, now that you have a well-written blog post that touches on trending industry themes of interest to key customer segments, it's time to share it. Post it to your blog, and then use a URL shortener like http://bitly.com/ or http://tinyurl.com/ to shorten your long blog URL. Then paste it into Hootsuite, summarize the topic, and post it strategically to your Twitter, Facebook, LinkedIn, and wherever else appropriate. (Hootsuite has its own built-in link shortener as well, here's a screenshot:)

To sum up, once you know a keyword theme, the process of creating a blog post is as follows:

1. **Identify the blog concept and relevant keywords**. These define what the blog post is about and which keywords people are likely to search for. Use a tool like Buzzsumo (http://buzzsumo.com) to see what's already being shared on social media sites.
2. **Outline the content and write a rough draft**. Just as in all writing, it's good to write out a rough draft. A good blog post should have about four to five paragraphs of text. "Less is more" when it comes to social media, so make the blog post pithy and informative.
3. **Identify a provocative image**. Whether it's on Instagram, Facebook, or LinkedIn, people respond to images. Use a free image site such as Foter (http://foter.com/) and find an image that conveys the essence of your blog post.
4. **Write a catchy, keyword-heavy headline**. It's no accident that popular sites like *Buzzfeed* and *Huffington Post* use shocking or provocative headlines! *Dog bites man, Read Donald Trump's Lastest Outrageous Tweet!, etc.* People react to, and share, content that hits an emotional nerve and the headline is the first step towards a strong emotional reaction.
5. **Finalize the content**. Review your content and make sure it is easy-to-read, preferably with lists and bullets.
6. **Share the content**. Identify the appropriate social media platform such as LinkedIn, Twitter, Facebook, Instagram, etc., and share your post. Use a tool like Hootsuite (https://hootsuite.com/) to organize and schedule your shares.

Your Blogging Objectives

In terms of social media marketing, your blog objectives are a) to stay "top of mind" among customers and their contacts, b) to substantiate your organization's brand image as a "helpful expert," and c) to encourage "social sharing" so that friends of friends, and colleagues of colleagues, can become aware of your company and its products or services. A strong blog post can be great as a trust indicator, great for SEO, or attractive for social media sharing, or all three! So, start blogging!

Create a Content Marketing Plan

Content, in sum, is both that of other people and that of your own company. It may take the form of a blog post, a video, an image, an infographic, a short quote, or other formulations. Regardless, your objective is to systematically build and turn on a **content marketing machine**. It's the foundation of your social media marketing strategy.

For your final **TODO**, download and complete the **Content Marketing Worksheet**. For the worksheet, go to https://www.jm-seo.org/workbooks (click on Social Media Workbook, enter the code 'smm2016' to register if you have not already done so), and click on the link to the "Content Marketing Worksheet."

» REMEMBER THE BIG PICTURE

At this point, you've begun your social media marketing journey. You've understood that social media marketing is about "throwing" the party more than "attending the party." You've realized you need to start "paying attention" with regard to what other marketers are doing on social media, with an eye to "reverse engineering" their marketing strategy so that you have ideas of what you like, and do not like, in terms of social media. You've started to brainstorm "discovery paths" and "goals" for your SMM efforts.

And you've realized that once you've identified your goals, identified relevant social media, set up your social accounts, the really hard work will be a) promoting your social media channels, and b) creating the kind of content that makes them want to "like you," keep coming back for more, and share your message with their friends, family, and/or business colleagues.

You've understood that **promotion** and **content creation** are the big on-going tasks of successful social media marketing.

>>>> DELIVERABLE: OUTLINE A SOCIAL MEDIA MARKETING PLAN

Now that we've come to the end of Chapter 1, your first **DELIVERABLE** has arrived. For the worksheet, go to https://www.jm-seo.org/workbooks (click on Social Media Workbook, enter the code 'smm2016' to register if you have not already done so), and click on the link to the "Social Media Marketing Plan Big Picture Worksheet." By filling out this plan, you and your team will establish a vision of what you want to achieve via social media marketing.

Once you've have a "big picture" plan, it's time to drill down into individual social media networks. We'll start with Facebook, the 800 pound gorilla of social media.

>> TOP CONTENT MARKETING TOOLS & RESOURCES

This Chapter has given you a conceptual framework to understand social media marketing. In addition, it's given you a task: to create a **content marketing machine**. Here are the top free tools and resources to assist you in identifying other people's content, creating your own content, and systematically sharing that content across social media platforms.

FEEDLY - http://feedly.com/

> Feedly is a newsreader integrated with Google+ or Facebook. It's useful for social media because you can follow important blogs or other content and share it with your followers. It can also spur great blog ideas.
>
> **Rating:** 5 Stars | **Category:** resource

BUZZSUMO - http://buzzsumo.com/

> Buzzsumo is a 'buzz' monitoring tool for social media. Input a website (domain) and/or a topic and see what people are sharing across Facebook, Twitter, Google+ and other social media. Great for link-building (because what people link to is what they share), and also for social media.
>
> **Rating:** 5 Stars | **Category:** tool

YOUTUBE TOOLS - http://bitly.com/ytcreatecorner

YouTube has done more and more to make it easier to publish and promote videos. This page lists six tools: YouTube Capture, YouTube Editor, Captions, Audio Library, Slideshow and YouTube Analytics. All of them are fantastic, free tools about YouTube by YouTube.

Rating: 5 Stars | **Category:** resource

PHOTOPIN - http://photopin.com

Get in the habit of creating blog posts with images by using PhotoPin. PhotoPin searches millions of Creative Commons photos and allows you to preview, download any of multiple sizes to upload into your posts, and provides handy cut and paste HTML for attribution, a small price to pay for royalty-free images. Adding images to your blog posts doesn't get any easier than this.

Rating: 4 Stars | **Category:** service

FOTER - http://foter.com

Add some color (or monochrome) to your blog posts with Foter. Search over 200 million high-quality, free, downloadable stock photos. Don't forget to copy and paste photo attribution credits included with the images details into your blog post.

Rating: 4 Stars | **Category:** resource

PABLO - https://buffer.com/pablo

Take an image, add some text. Presto! You have an engaging image for your blog post or social sharing. Memes, anyone?

Rating: 4 Stars | **Category:** tool

STORYBASE - https://www.storybase.com/

This is a brainstorming tool to help you with blogging and other types of content, both for social and for search engine optimization. Enter a phrase like 'wedding flowers,' or 'industrial fans,' and it gives you 'questions' being asked across the Internet. Then, you can write a blog post that 'answers' these 'questions.'

Rating: 4 Stars | **Category:** tool

GOOGLE EMAIL ALERTS - https://www.google.com/alerts

Use Google to alert you by email for search results that matter to you. Input your company name, for example, to see when new web pages, blog posts, or other items surface on the web. Enter your target keywords to keep an eye on yourself and your competitors. Part of the Gmail system.

Rating: 4 Stars | **Category:** service

GOOGLE NEWS - https://news.google.com/

Excellent for reputation management as well as keeping up-to-date on specific keywords that matter to you and your business. First, sign in to your Google account or gmail. Second, customize Google news for your interest. Third, monitor your reputation as well as topics that matter to you. Go Google!

Rating: 4 Stars | **Category:** service

REBATE OFFER

CLAIM YOUR $39.99 REBATE! HERE'S HOW -

1. Go to Amazon.com and search for **'Social Media Marketing Workbook'** or click http://jmlinks.com/smm.
2. Write a short, honest **review of the book** and indicate you've been gifted a 'review copy'.
3. Click https://jm-seo.org/rebate/ and fill out the **REBATE FORM**.

WE WILL THEN -

- **Refund** you the full price of the print edition (**$39.99**), so that you will have received a **FREE** review copy

~ $39.99 REBATE OFFER ~

~ LIMITED TO ONE PER CUSTOMER ~

EXPIRES: 10/1/2016

SUBJECT TO CHANGE WITHOUT NOTICE

GOT QUESTIONS? CALL 800-298-4065

2

FACEBOOK

Facebook is a great place to begin your Social Media Marketing journey! Let me give you four good reasons.

First, Facebook is – by far – the **largest social media platform**, with over one billion active users and countless profiles, Pages, and groups. Nearly every person has a Facebook account ("profile"), many businesses have Pages, and survey after survey ranks Facebook as the most used social media platform.

Second, once you **understand the dynamics of Facebook** – *Profiles and Pages, Timelines and Posts, Likes, Comments, and Shares...* you'll more easily **understand the dynamics of other social media** like LinkedIn, Twitter, or Instagram.

Third, Facebook has a component in its algorithm called **_Edgerank_**, which essentially **rewards** you for posting items that users interact with (as measured by *likes*, *comments*, and *shares*). Understanding what *Edgerank* is, and how to improve your *Edgerank* will help you be a better marketer on Facebook. Understanding *Edgerank* will also help you market better on the other platforms, as all of them use something similar in their own proprietary algorithms.

Finally, Facebook is **fun**! Social media marketing should not be thought of as a chore, but as a way to get closer to your customers and build a community of evangelists around your company, product, or service.

Let's get started!

TODO LIST:

>> Explore how Facebook Works

» Inventory Companies on Facebook

» Understand the Importance of Like & Edgerank

» Set up and Optimize Your Page

» Brainstorm and Execute a Posting Strategy

» Promote Your Facebook Page and Posts

» Measure your Results

» » Deliverable: a Facebook Marketing Plan

» Appendix: Top Facebook Marketing Tools and Resources

» EXPLORE HOW FACEBOOK WORKS

To understand Facebook as a marketer is to understand the "F's": friends, family, fun, photos, and "fake." Before you set up (or optimize) a Facebook Page for your business, before you start posting, before you start advertising, and before you start measuring your successes and failures, take some time to research how Facebook works.

> *What are people doing on Facebook? Why do they like it? What are they sharing and interacting with? Are your customers on it, and if so, what are they doing? How might you interact with customers in a compelling, fun and non-obtrusive way?*

First, I'm assuming you have a personal Facebook profile; *if not,* simply go to https://www.facebook.com/ and sign up. Facebook has a wonderful help section at https://www.facebook.com/help/ - just click on "get started on Facebook." Once you sign up – as an individual – you'll have a **profile**.

Next, I'm assuming you have a few friends and family. (*If not, find some – friends are good).* Send them "friend requests," and vice-versa. Next, post some photos of your family, your dog, your trip to Las Vegas or whatever to your "timeline," and when you login to Facebook on your desktop or your phone, look at your "news feed." Your news feed will show you the posts of the friends and family with whom you are connected: when they post to their "timeline," it will show in your "newsfeed" (with some caveats about *Edgerank*, more about this later). Similarly, when you post to your timeline, those posts will show on the news feed of your friends when / if they log into Facebook whether on their computers or their phones.

Here it is:

Hannah and I are **friends** on Facebook.

Hannah **posts** a picture of her victory in Texas Hold 'em on her Facebook **timeline**.

I see that picture when I log in on my Facebook **news feed**.

Here's a screenshot, with #1 pointing to my "timeline," where I can share a status update with text and/or photos with my friends, and #2 pointing to my "news feed," where I see what my friends or contacts (such as Hannah) have shared:

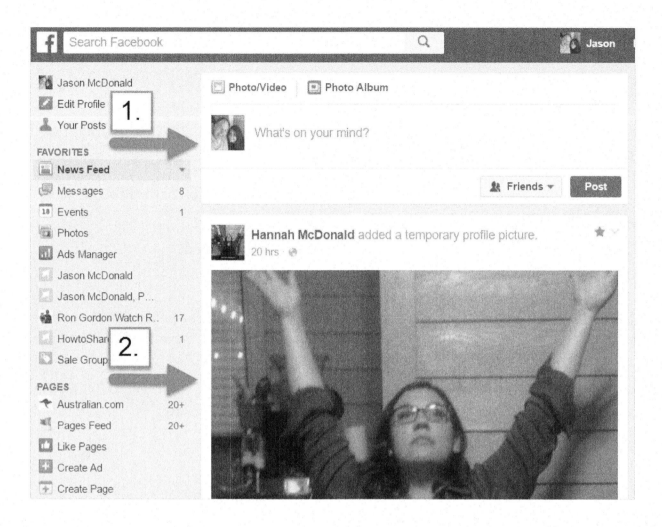

Essentially Facebook is a **huge interactive scrapbook**. You post photos and writings to your *timeline*, and your friends and family see them in their *news feed*, where they can like, comment, or share them. And vice-versa: your friends post to their timeline, and you see it in your news feed.

FACEBOOK IS A SOCIAL SCRAPBOOK

Facebook is also like a big family and friends party: 24/7. People post messages about their lives and families, social events, causes they like/dislike, etc.

Pay attention to what people are sharing on Facebook. Generally, you'll see it falls into the themes of fun, family, friends, and photos:

- **Photos.** Photos dominate Facebook! Photos of friends at the beach, at Disneyland, graduating from High School, new babies. People are constantly posting photos with short commentaries, generally about friends, family, and fun.
- **Friends, Family, Fun.** Whether shared in photo format, as an image, or as plain text, Facebook is a place where people share stuff about their friends and family.
- **Games, Social Contests, Groups.** For some people, Facebook is a place for social games. There are also groups on Facebook which allow people to collaborate and communicate, as for example a "group" of people taking a High School class in US History or a "group" of people who share a passion for duck hunting.
- **Social Causes and Endorsements.** People often "endorse" causes they care about (e.g., Breast Cancer awareness, Gay & Lesbian issues, Save the Whales) and share "outrage" about issues that they disagree with.
- **News & Commentary.** Increasingly, Facebook is becoming a major source of news. Thus, people log in, and see news posts (often by the media, often shared by friends), and "like," "comment," or "share" these news items.

So, next, using your own personal Facebook account, spend some quality time (ideally with your marketing team), just bopping around Facebook, observing what people are "doing" at this party. The marketing goal is to understand the *vibe* or *culture*, of Facebook so that your company's marketing message can blend in and build on this culture to nurture your brand image, grow your customer connections, and ultimately sell more stuff.

> **Research** a) *whether your customers are on Facebook, b) what they are posting, liking, commenting on, and/or sharing, and c) what companies like yours are doing on Facebook that connects to potential customers.*

It's very important to start to look at Facebook through the "**lens**" of a **marketer**, because you will be participating not as a person but as a **company**; you'll have a goal of building your brand image and ultimately "selling more stuff." Consequently, pay close attention to competitors and similar companies on Facebook. Begin to "reverse engineer" what they are doing, and why.

Facebook and Fake

Notice, also, that Facebook is also about "fake." By "fake," I mean that people generally do not share embarrassing news on Facebook. People are very likely to share photos of their family trip to Disneyland, their new Labrador puppy, or their endorsement of the San Francisco Red Cross. If they climb Mount Everest, you can be sure they'll take a selfie at the summit and post it to Facebook. They are not likely, however, to share news about their family struggles, their pending divorce, or their shameful addiction to candy corn and weight problems. In general, people put their best foot forward on Facebook: it's a social scrapbook in many ways about how life "should" be, rather than how life "is."

> *The tone and culture of Facebook are very upbeat, even artificially so. Consequently, the most effective marketing programs on Facebook are upbeat as well.*

Your Specific Customers

As you begin to categorize what people are posting and the tone of these posts, try to conceptualize not just Facebook's general culture but the specific tone or culture of your target customers. If you sell to High Schoolers, you'll find a different tone than if you sell to middle age women who are passionate about knitting, and still another tone if you sell to people passionate about outdoor camping and fishing. Each social medium is different, and you'll quickly realize that if LinkedIn is a serious platform for job searches and business-to-business information, Facebook is a fun platform for sharing photos with friends and family; even its subcultures focus on friends, family, fun, and fake albeit with different nuances in tone.

Once you grasp that Facebook is friends, family, fun, photos, and fake (in general), and once you grasp the unique tone of your target customers, you'll be better positioned to brainstorm how to take your company or brand and make the message fit the medium. Because Facebook is about fun, it's a natural place for fun consumer brands like Whole Foods, REI, and Disney Cruises. It's not such a great place for more "serious" or "boring" companies like Bank of America, the IRS, or Terminex Termite Services. Some companies will blend easily into the vibe of Facebook, while others will blend only with some brainstorming about how to be "fun" even if the product or service isn't that fun (dentistry? plastic surgery? insurance? termite protection? taxes?). And some products or services just do not work on Facebook.

Dentistry Can Be Fun

For example, take a look at the Super Dentists page at Facebook at https://jmlinks.com/12x. Now, dental work isn't exactly fun, is it? Who enjoys getting their teeth cleaned, getting a filling fixed, or having a root canal? Not many of us. The Super Dentists on Facebook, accordingly, is not a Facebook Page about the "serious" side of dentistry, something we all know is "good for us" but we don't exactly enjoy. Rather, their Page is about *fun, fun, fun, fun*, and then an occasional post about something serious with respect to dental care.

Here's a screenshot and link:

See http://jmlinks.com/12x.

What about Your Company and Your Customers?

Returning to Facebook, here are some questions to ask yourself as you investigate the social media giant:

- Are your target customers on Facebook in any capacity?
- If so, are they engaging in topics that directly touch on your company's brand objectives or are they only indirectly touching on those elements?
- What types of posts are your potential customers posting, liking, commenting on, and sharing? Which ones seem to be the most successful in generating interaction, and which the least?
- What are your competitors doing that seems to be working as measured by likes, comments, and shares?
- What other companies that are not competitors yet might act as models for your Facebook strategy doing, and what is working for them? Why or why not?

If you see your customers on Facebook and you see a way to "connect" with keyword themes that they care about, Facebook should be a high priority for you. If you research Facebook, and do not see your customers there, or you do not see a connection between your company's brand objectives and keyword themes being shared on Facebook, then it may not be a high priority for you.

Answer these questions -

1. Are your customers on Facebook? Yes | No (circle)
2. What are they doing on Facebook? Describe: _____
3. What do you see competitors doing on Facebook? Describe: _____
4. What can you post as content that will engage customers on Facebook? Describe:

_____

_____

_____

There is no right or wrong answer to these questions; there is no imperative to be active on Facebook (or Twitter, or Instagram, or LinkedIn), if your customers are not there! *Fish where the fish are! And if the fish aren't in this pond, go to the next one!*

▶▶ Make an Inventory of Likes & Dislikes on Facebook

Assuming you see potential in Facebook, it's time to dig deeper. But before you dive into the technical details of setting up your own Facebook Page and optimizing your posts, it's incredibly important to make a list of companies (whether competitors or more general consumer brands) that you admire on Facebook. You want to monitor them, and reverse engineer what they're doing that's working.

Imitation is the highest form of flattery, and identifying successful brands to reverse engineer is the easiest way to master marketing on Facebook.

So, now we are going to shift gears from **profiles** (individuals) to **Pages** (companies). You'll want to identify companies that are on Facebook, and reverse engineer their marketing strategy.

How do you find companies to "like" on Facebook?

Answer: By understanding how to be a power Facebook searcher.

Ways to Search Facebook

First identify the **keyword themes** that matter to you and your potential customers. For example, if you are a maker of organic baby food, you would use the key phrases "organic food" and "baby food" to identify companies that are already on Facebook. If you are a company that organizes bird-watching tours, then you'll be searching Facebook for keywords like "birding," "birding tourism," or perhaps "ecotourism." As you find companies that seem to be doing a good job with Facebook marketing, you'll be making an inventory of what you like / dislike about their Facebook marketing in terms of their cover photo, profile picture, tabs, and their posting strategy above all else. Remember: if you're going to throw a party, you'll inventory the party theme, decorations, invitations, and all the things you like / dislike to make an inventory for your own party planning.

Your **Todos** here are to identify companies that seem to "get" Facebook, and to inventory what you like or dislike about how they have set up their Facebook Page, and how they are posting content to Facebook.

Returning to the first step, here are the two best ways to find commercial Pages to inventory for your Facebook marketing plan:

Method #1 Search On Facebook Directly. Simply type into the search box your keyword as in "organic food." Next at the bottom click on where it says "See all results." Next at the top tab click on "Pages." Facebook is not the most elegant search engine (it's Facebook, and not Google). But in this way you can find Pages to browse in your industry. Here are screenshots:

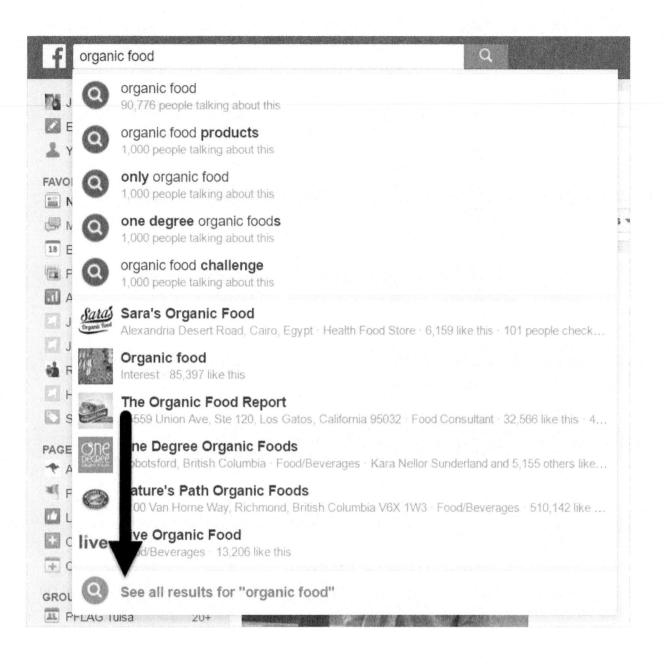

organic food

	organic food 90,776 people talking about this
	organic food **products** 1,000 people talking about this
	only organic food 1,000 people talking about this
	one degree organic food**s** 1,000 people talking about this
	organic food **challenge** 1,000 people talking about this

Sara's Organic Food
Alexandria Desert Road, Cairo, Egypt · Health Food Store · 6,159 like this · 101 people check…

Organic food
Interest · 85,397 like this

The Organic Food Report
559 Union Ave, Ste 120, Los Gatos, California 95032 · Food Consultant · 32,566 like this · 4…

ne Degree Organic Foods
botsford, British Columbia · Food/Beverages · Kara Nellor Sunderland and 5,155 others like…

ature's Path Organic Foods
00 Van Horne Way, Richmond, British Columbia V6X 1W3 · Food/Beverages · 510,142 like …

ve Organic Food
d/Beverages · 13,206 like this

See all results for "organic food"

And then, after you click on "See all results" -

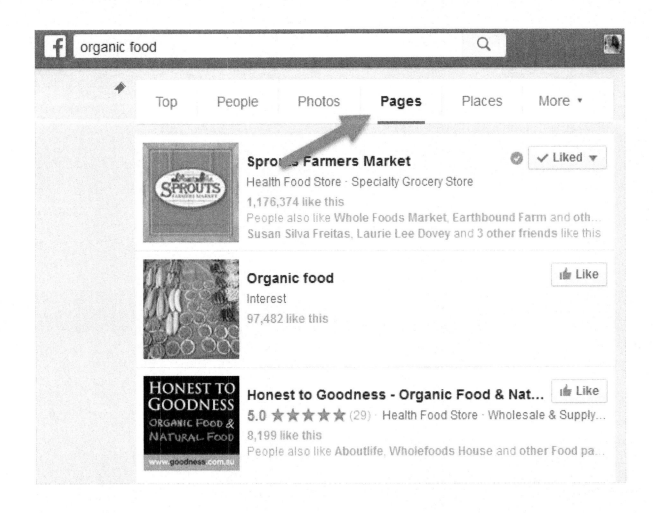

Then you'll see a list of relevant commercial Pages. You can click on each one, identify companies that seem to "get" Facebook, "like" them in your personal profile (so you can keep an eye on them), and begin to inventory your likes / dislikes.

Method #2 Identify Facebook Pages via Google Search. Go to Google (https://www.google.com/). Type into the Google search box *site:facebook.com "organic food"*. Google will then return to you a list of commercial Pages on Facebook with that term in it. To see this in action, go to http://jmlinks.com/2i.

Here's a screenshot:

Google   site:facebook.com "organic food"

Web   News   Maps   Images   Books   More ▾   Search tools

About 386,000 results (0.40 seconds)

Organic Food Truck - San Diego, California ... - Facebook
https://www.facebook.com/**OrganicFood**Truck ▾
Organic Food Truck, San Diego, California. 7533 likes · 14 talking about this. Organic
Food Truck.

It's very important that there be no space between *site* and *the colon*. It's *site:facebook.com* not *site: facebook.com.* You can use this tactic on Google for any social media; as for example, *site:yelp.com massage therapists boston,* or *site:twitter.com industrial fans.* Once you know your keyword themes, using Google in this fashion is a great way to browse a social media to find relevant companies to reverse engineer.

To see this in action, go to http://jmlinks.com/2i.

IDENTIFY COMPANIES WHO DO FACEBOOK WELL AND INVENTORY THEM

Don't be afraid to "like" companies via Facebook (even your competitors). In fact, I strongly encourage it: by "liking" companies you actually "like," you'll experience them marketing to you, and you can then reverse engineer this for your own company. Indeed, Facebook itself encourages companies to "spy" on other companies. Once you've set up a Page for your company, for example, click on the Insights tab, and Facebook will suggest companies similar to your own to monitor. Simply click on on "Pages to watch."

Here's a screenshot:

Returning to the regular Facebook interface, once you "like" a company, its posts will show up in your news feed (depending on *Edgerank*). However, Facebook gives priority to posts by humans (friends and family), so to find posts from brands you have liked, scan the left column of Facebook and look for a link to what is called "Pages Feed." Click on that, and you'll see posts from companies that you have liked. Here's a screenshot:

PAGES

- Moreno Ranches, ... 20+
- Wireless Safety So...
- Pages Feed
- Like Pages
- Create Ad
- Create Page

If you are logged into Facebook, you can also click on this link: https://www.facebook.com/pages/feed.

For your second **TODO**, download the **Facebook Research Worksheet**. For the worksheet, go to https://www.jm-seo.org/workbooks (click on Social Media Workbook, enter the code 'smm2016' to register if you have not already done so), and click on the link to the "Facebook Research Worksheet." You'll answer questions as to whether your potential customers are on Facebook, identify brands to follow, and inventory what you like and dislike about their Facebook set up and marketing strategy.

» UNDERSTAND THE IMPORTANCE OF LIKE AND EDGERANK

To market successfully on Facebook, you need a detailed understanding of its **structure** and how it works. Most importantly, you need to understand the difference between a profile and a Page, and what "like" means vis-a-vis a Page and/or a post, as well as comment and share.

For your inventory, you'll need to know some vocabulary about what is what on Facebook. Here's a synopsis:

- **People have "profiles."** This is *Jason McDonald*, a real person, for example. I have a *profile* (not a *Page*) on Facebook.
- **When two people "friend" each other by exchanging a "friend request," Facebook puts them in a "like" relationship.** If I "friend" my friend, Tom Jones, and he accepts this request, then he and I are connected via Facebook.
- **When two profiles are connected, if person A posts to his timeline, person B will see that post on his news feed** (with the *Edgerank* caveat that the news feed can be very busy, and Facebook prioritizes the posts of friends with whom you interact over those whom you ignore).
  - **People interact with a post** by "liking" the post, "commenting" on the post, and/or "sharing" the post, thereby essentially re-posting it to their own timeline so that their own friends can see / interact with the post. In the background Facebook ***Edgerank*** keeps track of which profiles, Pages, and posts are the most interactive, and favors them in the newsfeed across the social network.
- **Companies have Pages, not profiles.** A *profile* (person) creates a *Page* (company) and then manages it as an Admin. A Facebook Page can (and should) have more than one Admin. The *Page* for the JM Internet Group (https://www.facebook.com/jm.internet) is managed by me (a *profile*) for example.
  - Pages can NOT exist without sponsorship by at least one profile!
  - Any Admin can delete / change / post to a Page!
  - Therefore, have at least two reliable, trustworthy Page Admins at all times.
  - Before you fire someone, REMOVE him or her as a Page Admin!

- **When a person ("profile") "likes" a business "Page" that creates a Facebook relationship between the "profile" and the "Page."** When I "like" Safeway (https://www.facebook.com/Safeway), that means that when Safeway posts to its timeline, it might show on my news feed. By "liking" Safeway, I have given it permission to talk to me via Facebook.
  - **People interact with a post** by a Page by "liking" the post, "commenting" on the post, and/or "sharing" the post, thereby essentially re-posting it to their own timeline so that their own friends can see / interact with the post. In the background Facebook *Edgerank* keeps track of which posts are the most interactive, and favors them in the newsfeed across the social network.

To read the Facebook help files on setting up a business Page, go to http://www.jmlinks.com/1c. Note that you can technically create not just "Pages" for local businesses or places, companies, organizations, or institutions, and brands or products. You can create "public figure Pages" for artists, bands, or public figures (think CEO of your company, a la Martha Stewart), or even Pages for causes or communities. For most companies, you'll choose either the local business option, the company option, or the brand / product option. To see the options, go to https://www.facebook.com/pages/create/.

It Gets Complicated

Here's where it gets complicated. Remember our Social Media Marketing goals? Among them: staying top of mind, and encouraging social sharing? *Edgerank*, which is part of the Facebook algorithm, intervenes at this point. When a Page posts to its timeline, that post will show up on the news feed of "profiles" (people) who have liked it based on several factors:

- The individual ("profile") must have "liked" the Page in advance.
- If the individual previously "liked" the Page, and generally "liked" posts by the Page and/or commented on them and/or shared them, then the *Edgerank* of that Page is improved. The higher the *Edgerank* (based on more interaction between me and that Page), the more likely it is that the post by the Page will show in my timeline.
- A realtime analysis of the post: the faster and wider a post gets interactivity (likes, comments, and shares), the larger its Edgerank and it, therefore, gets even more publicity.

In essence, Facebook monitors whether users interact with the posts of a Page: the more users who interact with the posts of a Page, the higher the Edgerank of that Page and its posts, and the more likely users are to continue to see posts by the Page in their news feed.

Encouraging interactivity is the #1 goal of your Facebook marketing!

To use an example, let's look at the Mayo Clinic and me on Facebook.

1. I "like" the Mayo Clinic Page on Facebook (https://www.facebook.com/MayoClinic), giving it permission to talk to me via Facebook.
2. The Mayo Clinic posts images, photos, blog post summaries, etc., to its Facebook Page timeline, such as tips on how to live healthy, information on diseases, and even information on how to keep your pets healthy.
3. I "like" these posts, I "comment" on these posts (*"Oh, yes, I am going to eat more kale!"*), and even better I "share" these posts on my own timeline by clicking the share button.

Here's a screenshot of a post by the Mayo Clinic appearing on my Facebook news feed. I have highlighted in yellow the like / comment / share buttons at the bottom:

Mayo Clinic
4 hrs · 🌐

"The presence of Mayo Clinic has turned Rochester, Minnesota into a thriving destination for reluctant tourists from every state and 140 countries. Roughly 40 percent of the 400,000 patients seen at Mayo's main campus here each year come from outside a 500-mile radius, including more than 8,500 international patients. They are traveling not to tropical beaches or ski slopes but to doctors, nurses, and expertise."
http://bit.ly/1g2SlI3

Rochester thrives as destination medical center for reluctant tourists flocking to Mayo Clinic

Rochester, Minn., with its population of just over 100,000 and its iconic water tower painted like an oversized ear of corn, may not be a place many would...

WWW.BOSTONG...COM

Like · Comment · Share · 👍 2,662 💬 157 ↪ 441

By "liking," "commenting," or "sharing" this post, I am telling Facebook I am engaged with the Mayo Clinic Page. The more I do this, the more I will see its posts in my news feed.

Now, flip this around as marketers, your goals become:

- To increase your *Edgerank* (and the probability that people will see your posts in their newsfeed), you MUST get more likes, comments, and shares of your posts!

- To increase your *Edgerank*, we must get **interactivity**!

Encouraging interactivity is the name of the game when it comes to Facebook marketing.

INTERACTIVITY IS GOAL #1 FOR YOUR FACEBOOK POSTS

Posting strategy is all about what you post, and using those posts to drive up interactivity, and improve your Edgerank.

Be Emotional and Succeed on Facebook

What kind of posts do people generally interact with? As marketers, we want to reverse engineer what gets interactivity on Facebook. For the most part there is one constant among all highly liked, commented on, and shared posts: **emotion, emotion, emotion**. Posts that create emotional engagement tend to get the most interaction.

BE EMOTIONAL!

Here are example categories of posts that are likely to spur customer interactions:

- **Sentimental Posts**. Posts of kittens and puppies, posts of kids, posts of moms and dads, posts of moms and dads holding kittens and puppies. Posts about the

4th of July, posts about how much you love a cause… Brands on Facebook often post "sentimentality bait": posts that people click "like" on to indicate that they "agree" with the cause. So every mother's day, you can see brands posting pictures of mothers and their kids, and people clicking "like" on these posts because the "like" their mothers… which is increasing the Edgerank of these Pages.

- **Utility**. Posts that explain "how to do" stuff, especially things that are counterintuitive or funny. Such as "Ten Ways Not to Ask a Girl Out," or "Five New Ways to Lose Weight While on a Vacation."
- **Counterintuitive**. Posts that take things you "think" you know, and explain that they don't really work like you think they do. Especially common are things that people "think" are safe, but in fact are dangerous such as rawhide dog chews (who knew that they were dangerous?).
- **Funny**. Humor is big on Facebook. Posting jokes, funny quotes, videos, images (memes), etc. Things that make people laugh, get them to click like, comment, or share. Queue the funny babies, babies with dogs, and of course cat videos.
- **Surveys, Polls, Contests**. Asking your audience a question, and getting them to use the comments as a way to interact with that. Take this quiz and learn which Star Trek character best describes your love life.
- **Quotes**. Sentimental, humorous, make-you-think quotes.
- **Outrage**. Things that make people mad: mad enough to comment, "like" in the sense of opposing the thing that outrages them, and even share. Outrage is very big on Facebook, and brands (rather cynically) leverage this outrage to increase their Edgerank. Click "like" if you think dolphins shouldn't die in Tuna nets, animals shouldn't be abused, etc., for example.
- **Controversy**. Controversy, but in a good way, can be very good for your posts to Facebook. For example, avoid posting touchy subjects like abortion or gun control, but do post on "fun" controversies such as "Is a bikini or a one-piece a better bathing suit?," "Is it OK not to serve turkey on Thanksgiving," or "Which is better a cat or a dog?"

Thus in terms of **posting strategy**, brands will post items that are specifically engineered to increase engagement and thereby increase their *Edgerank*. Look back at the brands you like, and begin to notice how they are using the strategies above to increase interaction.

EDGERANK REWARDS YOU

FOR INTERACTIVE POSTS

Here are some brands that I admire in terms of their Facebook marketing, all of which build Edgerank by sharing interactive content on a regular basis:

Bishop Robert Barron (https://www.facebook.com/BishopRobertBarron) – known as the Catholic social media superstar, Bishop Barron shares history and theological insights, and shows how something as ancient as Catholicism can leverage new media to grow its reach and build its brand.

Navy Federal Credit Union (https://www.facebook.com/NavyFederal) – if you monitor its Page, you'll see a steady dose of sentimentality, especially pictures of military men with babies (a double whammy: *yes, I support our troops, and, yes, I like babies*!).

The Super Dentists (https://www.facebook.com/TheSuperDentists) – similarly to Metamucil, this San Diego kids dentists takes something not-so-fun (dentistry) and effectively builds eWom, one-touch-to-many, and even social sharing via pictures, contests, sentimentality posts and the like.

REI (https://www.facebook.com/REI). REI is an outdoor, sports retailer and uses Facebook to share "how to" information about hiking, campaign, and other outdoor sports, promote its products, and build a community around people who like the outdoors (and love its products).

The White House (https://www.facebook.com/WhiteHouse) – like him, hate him, I don't care, Barack Obama is our first "social media" president, and you can learn a ton from watching how his White House uses Facebook to spread its message, grow its political base, and just generally be cool.

Taco Bell (https://www.facebook.com/tacobell) – the edgy, youth brand is a master at building awareness, creating the "fourth meal" (just what obese America needed), and making factory food fun.

Metamucil (https://www.facebook.com/MetaWellness1) – there, I admit it. I use Metamucil! Any brand that can take something so, private, and grow a Facebook page to 209, 000 fans, has got to be doing something right. "Reverse engineer" how a product you probably didn't think of as friends, family, and fun uses social media on a regular basis (pun intended).

Make a list of your own favorite brands, "like" them on Facebook, and constantly "reverse engineer" their marketing strategy. Imitation, after all, is the highest form of flattery.

Posting Rhythm

Now the point of all this, as marketers, isn't that we really love babies and military personnel (although we probably do). It's to

- Increase our *Edgerank* to increase the probability that our Facebook fans will see our posts.
- Use our built-up *Edgerank* to propel posts that market our products or services into the news feeds of our fans, for free.

This gets to **posting rhythm**. Smart marketers will post ten or twenty "fun, fun, fun" posts to drive UP their Edgerank, and then one "buy, buy, buy my stuff" post that has a good chance of showing in the newsfeed. So the posting rhythm can be: *fun, fun, fun, fun, fun, fun, buy my stuff, fun, fun, fun, fun, fun, fun.*

FUN, FUN, FUN, BUY MY STUFF

Get Your Fans to Share

Even better, business Pages on Facebook will post items that their fans are likely to share with their own friends. If you post something to your Facebook Page (e.g., a contest to win a free week's supply of your products or a quote that is inspiring), and your Facebook fans share it with their friends and family, well, you've hit a home run. Why? Because Facebook (and people) pay a heck of a lot more attention to posts by people than to posts by Pages. So by all means, post stuff to your business Page that excites your fans so much that they do the sharing!

Facebook Rewards Posts by People over Posts by Pages

The reason for this tactic is that the *Edgerank* of people is much, much higher than the *Edgerank* of company Pages. So, to the extent that you can create a post that will be shared on Facebook, you can get your fans to market your company's products. Don't think in terms of only the *Edgerank* of your Page, but in the *Edgerank* of your customer evangelists (those people who not only like your Page, but interact heavily with your posts by liking them, commenting on them, and even sharing them to their own friends and family).

Let me repeat that:

> The *Edgerank* of people is much higher than the Edgerank of company Pages. **So getting your customers to share your posts is a fundamental component of an effective Facebook marketing strategy.**

To find out what's being shared in your industry, I recommend using Buzzsumo (http://www.buzzsumo.com/). Enter a keyword phrase, and Buzzsumo will tell you the highest shared content on Facebook in the past year, month, week or even day.

For example, here's a post of a military dad with a baby by Navy Federal Credit Union that got 854 "likes," 15 "comments," and 43 "shares":

Navy Federal Credit Union with Timothy Jump and 2 others

June 21 at 5:09am · 🌐

Tag your hero to wish him a Happy Father's Day!

Like · Comment · Share

👍 854 people like this.

Most Relevant ▾

↪ 43 shares

Write a comment...

💬 View all 15 comments

And here's a shameless "buy our stuff" post. Notice how few likes, comments, and shares it garnered:

Navy Federal Credit Union created an event.
June 12 at 11:00am · 🌐

Live Q&A
Let's Talk Autos and More!

Let's Talk Autos & More
June 24
37 people went   Join

Like · Comment · Share

👍 51 people like this.

💬 View 4 more comments

If you reverse engineer what Navy Federal Credit Union is doing on Facebook, it's posting items to drive up interactivity (fun stuff), and then occasionally posting items that are aimed to sell its products or services (serious stuff). So the posting rhythm is:

fun, fun, fun, fun, fun, fun, fun, fun, fun, **buy our stuff**, *fun, fun, fun, fun, fun, fun, fun,* **buy our stuff**, *fun, fun, fun, etc.*

There are two factors at work here:

> **Edgerank**: improving the *Edgerank* of posts by a Page, improves the *Edgerank* of its posts. (Note: this is also a reason to pay attention to the time of day, because *Edgerank* is determined "on the fly," and if a post does well "out of the gate," it will tend to do better over time).
>
> **Social Sharing**. Getting the fans of a Page to share the posts to their own friends and family.

Generally speaking, posts that are highly interactive get boosts on both measures. As you reverse engineer the posting strategy of competitors and/or brands you admire on Facebook, notice how they try to spur either one or both of the above.

⏩ SET UP AND OPTIMIZE YOUR FACEBOOK PAGE

Now that you've got the basics of Facebook down, it's time to set up or optimize your own company Page. A good way to do this is to compare / contrast Pages that you like and use your inventory list to identify ToDos. So, comparing Taco Bell (https://www.facebook.com/tacobell) the White House (https://www.facebook.com/WhiteHouse), and The Super Dentists (https://www.facebook.com/TheSuperDentists), let's go down item by item to see things you need to do in terms of Facebook Page setup.

Login to your Facebook Page, and then use the top menu.

- **Page Roles > Admins**. Your Page needs at least one Admin (you), but I recommend more than one. Realize that anyone who is an Admin can post to the Page, and also delete any other Admins. Your Admins should be reliable, and if you ever part ways (e.g., fire them), be sure to remove them as an Admin. *Located under Settings > Page Roles*
- **General Settings** (*Located under Settings > General*)
  - **Visitor Posts**. This setting allows users to post to the Page as well as add photos or videos. Note that Taco Bell has this "on" (anyone can post to the Page) vs. the White House, which has this "off." If you trust your fans, turn it on. If you're concerned about spam and controversy, turn it off.

- o **Tagging Ability**. Similar to the above, allows users to "tag" others in photos.
  - o **Page Moderation and Profanity Filter**. You can turn on filters that block naughty words like the "f" word, and/or enter specific words. If a user attempts to post or comment using these words, they will be blocked from your Page.
  - o **Other items**. Scroll through the list, and you can find other miscellaneous items such as banned users, post attribution, and notifications. For most of these, the default settings are fine.
- **About Your Page**. *Located under Settings > General > Page Info or click on the About Tab*. Fill out this information in detail. Note that if you are a "local Page" and you have a physical "address," this will turn on the **Review tab** and allow users to review your Page.
- **Tabs**. As you activate various components of your Facebook Page, you can reorganize your "tabs" by clicking on the "more" tab and then scrolling down to "manage tabs."

Among important Page set up issues are:

- **Visitor Posts**. If you are confident that your user community will help your brand, I recommend turning this "on," as this allows users to post information to your Page, and thereby encourages social sharing and spread. If you are worried about hostile or naughty users, turn this off. Taco Bell has this on; the White House has this off. You can see this by looking at their Facebook Pages, and notice that on Taco Bell's it shows you a Post box and says "write something."
- **Local Business Address**. If you enter a physical address (on the "about" tab) and your Page type is local business, then the **review tab** will be enabled. This allows users to review your Page and/or business. Turn it "on," if you think reviews will help you. If mobile users are important, this will also enable them to "**check in**" when they are at your business – and remember, when they "check in," Facebook will alert their friends (social sharing). (The Super Dentists (https://www.facebook.com/TheSuperDentists) has this on).
- **Call to Action Button**. This allows you to promote an action such as sign up for our newsletter, watch a video, etc. For an explanation, visit http://jmlinks.com/1d. Taco Bell has this set up for "use app." Available actions are: *Book Now, Contact Us, Use App, Play Game, Shop Now, Sign Up, or Watch Video*.

Set up Your Cover Photo and Profile Picture

Now that you've completed the basic structural set up for your Page, it's time to think about the graphic elements: the **cover photo** and the **profile picture**. The cover photo, of course, is the long horizontal photo that visitors see when they visit your Page. The profile picture is the square box that identifies your Page, both when they visit your Page and as a small icon when you post something that shows in their news feed. If you pay attention to companies like Taco Bell, the White House, Navy Federal Credit Union and the like, you'll see that they systematically rotate their cover photos. When a new cover photo is uploaded, that creates a post and an opportunity to alert your fans. Any change in the cover photo in particular "broadcasts" that change to people who like the Page.

For the technical specifications on changing your cover photo and/or profile picture, visit http://jmlinks.com/1e. The cover photo in particular is an opportunity for fun, high-quality photos and for seasonal rotations. Follow a vendor like REI (https://www.facebook.com/REI), and you'll see not only seasonal rotation but also thematic unity among their cover photos on Twitter (https://twitter.com/rei), Facebook, Instagram (https://instagram.com/rei/), etc.

For your third **TODO**, download the **Facebook Setup Worksheet**. For the worksheet, go to https://www.jm-seo.org/workbooks (click on Social Media Workbook, enter the code 'smm2016' to register if you have not already done so), and click on the link to the "Facebook Setup Worksheet." You'll answer and outline the basic setup issues for your Facebook Page.

≫ BRAINSTORM AND EXECUTE A POSTING STRATEGY

Now that you've set up your Facebook Page, you need to think about **content marketing** and your **posting strategy**. Remember that social media marketing stands or falls ultimately in terms of content. You must systematically produce and share a ton of content to your Facebook page. A good goal is at least one post per day to your Facebook Page, if not two or even three.

Turn back to your Content Marketing plan, and remember you'll need both "other people's content" and "your own content" to post:

- **Photographs and Images**. Facebook is very visual, and you'll need to systematically identify photographs and images that fit with your brand message and ideally encourage likes, comments, and shares.

- **Blog Post Summaries**. To the extent that you have an active blog and are posting items that fit with friends, family, and fun, post headlines, short summaries and links to your blog.
  - Note that the first or "featured" image will become the shareable image, and that the META DESCRIPTION will become the default description when sharing. Choose striking, fun images for your blog posts!
- **Quotes**. People love quotes, and taking memorable quotes and pasting them on graphics is a win/win.
- **Infographics and Instructographics**. Factoids, how to articles, especially ones that are fun, are excellent for Facebook.
- **Quizzes, Surveys, and Response-provoking posts**. Ask a question, and get an answer or more. Great for encouraging interactivity.

Turn to the content marketing section of the *Social Media Toolbook* for a list of tools that will help you find other people's content and create your own. I recommend Hootsuite (https://www.hootsuite.com/) to manage all your social postings across platforms.

For your fourth **TODO**, download the **Facebook Posting Worksheet**. For the worksheet, go to https://www.jm-seo.org/workbooks (click on Social Media Workbook, enter the code 'smm2016' to register if you have not already done so), and click on the link to the "Facebook Posting Worksheet." You'll systematically built out a posting strategy based on other people's content and your own content.

Once you get this done, it's time to post. Remember that Facebook marketing requires a commitment of time and resources. You can even create an editorial calendar and assigned **TODOS** for your team so that every week you are posting to Facebook on a regular basis.

How frequently should you post?

Because the Facebook news feed is very crowded, you can safely post quite frequently; even several times a day. But this differs with your audience, so pay attention using the Insights tab as to what posts get the best response, and whether the time of day matters. Pay attention as well to your Page likes and unlikes, to see if your posts are delighting or annoying your followers.

Experiment and measure, and you'll figure out a posting rhythm that works for you.

POST 80% OR MORE ABOUT "FUN," AND 20% OR LESS ABOUT "BUY MY STUFF."

Don't forget that most of your posts (80% or more) should be about friends, family, and fun, and only a few (20% or less) should be direct pitches to buy your stuff. If you oversell your stuff, your *Edgerank* will suffer and your fans will unlike your Page.

Finally, you can "pin" a post to the top of your Page, so that it is the first post people will see when they visit your Page. Just click on the down chevron on the top right corner of Facebook, and select "Pin to top" to "pin" a post to the top of your Page.

Here's a screenshot:

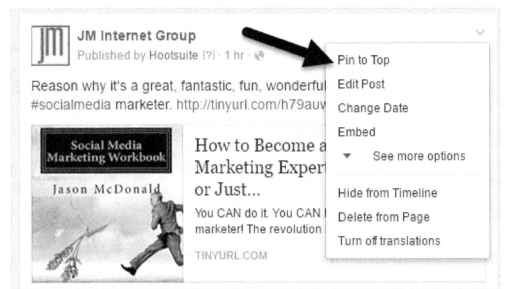

» PROMOTE YOUR FACEBOOK PAGE AND POSTS

Once you've set up your Page, and begun to populate it with posts on a regular basis, you've essential "set up" your "party." You've created a good-looking Facebook Page for your business, and you're posting so frequently that when someone lands on the Page, they'll see there's a lot of interesting, fun content. These "trust indicators" will encourage them to "like" your Page, thereby allowing you to post to your timeline and thereby (hopefully) reach them when they check their news feed.

Now it's time to send out the "invitations," that is to promote your Facebook Page to users. In and of itself, a Facebook Page will not be self-promoting!

Remember: social media is a party. You must have yummy yummy food and entertainment for people to show up, and stick around. So as you promote your Facebook Page, always keep front and center "what's in it for them" – what will they get by "liking" your Facebook page, and checking it out on a regular basis?

Assuming your Page has lots of great content that users will like, here are some common ways to promote your Page:

- **Real World to Social.** Don't forget the real world! If you are a museum store, for example, be sure that the cashiers recommend to people that they "like" your Facebook Page? *Why? Because they'll get insider tips, fun do-it-yourself posts, announcements on upcoming museum and museum store events, etc.*
- **Facebook Checkins.** If you are a local business and have entered your local business address into Facebook, this will enable Facebook "check in" on the mobile phone. When a customer walks into your brick-and-mortar store, ask them to "check in" via Facebook. Give them an incentive, such as a weekly drawing for a $50 gift certificate chosen from among people who have "checked in." When they "check in," Facebook alerts their friends and family, thereby leveraging a current customer to reach new customers. You can even temporarily use "check in" at a trade show or real-world event by temporarily making your business address the same as the convention center.
- **Reviews.** By entering your address into Facebook, you enable the "reviews" tab. Ask customers to review you on Facebook; when they write a review, Facebook may alert their friends and family, thereby leveraging one happy customer to reach other new customers.
- **Cross-Promotion**. Link your website to your Facebook Page, your blog posts to your Facebook Page, your Twitter to your Facebook Page, etc. Notice how big brands like REI do this: one digital property promotes another digital property.
- **Email**. Email your customer list and ask them to "like" your Page. Again, you must have a reason why they'll like it: what's in it for them? Have a contest, give away something for free, or otherwise motivate them to click from the email to your Page, and then "like" the Page.

- **Facebook Internal**. Interact with other Pages, share their content, comment on timely topics using #hashtags, and reach out to complementary Pages to work with you on co-promotion.
- **Use Facebook Plugins**. Facebook has numerous plugins that allow you to "embed" your Facebook Page on your website, and thereby nurture cross promotion. To learn more about plugins, visit https://developers.facebook.com/docs/plugins. If you are using WordPress, you can use the official Facebook plugin at https://wordpress.org/plugins/facebook/. In this way, your blog can promote your Facebook Page, and your Facebook Page can promote your blog. Similarly, your YouTube videos can promote your Facebook Page, and your Facebook Page can promote your YouTube Videos.
- **Leverage your Fans**. People who like your Page are your best promoters. When they first like your Page, when they comment on a post, when they "check in" to your local business on Facebook, and especially when they share your posts, their friends see this. Remember, it's *social* (!) media, and encouraging your customers to share your content is the name of the game. Create content that your users will pro-actively want to share such as funny memes, contests with give-aways, scholarship opportunities, coupons, useful "how to" articles, etc.

GET YOUR FANS TO SHARE YOUR POSTS ON FACEBOOK

Advertise. Advertising is increasingly important to success on Facebook. Just a few years back, Pages could really grow organically and be seen organically in the news feed. With the news feed increasingly crowded, Facebook has clearly prioritized content from real people over content from brands, and all but hidden posts by brand Pages. In many ways, Facebook has become **pay to play**. Here are ways you can promote your Page and posts through **advertising**.

Promote Your Page. When you log in as a Page administrator, you'll see a blue button called "promote your Page." Click on that, and then follow the instructions to demographically target potential customers. Facebook will then suggest your

Page to people, as a Page to "like." You can even specifically target certain demographic groups (such as your competitor's customers).

Boost your Posts. When you make a post to Facebook, a blue boost button will appear on the bottom. If you click boost, you can demographically target an audience as well as "boost" your Post to people who already like your Page.

Advertise Directly. You can advertise anything on Facebook – either your Facebook Page, a post by your Page, or cross-links to items on your website. Simply click on the "advertising" tab at the top right of the page, and set up an advertising campaign.

The great thing about Facebook advertising is that it is demographically targeted. You can even target a competitor's Facebook audience to grow your own Page. *(Note: this is a growing criticism of Facebook by companies: Facebook "sells" your user community to the highest bidder, so you build up your audience and then they sell it to your competition).*

To learn more about Facebook advertising, visit https://www.facebook.com/business.

▶▶ MEASURE YOUR RESULTS

Facebook marketing offers pretty good metrics. Inside of Facebook, click on the **Insights** tab at the top of your Facebook Page (when you're logged in, of course). Here you'll find an overview to your Facebook activity, and a post-by-post breakdown of the reach of a post and the engagement. A graph will tell you when your fans are most engaged. You can select "Pages to watch," and keep an eye on your competitors – even down to which posts of theirs were the most interactive.

For any of your posts, click on the post, and a popup window will give you drill-down information. Remember: you are trying to improve *Edgerank*, so pay attention to the positive and negative interactivity. Here's a screenshot of a post of "other people's content" to the JM Internet Group Facebook Page:

JM Internet Group
Published by Hootsuite [?] · June 22 at 5:55pm · 🌐

Tips for better #LinkedIn profile pictures. The rule of 3rds? http://read.bi
/1RXwtC7

7 simple LinkedIn photo tricks that will dramatically increase your...

LinkedIn is a great place to connect with...

READ.BI | BY PRAVEEN PATEL

232 people reached

Boost Post

Like · Comment · Share · 👍 7 ↪ 1

232 People Reached

8 Likes, Comments & Shares

7 Likes	**7** On Post	**0** On Shares
0 Comments	**0** On Post	**0** On Shares
1 Shares	**1** On Post	**0** On Shares

10 Post Clicks

0 Photo Views	**8** Link Clicks	**2** Other Clicks ℹ

NEGATIVE FEEDBACK

0 Hide Post	**0** Hide All Posts
0 Report as Spam	**0** Unlike Page

And here's a screenshot of a post of our own content that was boosted for $200.00

Pay attention to the *reach*, *likes*, *comments*, *shares*, and *clicks* of all your posts (both organic and advertised). All of this is influencing *Edgerank*. The *more interactive* your Page and posts are, the *higher* your Edgerank, and the *higher* your Edgerank the *more* people will see your posts and Page.

Interactivity is where it's "at" on Facebook!

Back to the top tabs, you can also drill down into people, to see the demographics of who is interacting with your Page. All in all, Facebook provides excellent insights into who is interacting with your Page. Use this information to make your Page better and better!

Google Analytics

For many of us, we want to drive traffic from Facebook to our website, even to our ecommerce store or to download a free eBook or software package to get a sales lead. Sign up for Google Analytics (https://www.google.com/analytics) and install the required tracking code. Inside of your Google Analytics account on the left column, drill down by clicking on Acquisition > Social > Overview. Then on the right hand side of the screen you'll see a list of Social Networks. Find Facebook on that list, and click on that. Google Analytics will tell you what URLs people clicked to from Facebook to your Website, giving you insights into what types of web content people find attractive.

You can also create a custom Advanced Segment to look at only Facebook traffic and its behavior. For information on how to create custom Advanced Segments in Google Analytics, go to http://jmlinks.com/1f. For the Google help files on Advanced Segments go to http://jmlinks.com/1g.

In sum, inside of Facebook you can see how people interact with your Page and posts. Inside of Google Analytics, you can see where they land on your website and what they do after they arrive.

≫≫ DELIVERABLE: A FACEBOOK MARKETING PLAN

We've come to the end our chapter on Facebook, and your **DELIVERABLE** has arrived. For the worksheet, go to https://www.jm-seo.org/workbooks (click on Social Media Workbook, enter the code 'smm2016' to register if you have not already done so), and click on the link to the "Facebook Marketing Plan." By filling out this plan, you and your team will establish a vision of what you want to achieve via Facebook.

≫ TOP FACEBOOK MARKETING TOOLS AND RESOURCES

Here are the top tools and resources to help you with Facebook marketing. For an up-to-date list, go to https://www.jm-seo.org/workbooks (click on Social Media Workbook, enter the code 'smm2016' to register if you have not already done so), and click on the link to the *Social Media Toolbook* link, and drill down to the Facebook chapter.

FACEBOOK LIKE BUTTON FOR WEB -
https://developers.facebook.com/docs/plugins/like-button

> The Facebook Like button lets a user share your content with friends on Facebook. When the user clicks the Like button on your site, a story appears in the user's friends' News Feeds with a link back to your website.
>
> **Rating:** 5 Stars | **Category:** tool

FACEBOOK HELP CENTER - http://facebook.com/help

The 'missing' help pages on Facebook. Useful for learning everything on the king of social media. Links on advertising, business accounts, connect, Facebook places and more.

Rating: 5 Stars | **Category:** overview

FACEBOOK SOCIAL PLUGINS (LIKE BOXES AND BUTTONS) -
http://developers.facebook.com/docs/plugins

Make it easy for your Facebook fans and fans-to-be to 'like' your company and Facebook pages you create. The best Facebook resource for all plugins to integrate Facebook with your website, including the Like, Share & Send Button, Comments, Follow Button and others.

Rating: 5 Stars | **Category:** tool

HOOTSUITE - https://hootsuite.com/

Manage all of your social media accounts, including multiple Twitter profiles through HootSuite. HootSuite makes it easy to manage multiple users over various social media accounts and allows you to track statistics. LOVE THIS TOOL!

Rating: 5 Stars | **Category:** vendor

KEYHOLE - http://keyhole.co

This tool provides real-time social conversation tracking for Twitter, Facebook, and Instagram. Use this tool to measure conversations around your business, identify prospective clients and influencers talking about your services, and find relevant content. Enables tracking of hashtags, keywords, and URLs.

Rating: 4 Stars | **Category:** tool

FACEBOOK ADVERTISING - http://facebook.com/advertising

Facebook advertising opportunities. Run text ads on Facebook by selecting the demographics of who you want to reach. Pay-per-click model.

Rating: 4 Stars | **Category:** overview

LikeAlyzer - http://likealyzer.com

LikeAlyzer analyzes the Facebook Page you enter and provides a very simple, easy to read report even the most statistically averse will understand. Best of all, LikeAlyzer provides an overall score and recommendations on where/how to improve. Recommendations are customized and analysis is based on the metrics the company has found to be important: presence, dialogue, action and information.

Rating: 4 Stars | **Category:** tool

Buffer - https://buffer.com/

Schedule tweets and other social media activity in the future. Competitor to Hootsuite.

Rating: 4 Stars | **Category:** tool

ShortStack - http://www.shortstack.com/

ShortStack is a nifty program to optimize your social media campaigns on platforms like Facebook, Twitter, Instagram and Pinterest. On Facebook, ShortStack provides polls and surveys, contents, and forms for newsletter signups, contact us, etc. and is free for Business Pages up to a certain number of Likes. No expiring trials. No credit card required.

Rating: 4 Stars | **Category:** service

Facebook Pages Help Center - https://facebook.com/help/281592001947683

Here it is. The help center for Facebook 'pages', where businesses, organizations, and brands live. Use this handy dandy resource from Facebook to answer your most basic questions - such as how to set up a page for a business, how to administer your page (e.g., comments, kicking users off and all that fun stuff), as well as how to manage admins. It is the first 'goto' page for help with Facebook Pages for business.

Rating: 4 Stars | **Category:** resource

IFTTT - https://ifttt.com

This app, If Then Then That, is a great tool for linking multiple social media accounts. It allows you to create 'recipes' that link your tools exactly the way you like them! For example: make a recipe that adds to a Google Apps spreadsheet every time a particular user uploads to Instagram - a great way to keep up with your competitors SMM strategies! With over 120 supported applications, the 'recipes' are endless, making this a good tool for your SMM strategies.

Rating: 4 Stars | **Category:** tool

TAG BOARD - https://tagboard.com/

Hashtags have moved beyond Twitter. This amazing cool tool allows you to take a hashtag and browse Facebook and Twitter and Instagram, etc., so see posts that relate to that hashtag. Then you can find related tags. Oh, and you can use it as a content discovery tool, too.

Rating: 4 Stars | **Category:** tool

FACEBOOK PAGE BASICS (FOR BUSINESS) - https://www.facebook.com/business/learn/facebook-page-basics

Confused by Facebook for Business? Have no fear, Learn How, Facebook's online learning center for businesses, is here. This easy-to-use resource, complete with videos, images and step-by-step instructions, answers businesses' frequently asked questions, like how to create a Page, and how to create a Custom Audience. Learn How content is organized to be flexible: use it in-depth, or as a reference library as questions arise.

Rating: 4 Stars | **Category:** tutorial

FACEBOOK FOR BUSINESS: MARKETING SOLUTIONS - https://www.facebook.com/marketing

Official pages on Facebook-approved 'best practices' for marketing your company on Facebook.

Rating: 4 Stars | **Category:** overview

REBATE OFFER

CLAIM YOUR $39.99 REBATE! HERE'S HOW -

4. Go to Amazon.com and search for 'Social Media Marketing Workbook' or click http://jmlinks.com/smm.
5. Write a short, honest **review of the book** and indicate you've been gifted a 'review copy'.
6. Click https://jm-seo.org/rebate/ and fill out the **REBATE FORM**.

WE WILL THEN -

- **Refund** you the full price of the print edition (**$39.99**), so that you will have received a **FREE** review copy

~ $39.99 REBATE OFFER ~

~ LIMITED TO ONE PER CUSTOMER ~

EXPIRES: 10/1/2016

SUBJECT TO CHANGE WITHOUT NOTICE

GOT QUESTIONS? CALL 800-298-4065

3

LINKEDIN

If **Facebook** is all about *friends, family*, and *fun* – a kind of 24/7 *company picnic*, **LinkedIn** is all about *business networking* – a kind of 24/7 online *industry conference* or *trade show*. Indeed, if you've ever been to a big trade show such as the *Consumer Electronics Show* in Las Vegas, or the annual *Direct Marketing Association (DMA) show* in Boston, you've likely attended corporate *meet-and-greets, wine and cheese* events, or *breakout learning sessions* on important industry topics. These industry conference events feature free food and entertainment, a speech or two by the CEO, and lots of *business networking* between vendors and potential customers. Dressed in business casual, people listen attentively, are in "learning" mode, and are also ready to introduce themselves and their products to you and others.

Business networking, in short, is the No. 1 activity via LinkedIn marketing!

It's totally appropriate to walk up to total strangers and introduce your (business) self; even better is to get one business contact to introduce you to another. To "schmooze" on LinkedIn is to succeed. (*If you don't know what schmoozing is, see* http://jmlinks.com/3f).

Accordingly, at a real world trade show, we'd have –

> "*Hi, my name is Jason McDonald, what's yours?*"

Or

> "*Hey, Sue, this is Jason McDonald, my social media expert friend. You and he have a lot in common because you're crazy for Twitter, so I'd thought I'd introduce you.*"

Or

Welcome to our booth, we're showcasing our latest embedded systems technologies. Would you like a demo?

Or

Our CEO is presenting a talk in ten minutes at the technical conference on the new ways in which cybersecurity can impact your brand. Would you like to attend?

And on LinkedIn, we have

Connections requests between people.

Introductions by one business contact to another

Updates on one's profile, sharing news, events, and insights.

Learning sessions occurring on LinkedIn groups that discuss industry trends and technologies.

And, company Pages on LinkedIn, which are the functional equivalent of a booth at a trade show.

In short, the "virtual world" of LinkedIn mirrors the "real world" of in industry conference or trade show.

This chapter will explore **LinkedIn for business**, with one important exception: **job search**. (While LinkedIn is THE social platform for job search, we will confine our explanation to the use of LinkedIn by an established company, or employed individual, seeking to reach out to existing and new customers through social media.) Our focus is on you as an employee / owner, or you as a company (or you and your employees acting as a team) using LinkedIn to **advance your company marketing goals**: building brand identity, staying in contact with prospects and customers, encouraging social spread, putting your best foot forward so that you are perceived as a trustworthy business partner, and using LinkedIn to sell more stuff. (For information on LinkedIn for personal branding, job search, and career-building, see http://jmlinks.com/jobsbook.)

In this Chapter, will explore the four big marketing opportunities on LinkedIn: 1) setting up your **profile** (as well as those of your employees) as a public resume, 2) using

LinkedIn to **network** with customers and prospects, 3) participating in LinkedIn **groups**, and 4) leveraging a LinkedIn **company page** for your business.

Let's get started!

ToDo List:

» Explore how LinkedIn Works

» The LinkedIn Profile as Public Resume

» Schmoozing on LinkedIn: Your Social Rolodex

» Being Active on LinkedIn: Posting and Groups

» LinkedIn Company Pages

» Promoting Your LinkedIn Profile, Posts, and Pages

» Measuring your Results

»» Deliverable: A LinkedIn Marketing Plan

»» Appendix: Top LinkedIn Marketing Tools and Resources

» Explore How LinkedIn Works

Let's review the basic structure of LinkedIn:

- **Individuals have LinkedIn profiles**, which function as online resumes listing skills, education, and interests. Profiles allow one individual to "connect" with another individual; once connected, any post by individual No. 1 will show in the news feed of individual No. 2. In this sense, LinkedIn profiles function structurally in exactly the same way as Facebook profiles: you send connection requests (friend requests), and once accepted and connected, you and the other individual can directly check each other out, communicate via LinkedIn messaging, and see posts to each other's news feed.
- **Individuals can join groups.** While groups on Facebook are of limited business interest, groups on LinkedIn are very important. As at a major trade show, LinkedIn has "break out" groups by topic (from petroleum engineering to marketing to advertising to WordPress web design and beyond), that bring like-

minded people together in a professional way. Note, however, that it is people (and not business Pages!) that participate in groups.

- **Companies can have LinkedIn Pages.** As on Facebook, companies can create business Pages on LinkedIn. Individuals can follow companies, and by doing so, give permission to that company to converse. Posts by the company have a chance to show in the news feed of individuals who have "followed" a particular company.
- **Posts and the News Feed.** When an individual shares an update to his or her LinkedIn profile, or a company shares an update to its LinkedIn Page, those updates (similar to Facebook posts) show up in the news feed of connected individuals. LinkedIn, like Facebook, therefore has a posting rhythm in which individuals and businesses compete for eyeballs and attention.

Structurally, therefore, LinkedIn is very similar to Facebook. *Profiles and connection requests, Pages and following, posts and news feeds.*

However, the **structural** similarities hide a very different **culture** on LinkedIn. Whereas on Facebook, the center of marketing is the business Page. On LinkedIn, the center of gravity lies with the personal profiles of employees. Whereas on Facebook, you primarily interact with business pages in terms of marketing, on LinkedIn you primarily interact with the employees of various businesses.

LINKEDIN'S CENTER OF GRAVITY IS THE PERSONAL PROFILE

LinkedIn's center of gravity is person-to-person interaction. This makes sense if you compare a company picnic (Facebook) with a business networking event (LinkedIn). Whereas at the former, you interact with the company (who brings the food and entertainment, and pays for the party), at the latter, you interact with the employees of the company, talking about industry events and schmoozing about shared interests. You don't business network with *companies*, after all. You business network with *individuals.*

Whereas on Facebook, it's impolite to ask what one "does for a living" or to "pitch business ideas," on LinkedIn this is so important as to be the core function. People on

LinkedIn, in short, are in **business networking mode**. This makes it a fantastic social medium for business-to-business marketing!

LINKEDIN IS THE 24/7 BUSINESS NETWORKING EVENT

In addition, LinkedIn groups are rather robust, especially in technical areas. For a technical industry such as oil and gas, people increasingly use LinkedIn groups as a way to stay professionally educated. LinkedIn's acquisition of Lynda.com (https://www.lynda.com/) speaks to this growing trend to use LinkedIn as a way to stay up-to-date about an industry. Finally, although business Pages do exist on LinkedIn and are increasingly important for business-to-business companies, their utility is much weaker than on Facebook for business-to-consumer companies.

LinkedIn is a Team Sport

Perhaps the most important distinction of all is to think of Facebook as a *company-first* marketing platform and LinkedIn as an *employee team-first* marketing platform. Whereas on Facebook, you can manage your marketing "top down," using your company Page as your primary customer interaction vehicle, on LinkedIn you must rely heavily on your employees. Every customer-facing employee needs to be "on board" with your LinkedIn marketing: he or she needs a robust LinkedIn profile, and a passionate commitment to schmooze with other LinkedIn members through outreach, posting, and group participation. To really succeed at LinkedIn as a business, each and every customer-facing employee must actively participate as an individual, and your company should manage its own LinkedIn business page in tandem. LinkedIn, in sum, is an **employee team sport** (more on this later).

> ***Employee participation*** *+ an active **LinkedIn business page** = LinkedIn marketing **success**.*

Throughout this Chapter, I will often refer to an individual "you" as participating in LinkedIn, but remember when I say "you," I mean "you" as an individual as well as "you" as a team of like-minded, enthusiastic employees. If your company is one employee, five employees, or five hundred employees, the real key to LinkedIn success is to get everyone "on board" and participating!

Search LinkedIn

First, you'll need to research LinkedIn to estimate its value to your business marketing efforts. (We'll assume you've already set up a basic personal profile on LinkedIn. If not, visit https://www.linkedin.com/ and sign up). For your first **TODO**, log on to LinkedIn, and search by keywords that are relevant to your company or industry. Identify persons, groups, and companies that are active on these topics.

Simply type a keyword of interest into the search bar at the top of the LinkedIn page (e.g., "organic food" if your company is involved in the organic industry, or "oil and gas," if your company works in the petroleum industry). On the left, click on people, jobs, companies, groups, universities, or posts, to narrow down your search and browse what's going on.

Here's a screenshot:

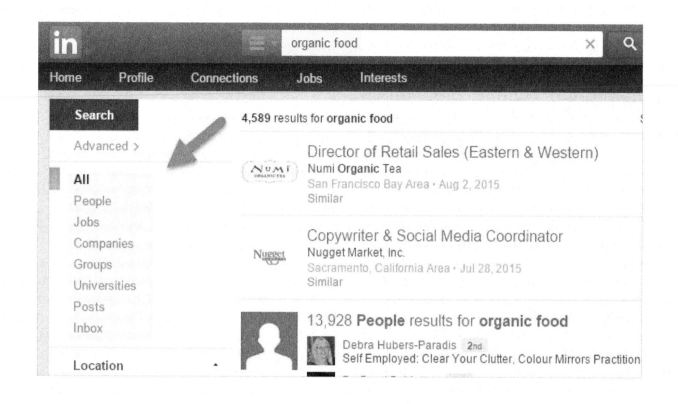

As you begin touring LinkedIn with the question of whether (or not) your potential customers actively use it, narrow your search by type, and ask these questions:

People. Do you see many people with relevant job skills and active profiles on LinkedIn? You're not looking to hire them; you're looking to see if your target customers are engaged enough on LinkedIn to be actively updating their profiles and posting to their accounts. Are they active on LinkedIn?

Companies. Especially for business-to-business sectors, LinkedIn company pages can be quite robust. Are your competitors on LinkedIn? Are similar companies? If so, what are they doing? If not, why not? Do you see a lot (or a little) interaction on the company pages?

Groups. LinkedIn groups act like breakout sessions at a trade show. Do you see relevant groups on LinkedIn? Are they active with many members, or dormant with few? What kinds of discussions are going on?

Posts. Who is posting on relevant topics on LinkedIn and why? What is the quality of the posts, and are there many comments, and reshares to specific posts?

As is always the case in social media, there's no point in pouring time, treasure, and talent into LinkedIn marketing if you don't see your customers online. But if you do, then it will be well worth the effort.

For your first **TODO**, download the **LinkedIn Research Worksheet**. For the worksheet, go to https://www.jm-seo.org/workbooks (click on Social Media Workbook, enter the code 'smm2016' to register if you have not already done so), and click on the link to the "LinkedIn Research Worksheet." You'll answer questions as to whether your potential customers are on LinkedIn, identify individuals and companies to follow, and inventory what you like and dislike about their LinkedIn set up and marketing strategy.

» THE LINKEDIN PROFILE AS PUBLIC RESUME

The personal profile is the foundation of LinkedIn. Just as on Facebook, an individual needs to set up a LinkedIn profile and populate it with information about him or herself. Unlike on Facebook, however, this personal profile is highly visible and acts as a kind of "public resume." As a business owner or marketer, you'll want your own well-optimized profile, but you'll also want to motivate your CEO, other key executives, and any employees that are customer-facing to potential clients to also set up and optimize their LinkedIn profiles.

The **TODOS** here are:

1. **Sign up** for LinkedIn as a personal profile (and encourage everyone else in the company to sign up as well!)
2. Identify the **keywords** that represent your business value to other people, that is keywords that "describe you" as a businessperson and/or a company or non-profit, such as "WordPress web designer," "CPA," or "Business Coach for startups," or "Apple iPhone App development firm."
3. **Optimize** your personal profile so that it –
   a. Clearly and quickly represents your **personal business value proposition** as well as that of your **company**.
   b. Is **findable** via LinkedIn search by **keywords**.
   c. Establishes **trust** in you and your company as an authority and someone who is worthy of a business partnership.

First and foremost, think of **search** and **trust**. By search, we mean that people will go to Google and/or LinkedIn after they have met you or a key employee. They'll "search" you on the Internet with an eye to deciding whether you have any skeletons in your closet, whether you seem knowledgeable about your subject, and whether you seem like a good person to do business with. This trust will flow "up" to the company as well. Nowadays, people go to networking events such as trade shows, and return with business cards and email addresses. They then "vet" these people and their companies by searching them on Google and on LinkedIn. Indeed, you can optimize your LinkedIn profile to show high on searches for your own name plus keywords.

Think of your LinkedIn profile as your public resume. Think of your employees' profiles' as their business cards to exchange at an industry trade show.

To see mine, visit http://jmlinks.com/3g. Note that my LinkedIn profile appears in about position four on a Google search for *Jason McDonald SEO*. Here's a screenshot:

Jason McDonald | LinkedIn
https://www.linkedin.com/in/**jason**eg3 ▾
San Francisco Bay Area - SEO, AdWords & Social Media Consulting & Expert Witness
- San Francisco Bay Area
View Jason McDonald's professional profile on LinkedIn. LinkedIn is the ... SEO,
AdWords & Social Media Consulting & Expert Witness - San Francisco Bay Area.

The concept here is when someone meets me (or meets you, or meets a key employee), you want to use LinkedIn to show prominently in a search for your name plus keywords, plus you want your LinkedIn profile to show off your expertise and talents. Just like a "real" resume, your LinkedIn "resume" should be optimized to be found and to put your best foot forward. It should also be publically viewable without the necessity of being logged into LinkedIn.

Having optimized your own profile, now it's time to call a "group meeting" of your employee team. Have them each optimize their LinkedIn profiles vis-à-vis your target keywords and target customers. It is essential that **all** key, customer-facing employees optimize their LinkedIn profiles.

LinkedIn is a team sport: you need every employee "on board" with full and eager participation!

As you work with key employees, let's turn to the steps to **optimize** a LinkedIn profile for search and trust.

Define your target keywords. What value do you provide for others in a business relationship? Remember: you are NOT looking for a job. Generally, you are positioning yourself as a "helpful expert" in a defined area. Are you a WordPress expert? An expert CPA for small business? An architect with a focus on ecofriendly design? Brainstorm and define the logical keywords that someone would append to your name. There are, for example, many "Jason McDonalds" in this world. But I want to rank, and be trusted as the Jason McDonald that can help you with **SEO**, **Social Media**, and **AdWords**. Thus, I embed those keywords in my profile, and write it well enough to convey my value as a helpful expert in those endeavors.

Once you have identified your keywords, weave them strategically into your LinkedIn profile.

To access these features, click on *profile > edit profile* while logged in to LinkedIn. Hover over an area, and click on the pencil to edit.

Professional Headline. This is the most important text on your LinkedIn profile for search discoverability. It should answer the question, "What can you do for me." Here's a screenshot of mine:

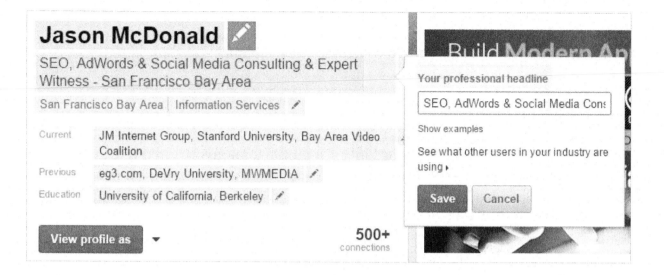

Current (Position). This is your current job, so state it well.

Summary. Like a real resume, this describes your skills and experience. *Do NOT write this like you are looking for a job, if you are NOT looking for a job!* Instead, use ALL CAPS and other ways to break up the content. Populate it with relevant keywords that people might search on LinkedIn, and make it easy to read. It should state your business value proposition succinctly. Write this "as if" you were explaining to someone at a business networking event what you do, and how this is relevant for what they might need.

Experience. Here's where you input your current and past employment. If your company is on LinkedIn with a company page (and, of course, it should be), a logo will be available. Again, write succinct summaries of current and past employment that contain logical keywords (do not overdo this), and explain how you can help an interested party to accomplish something of business value.

Languages. Input any languages you speak.

Education. Don't be shy. Populate your education section with your educational achievements, not only degrees but any awards or extra-curricular activities.

Additional Info. Fill out as indicated, especially the "advice for contacting" so that it's easy for prospects to find you.

Honors and Awards. Got any? Add them.

Groups. LinkedIn groups to which you are a member will show here.

A Word about Groups

At this point, we are optimizing your LinkedIn profile for **search** and **trust**. In terms of groups, therefore, you might consider joining groups not because you plan to actively participate in them but because they convey your interests and skills. For example, I am a member of both the Harvard and UC Berkeley alumni associations really just to convey that I am smart, and attended these prestigious institutions. Similarly, I am a member of Ad Age and WordPress experts groups to convey my interest and expertise in those topics. (I don't actually participate in these groups in any serious way – I'm too busy!) Think of groups as you would think of college extracurricular activities on your resume: to convey interests and skill.

Profile Visibility

At this point, scroll back up, just under the blue "View profile as" button and click on gear icon, next to the the little LinkedIn logo on the left with the https:// web link. Here's a screenshot:

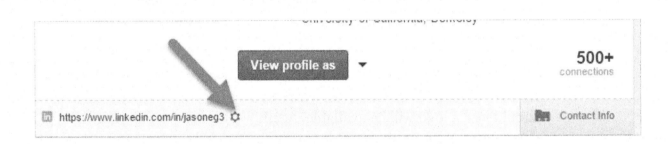

By clicking on the gear icon, you open up the privacy settings of LinkedIn. These appear on the right hand side.

Your public profile URL. Set this to be something short and easy to remember; this becomes what is visible on a Google search.

Customize your Public Profile. Here, you can control what is viewable to anyone either on LinkedIn or via a Google search.

Your public profile badge. Click here, and LinkedIn will give you the code to place on your blog or website, so people can easily view your profile. To see it in action, visit https://www.jasonmcdonald.org/ and click on the LinkedIn icon on the right.

If you click on "Create a public profile badge," which is right underneath "Your public profile badge," LinkedIn will give you the HTML code so that you can put a direct link on your personal blog, company website, etc., to your LinkedIn profile. This is great for cross-fertilization, and to establish yourself as a "helpful expert" on other venues. Here's a screenshot:

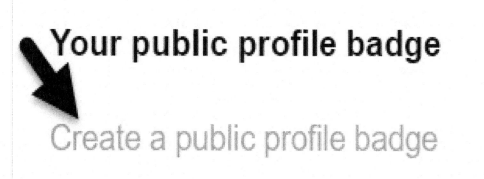

A word about privacy. For most of us, we want to be highly **visible** *(non-private)* on LinkedIn. We want potential customers, friends, and business associates to easily find us. Therefore, set your public profile as "visible to everyone," and check all of the boxes below. *If, for some reason, you do NOT want to be publically visible on LinkedIn, then set the visibility and check boxes accordingly.*

One of the more common mistakes people make is to think of the LinkedIn profile like the Facebook profile: whereas on Facebook, you often want to be *invisible / private* to strangers, on LinkedIn you often want to be *visible / public* to strangers. Accordingly, setting your LinkedIn to *private* defeats the purposes of search and trust as part of your LinkedIn marketing.

For most people, therefore, I recommend to set LinkedIn to fully *visible / public*.

GENERALLY, LINKEDIN IS *PUBLIC* PROFILE & *PUBLIC* COMPANY, WHILE FACEBOOK IS *PRIVATE* PROFILE & *PUBLIC* COMPANY

Now close your settings window, go back to the basic profile page, and click on "Contact info" on the far right. Here, you'll see your email, phone, IM, and address as well as social media links. Here's a screenshot:

Visible to your connections

Email   jasoneg3@gmail.com   Phone   510-894-6169 (work)

IM   Address

Visible to everyone on LinkedIn

Twitter   jmgrp

WeChat

Websites   Contact Jason
           Read Jason's Blog
           Follow Jason on G+

https://www.linkedin.com/in/jasoneg3   Contact Info

Generally, I would not put your physical address here (*too many crazy stalkers on the Internet*), but I would put your email and phone. As for the social icons, LinkedIn has a direct link to your Twitter account. As for websites, you can either use their standard descriptions, or if you click "other" you can set these to what you like. I have set mine, for example, to "Contact Jason," "Read Jason's Blog," and "Follow Jason on G+." Here's a screenshot:

You'll need to know the http:// link for each. When enabled, this makes it easy for anyone to contact you on LinkedIn. Importantly, this means that anyone will be able to contact you: 1st level, 2nd level, and even 3rd level connections. If you leave these items blank, then only 1st-level connections will be able to easily contact you via LinkedIn.

Therefore:

> *If you want to be highly findable and easy-to-reach via LinkedIn, be sure to enable the Websites section under your contact information.*

At that point, you're done with populating and optimizing your LinkedIn profile for **search** and **trust**. Congratulate yourself: you've optimized your LinkedIn public resume!

For your second **TODO**, download the **LinkedIn Profile Worksheet**. For the worksheet, go to https://www.jm-seo.org/workbooks (click on Social Media Workbook, enter the code 'smm2016' to register if you have not already done so), and click on the link to the "LinkedIn Profile Worksheet." You'll answer questions to help you set up and optimize your LinkedIn Profile.

Note: as we will discuss below, if you have several "outward-facing" employees, it's an excellent idea to sit down as a company group and have a LinkedIn optimization workshop. Have each and every important employee optimize his or her LinkedIn profile.

Recommendations and Endorsements

While building out your profile, you'll notice that some people have many **recommendations** or **endorsements**. **Recommendations**, like references for a resume, are generally all positive. After all, you control them: why ask for a reference from a boss or coworker who won't give you a glowing endorsement? Similarly, LinkedIn will prompt you (and your connections) to complete **endorsements** for each other concerning relevant skills. These build out like "merit badges" on your profile, making you look trustworthy.

Note: you control whether recommendations show on your public profile; you can suppress any you do not like.

Solicit Recommendations and Endorsements

Your **TODO** here is to ask for recommendations and endorsements from friends, coworkers, and business colleagues. One of the best ways to get them is to pro-actively do them for other people. After completing a project with an outside vendor, for example, connect to that person on LinkedIn and write him or her a glowing recommendation and endorsement. Often, they will reciprocate. *(This is called "pre-emptive" recommendations in LinkedIn lingo.)* Regardless of how you get them, getting many positive recommendations and endorsements will make your LinkedIn profile shine.

» SCHMOOZING ON LINKEDIN: YOUR SOCIAL ROLODEX

Nearly everyone needs an optimized personal profile on LinkedIn, if for no other purpose than job search. For those whose job is "client or customer facing," meaning identifying, interacting, and schmoozing with potential clients, the primary purpose of LinkedIn is to schmooze. (Schmoozing, of course, is another word for business networking: expanding your circle of business contacts, nurturing their respect for you, and keeping top of mind so that when they have a business opportunity, they think of you).

By nurturing your 1st level contacts and being active on LinkedIn, you can use LinkedIn as your online social rolodex, extending beyond just people you actually know to people you'd like to know for your business needs. Let's investigate schmoozing on LinkedIn, namely:

1ˢᵗ level contacts: these are people who have accepted your connection requests on LinkedIn.

2ⁿᵈ level contacts: these are 1ˢᵗ level contacts of your 1ˢᵗ level contacts (friends of friends, as it were).

LinkedIn Connections: What's Your Bacon Number?

Your "bacon number" is a term coined to humorously point out that nearly everyone on the planet is connected to actor Kevin Bacon. Google, for example, has a funny hidden Easter egg: go to Google and type in a famous person's name followed by "bacon number," for example: "Cher Bacon Number" or visit http://jmlinks.com/12u. Cher has a Bacon number of two because she and Jack Nicholson appeared in *The Witches of Eastwick*, and Jack Nicholson and Kevin Bacon appeared in *A Few Good Men*.

So Cher is a 1ˢᵗ level connection with Jack Nicholson, and a 2ⁿᵈ level connection with Kevin Bacon. (*Which means that my Bacon Number is a four, because my Mom knows Cher, Cher knows Jack Nicholson, and Jack Nicholson knows Kevin Bacon*).

How does the Bacon number concept relate to LinkedIn? LinkedIn uses the same system universally: you can *direct message* or *see the email* of your 1ˢᵗ level connections, and you can use your 1ˢᵗ level connections to get introduced to your 2ⁿᵈ level, for example:

Cher can message via LinkedIn or email Jack Nicholson, directly.

Cher can "see" that Jack Nicholson is connected to Kevin Bacon, and ask Jack to "introduce" her to Kevin.

Similarly, on LinkedIn, you can directly message / find the email of anyone who is your 1ˢᵗ level connection. Or, you can ask a 1ˢᵗ level connection to introduce you to a 2ⁿᵈ level connection. For example, simply search on LinkedIn for the name of someone with whom you are already connected. Then:

Click on the **blue** "Send a message" box. This sends them a message via LinkedIn, and in most cases, will also send them an email alert that they have a message waiting on LinkedIn.

or –

Click on the "**Contact info**" tab and you can view their email address, phone number, and address.

Or, let's assume you're trying to find a connection that has a particular interest or skill. Rather than typing a person's name into the search box, type a keyword / keyphrase such as "WordPress," or "Joomla," or "Accountant for small business" and hit search. On the left, under search you can narrow your results by parameters. Here's a screenshot:

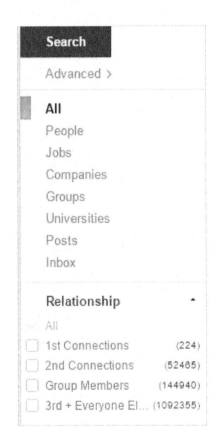

If, for example, you click on "People," you are only searching LinkedIn for people whose profiles contain that keyword. If you click on "People," and on "1ˢᵗ Connections," then you are searching for people whose profiles contain the keyword AND are in a 1st level connection with you. Remember: 1st level connections mean you can direct message them via LinkedIn and/or see their email address and other contact information.

You can "tag" 1st level connections by affixing keywords to individual connections. For example, you can create a "tag" that indicates a "real-world friend" or a "tag" that indicates an industry trade show connection or a "tag" that indicates they have a blog. Once tagged, you can then sort or filter your connections by tag. To "tag" a connection, simply click on a connection, click on the "relationship" tab, and next click on "Tag." Here's a screenshot:

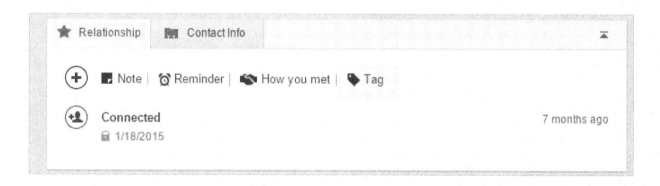

Once you've "tagged" your connections, you can then filter them. To do so, click on My Network > Connections, and then "Filter by." Here's a screenshot:

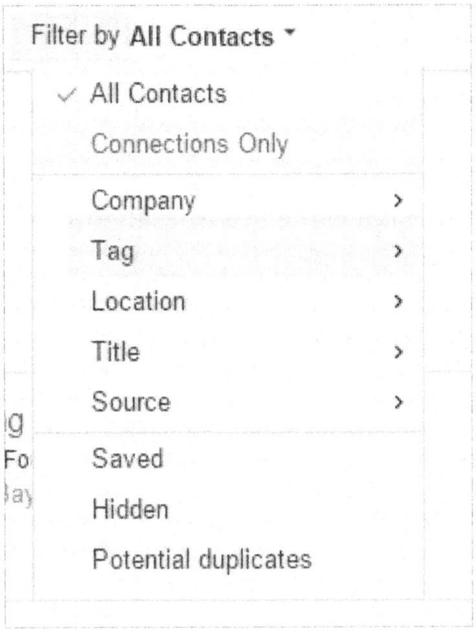

Filter by **All Contacts** ▾

✓ All Contacts

Connections Only

Company   ›

Tag   ›

Location   ›

Title   ›

Source   ›

Saved

Hidden

Potential duplicates

Now that you have them filtered by a "tag," you can do a "mass email" to them via LinkedIn. Simply filter them via your "tag," set up an email in a text file (so you can copy / paste it in), then go down your list, hover on each person's name in blue, click on message, and then paste your email and click "send message."

Here's a screenshot:

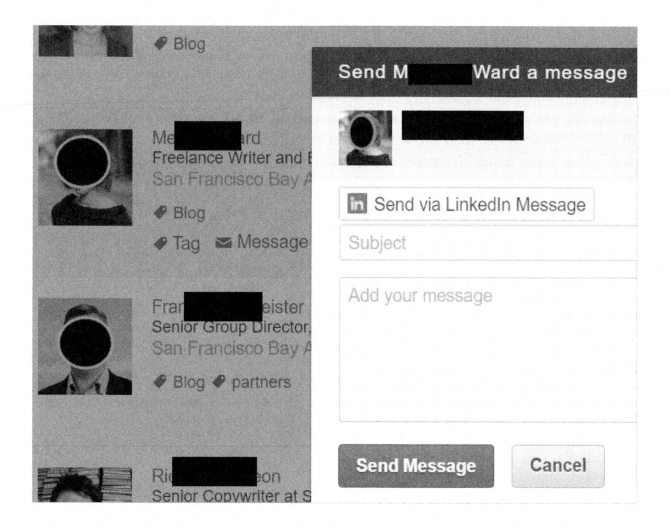

Essentially, you are able to use LinkedIn as a searchable rolodex of 1st and 2nd level business contacts: define what type of person you want to contact (or prospect), search for them, and reach out directly. For those who are 1st level connections, you can filter them by "tag" or "keyword," and then reach out to them via LinkedIn (which also generally causes an email to them).

Working with 2nd Level Connections

While you can direct message (send emails or see the email addresses of) 1st level connections, this is not true of 2nd level connections (who are the 1st level connections of your 1st level connections). However, LinkedIn allows you to ask for an "introduction" from a 1st level connection to a 2nd level connection.

Here's a typical scenario.

Let's suppose you are the sale manager for a company in the Proteomics industry. (*Proteomics is the large scale study of proteins and is used heavily in industry to analyze organic materials*). You're going to "Proteomics World" in Boston, and you'll be introducing your new "Proteomics 2000" product to the industry. You are planning on having one of those fun-filled wine and cheese parties, where your company will roll out the red carpet with free food and wine, and in exchange, attendees will be updated on your "Proteomics 2000." It's a business meeting with a little fun, a little free food and drink, and some salesy information about your new product.

Your job is to get people to attend. You go to LinkedIn and search for:

> *Proteomics*
> *Check: People*
> *Check: 1st level*

You can direct message all of these 1st level people and invite them to the wine and cheese event. Remember: social media is a *party*, not a *prison*, and in terms of content you have something *fun* and *interesting*: your *wine and cheese event*.

Secondarily, you can search for

> *Proteomics*
> *Check: People*
> *Check: 2nd level*

Here, although you cannot see the contact information on the 2nd level connections, you can ask for an introduction from a 1st level connection. This is akin to being at a trade show event, going up to a 1st level connection who knows someone whom you want to get to know, and asking for an introduction. Then your 1st level walks over to your 2nd level (his 1st level), and introduces you. Susan (your 1st level) introduces you to Bob (her 1st level, and your 2nd level connection):

> *"Hey Bob, I'd like you to meet Jason. He's the Proteomics marketing manager over at PT Inc. They're having some sort of a wine and cheese event, and I thought you two might get to know each other."*

Or structurally:

First level > reason to ask for an introduction > introduction to 2nd level > and (hopefully) the 2nd level becomes a 1st level (accepts your request).

Essentially, do your search by keyword, filter for 2nd level connections. Find a connection that interests you, and click on her name. Then, scroll down and on the far right hand column you'll see "How You're Connected." Choose a 1st level connection, and then click on the "Ask so-and-so for an introduction."

Here's a screenshot:

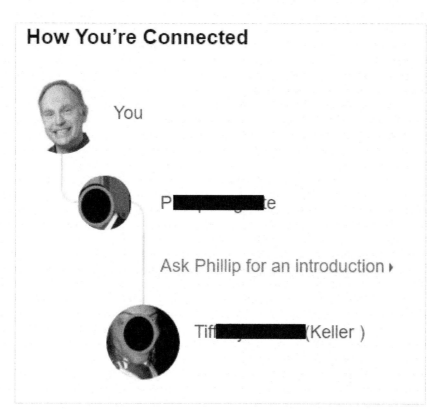

After you click on "Ask so-and-so for an introduction," LinkedIn will pop up a form email. You can (and should) customize this so that your 1st level introduction understands why you want to be connected to his 1st level connection, and what you have to offer to this friend / connection.

Here's a screenshot:

Alternatively, you can send an InMail (see http://jmlinks.com/3m) with a paid account, but it's probably more effective to "get introduced" as it would be in a real-world business encounter. After all, people trust people they know more than a "cold" call or a "cold" InMail / email.

> *It's not what you know (in business). It's who you know.*

The bottom line, therefore, is to use your 1st level connections to get to your 2nd levels, and the **TODO** for LinkedIn is to constantly be expanding your 1st level network, but how?

How to Expand Your LinkedIn Connections

If having many connections is the name of the game on LinkedIn, how do you grow your connections? Here are some strategies:

> **Ask.** Continually ask every business person you meet for their email, and then look them up on LinkedIn. Next click the Connect button and then fill out the

information as indicated (you'll need their email and then write a note as to how you met them). Here's a screenshot:

I recommend customizing your personal notes, such as *"Hi Sallie! You and I met at Proteomics world last week, and I'd like to contact with you on LinkedIn."* If she accepts, she becomes a 1st level connection.

No Spamming. Do not contact people you do not know because spamming LinkedIn can lead your account to be deactivated.

Lifetime Limit. Indeed, there is a lifetime limit of 5000 invitation requests, designed to prevent connection spamming.

Get People to Ask You. Even better than asking people to connect to you, is to get them to ask you. Ideas for this would be:

- **Real World to LinkedIn**. If you give a presentation at a trade show, ask attendees to connect with you on LinkedIn. Include LinkedIn on

your business cards, and literally mention LinkedIn when you meet business associates in real life.
- **Your Website or Blog**. Place the LinkedIn icon on your website or blog, and encourage visitors to connect. (To generate a personalized LinkedIn badge, visit http://jmlinks.com/12r).
- **Other Social Media**. Connect your LinkedIn to your Twitter, Facebook, Google+, etc., and encourage people who already follow you on Twitter, for example, to connect with you on LinkedIn.

The point is to do everything you can to encourage business contacts to connect with you on LinkedIn, because the more you grow your 1st level contacts, the more you can directly connect to them, and the more you can use them as introductions to their 1st level contacts, i.e., your 2nd level contacts. Schmooze, schmooze, schmooze to grow your LinkedIn network!

With Whom Should You Connect?

There are different strategies in terms of reaching out, or accepting, the connection requests of others on LinkedIn. There is no right answer. For someone who is in customer outreach (e.g. sales), he or she should probably accept every inbound request. For someone who is a venture capitalist, he or she might accept requests only from people they really know. Another strategy is to only accept requests from people for whom you'd actually do a favor in real life.

Are Paid LinkedIn Accounts Worth It?

Unless you are an active recruiter, an active job seeker, or an outbound sales person actively "cold calling" or prospecting, I do not generally recommend paid LinkedIn accounts. The main advantages of a paid LinkedIn account (of which there are several types) are:

- Enhanced cosmetics for your profile, such as a larger photo;
- Better positioning when applying for a job;
- Access to everyone who's viewed your profile in the last 90 days;
- Ability to see 3rd degree profiles;
- Additional search filters, and the ability to filter and save search results (great for sales prospectors);

- Up to 15-30 InMails per month to directly contact anyone on LinkedIn, even if you are not connected; and/or (depending on the package you get)
- More detailed analytics.

To learn more about LinkedIn Premium, visit https://premium.linkedin.com/. For a very helpful comparison of accounts, visit http://jmlinks.com/3n.

Your **TODO** here is to brainstorm a logical connection philosophy. If your purpose on LinkedIn is to use it for customer outreach and heavy schmoozing, then connecting with anyone or everyone makes sense. If your purpose is more passive or more secretive, perhaps just using LinkedIn as a public resume, and/or to keep up-to-date on industry trends, then connecting only with real-world connections makes sense. Remember: once you accept a connection request, you become a 1st level connection, meaning that person can directly contact you via LinkedIn and email, as well as see your contact information. Similarly, he or she can see your 2nd level connections (unless you block that in settings). So, if you need to be more secretive, then be more judicious about with whom you connect. If not, not. There is no right or wrong connection strategy: just pre-think a strategy that makes sense for your marketing objectives.

And, remember, it's not just about "you," it's about "you" and "your team." LinkedIn is a team networking sport at the corporate or business level!

Brainstorming a Schmoozing Strategy

For your third **TODO**, download the **LinkedIn Schmoozing Worksheet**. For the worksheet, go to https://www.jm-seo.org/workbooks (click on Social Media Workbook, enter the code 'smm2016' to register if you have not already done so), and click on the link to the "LinkedIn Schmoozing Worksheet." You'll brainstorm your strategy for growing your LinkedIn connections. (Remember to do this with each and every customer-facing employee).

▶▶ BEING ACTIVE ON LINKEDIN: UPDATES & POSTS

In the real world of business, it's a truism of marketing that you need to "look active." People respect people who are involved and engaged, and look down on people who seem to be doing nothing. Similarly, on LinkedIn it is important to present at least the appearance of activity. By being active, you "look active" (a **trust** indicator) plus you have new ways to reach out to prospects and customers to stay top-of-mind and generate business inquiries.

Posting frequently and being active in LinkedIn groups, in short: a) makes you seem active (and therefore trustworthy), and b) gives you more opportunities to be top of mind among prospects, thereby increasing opportunities for connections and business engagements. I'm not saying you should be fraudulent. But, just as at a business networking event, be active and engaged in a serious way. Participation is important!

Remember: LinkedIn is a team sport, and only individuals can post to their own accounts. Getting employees to post and be active is yet another example why getting all your customer-facing employees "on board" is a key element of LinkedIn success!

Updates and Posts

The first way to do this is to post informative content to LinkedIn on a regular basis via *updates* and *posts*, and the second, is to participate in LinkedIn Groups. Let's look at each in turn.

Just as on Facebook, if you share an update to your profile (what most of us would call a "post," although in LinkedIn lingo this is called an "update,") and I am a 1st level connection, then that post has a good chance of showing in my news feed. The news feed on LinkedIn is the first content that greets me when I login.

Here's a screenshot of my news feed highlighted in yellow:

David Amerland, with whom I am a 1st level contact, posted an update, namely a link on LinkedIn to his blog post on "Business Fatigue." He posted his update, and it showed in my news feed. So the process is:

Identify items of interest to your business contacts (your own content or that of others) > Post updates on them to LinkedIn > Your connections see them in their news feeds (and hopefully get excited about doing business with you and/or your company).

Content is king, and queen, and jack on LinkedIn as on all social media. Turn back to your Content Marketing plan, and remember you'll need both other people's content and your own content to post as updates or as posts to *Pulse* (more below):

- **Blog Post Summaries**. To the extent that you have an active blog and are posting items that fit with LinkedIn's professional focus, post headlines, short summaries and links to your blog.
  - Note that the first or "featured" image will become the shareable image, and that the META DESCRIPTION will become the default description when sharing. Choose striking, fun images for your blog posts!
- **Quotes**. People love quotes, and taking memorable quotes (on business themes) and pasting them on graphics is a win/win.
- **Infographics and Instructographics**. Factoids, how to articles, top ten lists, 7 things you didn't know lists, especially ones that are fun yet useful, are excellent for LinkedIn.
- **Quizzes, Surveys, and Response-provoking posts**. Ask a question, and get an answer or more. Great for encouraging interactivity, especially when the interaction is business-oriented. A great idea is to mention a project you are working on, and ask for feedback before, during, or after.

Turn to the content marketing section of the *Social Media Toolbook* for a list of tools that will help you find other people's content and create your own. I recommend Hootsuite (https://www.hootsuite.com/) to manage all your social postings across platforms. I recommend Feedly (http://www.feedly.com/) as a way to organize industry blogs and the content of other people, so that you can be a useful sharer of third-party information on LinkedIn.

LinkedIn *Pulse*

One opportunity not to be missed on LinkedIn in terms of posting is *LinkedIn Pulse* (https://www.linkedin.com/pulse). LinkedIn is aggressively trying to grow its role not only for job seekers but for the fully employed. *Pulse* is LinkedIn's internal blog, and anyone (including you) can easily post to *Pulse*. Think of posting to *Pulse* as you would posting to your own blog:

1. **Identify a topic** that will interest your prospects and customers, such as an industry trend or a common "pain point" in your industry or more generally in business.
2. **Brainstorm and identify keywords** using tools like Google suggest, Ubersuggest, or the Google Keyword Planner.
3. **Write a strong post with a great headline**, catchy first paragraph, and some substantial content that will be useful to readers and position you as a "helpful expert."
4. **Tag your *Pulse* post with relevant tags** – these influence whether your *Pulse* post will show in their news feed and/or relevant searches.

Inside of LinkedIn, *Pulse* lives under the beige button "+*Write a new post*". Here's a screenshot:

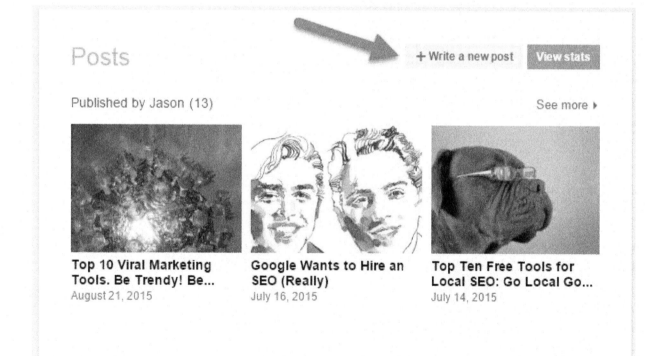

Pulse Reaches Beyond Your Connections

LinkedIn *Pulse* also allows individuals with whom you are NOT 1st level connections on LinkedIn to "follow you." Even better, when you share your *Pulse* Post on other social networks (e.g., Twitter, Facebook, Google+) and encourage people to cross over to LinkedIn, LinkedIn monitors this activity. If you get enough momentum, a *Pulse* Post can "go viral," and really supercharge your LinkedIn connections.

LinkedIn's own marketing team is keen to promote Pulse, so if you've written something substantial, be sure to tweet your Pulse post to LinkedIn Marketing at https://twitter.com/LinkedInMktg. You can find the official LinkedIn Pulse editorial calendar at http://jmlinks.com/12s.

Therefore, a strong *Pulse* posting strategy can position you as a "helpful expert" to new people, and is not an opportunity to be missed!

For your fourth **TODO**, download the **LinkedIn Posting Worksheet**. For the worksheet, go to https://www.jm-seo.org/workbooks (click on Social Media Workbook, enter the code 'smm2016' to register if you have not already done so), and click on the link to the "LinkedIn Posting Worksheet." You'll create a systematic plan for posts to LinkedIn, both your own content and the content of others.

As much as it is fun and easy to post, the reality of LinkedIn today is that outside of job seekers, not everybody checks LinkedIn on a daily or even weekly basis. So while posting frequently to LinkedIn is a good idea, it is not nearly as dynamic as Facebook in terms of active engagement. Keep that in mind when you measure the ROI of posting frequently on LinkedIn.

How frequently should you post?

Now that the LinkedIn news feed is very crowded (and the reality is that only few people outside of job seekers and outbound marketers check their feed daily), you can safely post quite frequently: even several times a day. But this differs with your audience, so pay attention to your updates, by monitoring thumbs up and comments (*for LinkedIn updates*) and stats (*for Pulse posts*). Your goal is to be interesting, informative, useful, and friendly as trust indicators and hopefully get social spread amongst new contacts, especially via *Pulse*. Note that you can see who responded to your *Pulse* posts, and this gives you an opportunity to connect with them

▶ BEING ACTIVE ON LINKEDIN: LINKEDIN GROUPS

With LinkedIn's growing emphasis on "professional learning," it should come as no surprise that LinkedIn has a growing ecosystem of groups on every topic imaginable. Compare LinkedIn groups to the "break out" sessions at your industry trade show: interested parties show up, listen to each other, participate in discussions, and showcase their questions (and answers) on professional topics. Oh, and occasionally, they use groups as yet another opportunity to **schmooze** *(surprise!)*. By participating tactfully in LinkedIn groups you can grow your prestige (and that of your company). It's a soft sell environment; however, anyone who is a member of a group that you are a member of is a good prospect to become a LinkedIn 1st level connection.

To find relevant groups, simply search LinkedIn by keyword and then click on "Groups" on the left hand column. LinkedIn will return a list of relevant groups; simply click on the group to learn more about it, or click the blue join group.

Note that there are two types of groups: **closed** and **open**. **Closed** groups are indicated by the word "join"; by clicking "join," you are requesting the group moderator to approve your membership. **Open** groups are indicted by the word "View," and you first click the blue "View" button and then "ask to join." Once you've successfully joined a group (either open or closed), you'll see a blue "**Post** icon."

Here's a screenshot of the three possibilities, after a keyword search for "content marketing" > groups:

Group Promotion Strategy

LinkedIn is a serious social media platform; so please don't "spam" groups with self-serving "buy my stuff" messages! Instead, join relevant groups, pay attention to the on-going discussions, and post informative and useful content. It's a soft sell environment. Let group members realize how smart and useful you are, and then reach out to you directly.

As you research (or join) groups, pay attention to the quality of the discussions. Some groups are fantastic: full of motivated, informed, honest people. Other groups are quite spammy with everyone talking, and few people listening. Just as at a professional trade show, be choosy with your time and efforts. Not all groups are created equally.

Your **Todo** for groups is simple:

- **Log on** to your LinkedIn account.
- **Search for relevant groups** by keyword.
- **Identify** interesting and useful **groups**, and join them (or apply to join if it's a closed group).

- **Monitor** and begin to **participate**.
- Diplomatically position yourself (and your company) as a **helpful expert**.

» LINKEDIN COMPANY PAGES

Like Facebook, LinkedIn offers company Pages. And like Facebook, you must first have an individual profile to create (or manage) a company page. To view the official LinkedIn information on company pages, visit http://jmlinks.com/3h. The steps to create a business Page on LinkedIn are:

1. Sign in to your personal profile.
2. Click on http://jmlinks.com/3j.
3. Add your company name, and your email address, matching the company website domain.
4. Enter your company name.
5. Enter your designated Admins.

Now that you have created a company Page, it's time to optimize it. Login in, first, to your personal profile. Then simply type your company name into the search box. Assuming you are an Admin for your company, LinkedIn will load your company page. On the far right, click on the blue "Edit" button.

Here's a screenshot:

Now you can edit / optimize:

- **Company Name**. Enter or adjust your company name, accordingly.

- **Company Description**. Enter a keyword-heavy yet relevant description of your company. Explain your value proposition: what can you do for LinkedIn members?
- **Designated Admins**. Here, you can add or remove Admins. Any Admin has full `control of the page; so if you terminate an employee, remove them first!
- **Image**. Similar to the Facebook cover photo, you can change your LinkedIn (cover) image.
- **Company Logo**. Similar to the Facebook profile picture, you can change your LinkedIn Profile picture.
- **Company Specialties**. These function as keywords for indexing purposes.
- **Featured Groups**. You can feature relevant groups, just as you would at the individual level.

The reality is that few people "search" LinkedIn to find companies. So the bread-and-butter of your company page is to post interesting items (both your own content and that of other people) to people who follow your page because externally they have already decided to follow you. For example, existing customers or people who find your blog interesting might "follow" your company on LinkedIn to stay updated.

For tips from LinkedIn on how to nurture effective company Pages, please visit http://jmlinks.com/3k.

Page Posting Strategy

Although most of the action on LinkedIn is at the profile to profile level, you can post via your company Page as well. Just as with a profile, the trick is to identify interesting, engaging content (both your own and that of others) to post to the Page. In reality, you can cross-post content on both employee profiles and the company page. For example, if the director of marketing writes an informative piece for LinkedIn *Pulse*, you can "cross post" this to your LinkedIn company feed. Similarly, you can identify interesting industry-related articles on Feedly, and share this content at both the profile and Page level.

Essentially, you are trying to position your company as a "helpful expert" on a relevant topic, by posting:

- **Your own content** such as blog posts, videos on YouTube, infographics / instructographics, reports, eBooks, industry studies that deal with industry issues in an informative way;

- **Other people's content** similar to the above.
- **Self-promotional content** like announcements of free Webinars, eBooks, upcoming trade shows, new products, etc.

Remember, of course, your **posting rhythm** of *fun, fun, fun, fun, buy my stuff* (on Facebook), which becomes on LinkedIn:

> *useful, useful, useful, useful, useful, useful, useful, attend our webinar, useful, useful, useful, useful, useful, useful, useful, download our free eBook, useful, useful, useful, useful, useful, useful, visit us at the tradeshow...*

Get Employees to Post Your Content as Well as Your Company Page

And remember, LinkedIn marketing is a **team sport**: if you have a great blog post, video, or infographic, have it posted not only to your company LinkedIn page but have key employees share it as an update on their own LinkedIn profiles as well!

In other words, make 80% or more of your posts useful, and only 20% or less, shameless, self-promotional announcements. If you like you can "pin" a company update to the top of your company Page. Simply find the update, and click "Pin to top" located beneath it.

Here are some examples of effective LinkedIn company pages:

- Thermo Fischer Scientific at https://www.linkedin.com/company/thermo-fisher-scientific.
- Intel Corporation at https://www.linkedin.com/company/intel-corporation
- Monsanto at https://www.linkedin.com/company/monsanto
- Social Media Examiner https://www.linkedin.com/company/social-media-examiner

To find companies to emulate, either search LinkedIn directly by keywords, or use this Google trick. Go to https://www.google.com/ and enter:

site:linkedin.com/company {keyword}

site:linkedin.com/company {company name}

as for example:

site:linkedin.com/company "organic food" at http://jmlinks.com/12t.

You'll find that LinkedIn is fast becoming a better home for more "serious" or even "boring" companies than Facebook; companies whose business value proposition is more *business-to-business* rather than *business-to-consumer*, and whose customers engage when they are in their work / professional / business mode.

In sum, if your business is *business-to-business* such as professional services like Web design, accounting, business attorneys, computer services, SEO, social media marketing, marketing services... any business-to-business, professional service, then a company Page on LinkedIn can be a very effective marketing tool.

» PROMOTING YOUR LINKEDIN PROFILES, POSTS, AND PAGES

Once you and your employees have established their individual profiles, begun to share updates or posts to LinkedIn *Pulse*, set up a company Page, and begun to populate it with posts on a regular basis, you've essentially "set up" the social media party. Now it's time to send out the invitations. In and of itself, nothing on LinkedIn is truly self-promotional.

Remember: social media is a **party**. You must have yummy yummy food and entertainment for people to show up, and stick around. So as you promote your LinkedIn **content**, always keep front and center "what's in it for them" – what will they get by connecting with your employees on LinkedIn or following your company LinkedIn page?

Generally speaking, people on LinkedIn are looking for informative, educational, useful, professional content relevant to their industry and job, so that they can stay informed and educated. If on Facebook the name of the game is *fun*, on LinkedIn the name of the game is *useful*.

FACEBOOK IS ABOUT FUN; LINKEDIN IS ABOUT USEFUL

Assuming your profiles and Page have lots of useful content, here are some common ways to promote your LinkedIn accounts:

- **Real World to Social.** Don't forget the real world! If you are a serious technology vendor of single board computers, and you're at the industry trade show, be sure that the folks manning the booth, recommend to booth visitors that they "connect" with your employees and "follow" your business LinkedIn Page. *Why? Because they'll get insider tips, industry news, free eBooks and webinars – stuff that will keep them abreast of the industry, and better informed at their jobs.*
- **Cross-Promotion**. Link your website to your LinkedIn profiles and Page, your blog posts to your profiles and Page, your Twitter to your profiles and Page, etc. Notice how big brands like Intel (http://www.intel.com/) do this: one digital property promotes another digital property.
- **Email**. Email your customer list and ask them to "connect" with key employees and/or "follow" your Page. Again, you must have a reason why they'll should do so: what's in it for them? Have a contest, give away something for free, or otherwise motivate them to click from the email to your profiles or Page, and then connect.
- **LinkedIn Internal**. More at the profile level than on the Page level, participation on LinkedIn in an authentic way can grow one's follower base. LinkedIn *Pulse* is especially useful for this, as are LinkedIn groups. Internal promotion is not particularly strong on LinkedIn, but it should still be in the mix.
- **Use LinkedIn Plugins**. LinkedIn has numerous plugins that allow you to "embed" your LinkedIn content on your website, and thereby nurture cross promotion. To learn more about plugins, visit https://developer.linkedin.com/plugins. In this way, your blog can promote your LinkedIn content, and your LinkedIn content can promote your blog. Similarly, your YouTube videos can promote your LinkedIn Page, and your LinkedIn updates and *Pulse* posts can promote your YouTube Videos and vice-versa.
- **Leverage your Customers**. People who already have connected with you and your company are your best promoters. Remember, it's *social* (!) media, and encouraging your customers to share your content is the name of the game. You want to leverage your connections as much as possible to share your content. On LinkedIn, it's all about being useful! Indeed, a timely post to LinkedIn *Pulse* can

be picked up by key influencers, go viral, and exponentially increase your personal and company reach.

GET YOUR CUSTOMERS TO HELP PROMOTE YOUR LINKEDIN CONTENT

Advertise. Advertising is increasingly important to success on LinkedIn. Visit LinkedIn's advertising center at https://www.linkedin.com/advertising to view their official information. Here are some ideas:

Promote your Page Updates. On your LinkedIn company page, find an update. At the bottom of the update, click on the gray "Sponsor Update" button and follow the instructions. You can demographically target advertising on LinkedIn in a very focused way: people who are members of a group, people who follow specific companies, etc.

Advertise Directly. You can create direct ads on LinkedIn to promote either offsite web content, or connect back to your Page or Posts. In terms of LinkedIn promotion, therefore, you can use LinkedIn advertising to grow your LinkedIn company followers by advertising your Page and/or posts.

Think Out of the Box on LinkedIn Advertising

LinkedIn does not currently allow you to promote individual profiles or the updates / posts of individuals via direct advertising. However, assuming you want to grow the LinkedIn presence of key company employees:

1. Have the employee **post** to his or her **blog**; and/or
   o Have the employee **post** to **LinkedIn** *Pulse*.
2. **Share** this content as an "**update**" via your LinkedIn Page.

3. **Pay to advertise** this content via your Company Account by clicking the "Sponsor Update" button.

In this way, you can use your company Page to grow the following of individual key employees as well as boost their content for thought-leadership and brand purposes.

>> MEASURING YOUR RESULTS

LinkedIn offers more metrics at the company level than at the personal profile level.

LinkedIn Profiles

First, let's look at the profile level. If you have a free account, login to your LinkedIn profile and then click the "Who's viewed your profile" section on the right. That gets you to LinkedIn stats, such as who has viewed your profile, your posts, and a comparison of how your rank for profile views compared with those of similar people on LinkedIn. Here's a screenshot:

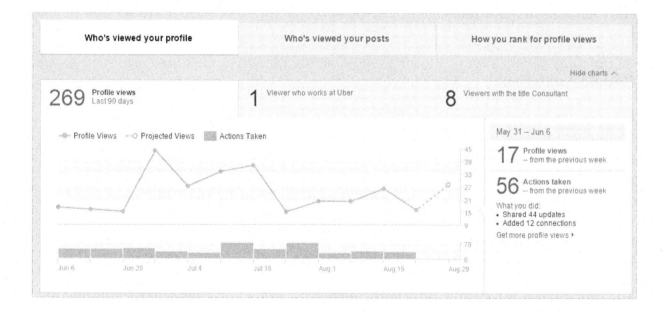

If you click on the center tab, "Who's viewed your posts," this gives you metrics for your LinkedIn Pulse posts. Here you find detailed information on their industries, job titles, locations, and traffic sources. If they interacted with your post by liking, commenting on, or sharing it, then you can also click up to their LinkedIn profile to learn more about them. Indeed, this even gives you an excuse to reach out and connect. By paying and joining LinkedIn premium (https://premium.linkedin.com/), you gain access to more detailed data.

As for your shared updates, the only data available is to look at each update and eyeball how many comments and likes an update received. By clicking on the like, comment, or share icon, you can see who interacted with an update.

LinkedIn Pages

LinkedIn Page data is more robust. If you are logged in as the company, simply scroll down to company updates. For each, you can see impressions, clicks, interactions, and engagement data.

Click on the "Analytics" tab and LinkedIn provides lots of graphical data about your Page and its reach. Click on "Notifications," and you can see likes, comments, shares, and mentions in more detail.

Google Analytics

For many of us, we want to drive traffic from LinkedIn to our website, even to our ecommerce store or to download a free eBook or software package to get a sales lead. Sign up for Google Analytics (https://www.google.com/analytics) and install the required tracking code. Inside of your Google Analytics account on the left column, drill down by clicking on Acquisition > Social > Overview. Then on the right hand side of the screen you'll see a list of Social Networks. Find LinkedIn on that list, and click on that. Google Analytics will tell you what URLs people clicked to from LinkedIn to your Website, giving you insights into what types of web content people find attractive.

You can also create a custom Advanced Segment to look at only LinkedIn traffic and its behavior. For information on how to create custom Advanced Segments in Google Analytics, go to http://jmlinks.com/1f. For the Google help files on Advanced Segments go to http://jmlinks.com/1g.

In sum, inside of LinkedIn you can see how people interact with your Page and updates as well as those made by individual profiles. Inside of Google Analytics, you can see where they land on your website and what they do after they arrive.

»» DELIVERABLE: A LINKEDIN MARKETING PLAN

Now that we've come to the end our chapter on LinkedIn, your **DELIVERABLE** has arrived. For your final **TODO**, download the **LinkedIn Marketing Plan Worksheet**. For the worksheet, go to https://www.jm-seo.org/workbooks (click on Social Media Workbook, enter the code 'smm2016' to register if you have not already done so), and click on the link to the "LinkedIn Marketing Plan Worksheet." You'll brainstorm your strategy for LinkedIn at both the employee (profile) and company (Page) level.

» TOP LINKEDIN MARKETING TOOLS AND RESOURCES

Here are the top tools and resources to help you with LinkedIn marketing. For an up-to-date list, go to https://www.jm-seo.org/workbooks (click on Social Media Workbook, enter the code 'smm2016' to register if you have not already done so), and click on the link to the *Social Media Toolbook* link, and drill down to the LinkedIn chapter.

LINKEDIN HELP CENTER - https://www.linkedin.com/help/linkedin

Learn about all the different features on LinkedIn. From a brief overview to detailed tips, you'll find them here. Learn about profiles. Find out how to get a new job. Use LinkedIn on your mobile phone. Learn how to build your network. Get answers to your questions with Answers.

Rating: 5 Stars | **Category:** overview

HOOTSUITE - https://hootsuite.com/

Manage all of your social media accounts, including multiple Twitter profiles through HootSuite. HootSuite makes it easy to manage multiple users over various social media accounts and allows you to track statistics. LOVE THIS TOOL!

Rating: 5 Stars | **Category:** vendor

LINKEDIN ENGINEERING - http://engineering.linkedin.com

LinkedIn Engineering hosts a small set of projects and experimental features built by the employees of LinkedIn. Some of these plugins can be good for your LinkedIn marketing efforts.

Rating: 4 Stars | **Category:** tool

LINKEDIN LEARNING WEBINARS - http://help.linkedin.com/app/answers/detail/a_id/530

LinkedIn hosts live learning webinars on a variety of timely LinkedIn topics. Alternatively, users can view pre-recorded sessions. Topics are designed for a variety of audiences including, job seekers, corporate communications professionals, and journalists.

Rating: 4 Stars | **Category:** resource

LINKEDIN COMPANY PAGES FAQ - http://linkd.in/1BbOokZ

Interested in setting up a business page on LinkedIn? Here's the official FAQ on LinkedIn company pages.

Rating: 4 Stars | **Category:** resource

OFFICIAL LINKEDIN BLOG - http://blog.linkedin.com

The official LinkedIn Blog...lots of detailed information on what's happening when, where, and how on LinkedIn by LinkedIn staff.

Rating: 4 Stars | **Category:** blog

RAPPORTIVE - http://rapportive.com

Rapportive is a Gmail plugin that works with LinkedIn (and other social media sites). So when you're exchanging email with someone, you can see their

LinkedIn profile details. It's sort of a bye-bye privacy app that helps you know how 'important' someone is with whom you are interacting.

Rating: 4 Stars | **Category:** tool

LinkedIn YouTube Channel - https://www.youtube.com/user/LinkedIn

LinkedIn has some novel advertising opportunities. This is their official YouTube channel. It's pretty salesy, but has some useful information especially on marketing and sales aspects of LinkedIn.

Rating: 4 Stars | **Category:** video

Buffer - https://buffer.com/

Schedule tweets and other social media activity in the future. Competitor to Hootsuite.

Rating: 4 Stars | **Category:** tool

LinkedIn Pulse - https://www.linkedin.com/pulse/

Need ideas for your next blog post? Look no further than LinkedIn Pulse where top business influencers post their thoughts daily. Even better, you can post to LinkedIin Pulse and become a LinkedIn superstar as well. Even even better: post to both LinkedIn Pulse and your own blog.

Rating: 4 Stars | **Category:** resource

4

TWITTER

Do you Tweet? Should you? Twitter is among the most misunderstood of all the social media. On the one hand, it dominates news and pop culture, giving Twitter a brand presence second only to Facebook. *Ellen DeGeneres tweets. Barack Obama tweets. CBS News tweets.* And so the logic goes: *you better tweet, too.* But, on the other hand, Twitter is full of noise, news and craziness: it isn't necessarily a good marketing venue for many businesses. In fact, many businesses tweet and no one is really listening, so Twitter can be a complete waste of time.

In short, Twitter can be an **effective marketing channel** for your business, or Twitter can be a **huge waste of time**. Which is it? Should you use Twitter, and if so, how? The answer, of course, is "it depends." It depends on whether your customers are on Twitter, and whether you can systematically implement a Twitter marketing strategy.

In this chapter, you'll learn how Twitter works, how to figure out if Twitter is a good opportunity for your business, how to set up your Twitter account, and – most importantly – how to tweet effectively. Throughout, I will point you to free tools and resources for more information as well as worksheets to guide you step-by-step. Even if you are already tweeting, you'll learn how to really use Twitter for marketing as opposed to just wasting your time.

By the end of this Chapter, you'll understand how Twitter works, be able to research whether Twitter has potential for your company, and be on your way to implementing a step-by-step Twitter marketing plan.

Let's get started!

To Do List:

>> Explore How Twitter Works

>> Inventory Likes and Dislikes on Twitter

» Brainstorm and Execute a Tweeting Strategy

» Promote Your Twitter Account and Tweets

» Measure your Results

»» Deliverable: A Twitter Marketing Plan

» Appendix: Top Twitter Marketing Tools and Resources

» EXPLORE HOW TWITTER WORKS

One way to understand **Twitter** is to think of Twitter as a **micro blogging** platform. Blogs are all about having an inspiration for a blog post, composing a strong headline, and writing some detailed paragraphs about the topic. Twitter is very similar, just a lot shorter - 140 characters, to be exact.

Let's compare writing a blog post and composing a tweet.

When you write a blog post, you a) conceptualize a **topic** (*hopefully of interest to your target audience*), b) write a **headline** and the **blog post** itself, and c) **promote** your blog post. Similarly, within the constraints of a 140 character tweet, you a) conceptualize a **topic** of interest to your (potential) followers, b) write a **headline / tweet** (they're basically one-and-the-same on Twitter), and c) **promote** your tweet.

TWITTER IS MICROBLOGGING

One difference apparent right from the start is that on Twitter a tweet often points outwards to an in-depth blog post, a video, an infographic, or an image. A tweet can often be just a "headline" pointing out to the "rest of the story," but many tweets are self-standing as well. But in either case, composing a tweet is very similar to composing a blog post.

Twitter is Like Facebook (and Instagram, LinkedIn and Pinterest...)

Structurally speaking, Twitter also shares many similarities with other social media. Like Facebook, LinkedIn, Pinterest and other social media, your Twitter account (a.k.a., "Page") can be "followed" ("liked") by others, who are alerted in their news feeds when you tweet new items. In addition, tweets can be discovered through *#hashtags* plus people can *retweet* (share) your tweets, respond to them, or favorite them, thereby drawing the attention of their followers to you.

In fact, as Twitter becomes more visual and Instagram becomes more textual, these two are on a "collision course," and the world may not be big enough for both of them!

The names may have changed, but the basic structure of Twitter works pretty much like that of other social media platforms:

- Individuals have *accounts* on Twitter ("profiles" on Facebook).
- Companies have *accounts* on Twitter ("pages" on Facebook).
- If an individual *follows* your account on Twittter ("likes" your Page on Facebook), then when that company tweets it will show up in the *news feed* of that individual.
- Individuals can
    - *favorite* a tweet – "like" a post on Facebook;
    - *respond* to a tweet – "comment" on Facebook; and/or
    - *re-tweet* a tweet to their followers (reshare posts on Facebook).

Tweets are short (less than 140 characters), and consist usually of text but can include links, graphics and videos.

The structure of Twitter is quite similar to that of Facebook; the big differences are that Twitter is shorter, faster, and noisier than Facebook.

Let's review the differences in detail.

How Twitter is Unique

First and foremost, Twitter is the most open of all the social media. Anyone can set up a Twitter account in literally minutes, and start tweeting – there's no real authentication. And anyone can listen in: there's no required friending or connecting as on Facebook or LinkedIn. Indeed, even people who do not follow you can easily find and read your tweets. They can even contact you, without your pre-approval. Let me repeat these facts:

anyone can instantly set up a Twitter account and start tweeting: no authentication required;

anyone can listen in to anyone on Twitter: no friending required; and

anyone can talk to **anyone** via Twitter: it's completely open!

Twitter is Open

Twitter is like a massive 24/7 talk radio station, or a water cooler conversation: anyone can talk, and anyone can listen, no authentication required and no requirement that the person talking have any expertise or intelligence on the matter.

> Twitter is as open as talk radio, even more so because not only can anyone listen in, anyone can broadcast!

So anyone can talk on Twitter, but is *anyone really listening*? That's a different question and the answer varies a great deal based on your industry, your status, and your skill at building an audience on Twitter. Also, because Twitter is short and news-oriented as well as open to any sort of broadcasting, it is incredibly noisy and full of silly Internet insanity.

Twitter is Noisy, Really Noisy

Because of its openness and because of its focus on short, newsy content, Twitter is a blizzard of information with lots and lots of noise obfuscating the interesting stuff. Whereas Facebook is all about friends, family, and fun "as if" you are at a company picnic or family reunion, Twitter is "as if" you were listening to all talk radio stations and all cable TV stations at the same time.

Amidst the noise of Twitter, the trick is to focus in on your customers and any marketing opportunities.

Twitter's Culture

For any social media, it's important to understand its culture. Twitter is fast-paced and used primarily to share news (about everything) and/or to share gossip (about pop culture and politics). If, for example, your business lives in an industry that thrives on news, Twitter may be great for you. If, for example, your business is connected to politics, news, or pop culture, Twitter may be essential to your marketing efforts. If your business is about coupons, special deals, and foodie events, Twitter may be an amazing marketing opportunity. If you attend industry trade shows or want to reach specific journalists hungry for story ideas, Twitter can be your secret marketing weapon. Throughout, keep your eye on how to "tune in" to the appropriate conversations on Twitter and "tune out" the blizzard of useless Twitter noise. Like talk radio or the 365 channels on cable TV, it's all about tuning in to an audience to succeed at Twitter marketing.

Untuned, your Twitter marketing will be a waste of time!

Sign up for Twitter

If you haven't already signed up for Twitter, simply go to http://jmlinks.com/1h. For more complete information on setting up your business, go to http://jmlinks.com/1i.

The basics of a business Twitter account are as follows:

- **Your Account / Your Username / Twitter Handle**. A username such as **@jmgrp** becomes your Twitter handle or URL (http://twitter.com/jmgrp) and shows up in your tweets. Choose a short user name that reflects your brand identity. **Shorter names are better** because tweets are limited to 140 characters and your username or "handle" counts as characters. As with most social media, you need an email address to sign up, or you can use a mobile phone number; unlike Facebook pages, you can only have one email address / password / user – or you can use third party apps like Hootsuite (http://www.hootsuite.com/) or Tweetdeck (https://tweetdeck.twitter.com/) to let multiple people access your account.
- **Profile Photo**. This is essentially the same as a profile photo on Facebook. The recommend images size is 400x400 pixels. It shows on your Tweets when viewed in a follower's news feed.
- **Bio**. You have 160 characters to explain your company brand, products, and/or services. Be sure to include a http:// URL link to your company website.
- **Header Image**. Similar to the Facebook cover photo, you get 1500x500 pixels to run as a banner across your account page.
- **Pinned Tweet**. You can "pin" a tweet to the top of your Twitter account, so that it shows first when users click up to your Twitter page. For example, compose a

tweet that promotes your email newsletter, and then "pin" this to the top of your Twitter account.

Here's a screenshot of how to "pin" a Tweet:

 Jason McDonald @jasoneg3 · 1h
Free tools for social media marketing.
Social Media Toolbook. Coupon code:
social3762 jm-seo.org/?p=1103

 Jason McDonald @jasoneg3 · 1
"Is Donald Trump   ian 4
Scam?" #market
jamesaltucher.co   n...

Share via Direct Message

Copy link to Tweet

Embed Tweet

Pin to your profile page

Delete Tweet

View

Essentially, find the tweet you want to pin, click on the dot dot dot icon, and then click on "pin to your profile page."

To access any of the other settings and features, go to your page on Twitter (as for example, http://twitter.com/jmgrp), be sure you are logged in, and click on the "edit profile" button in the far right of the screen. Also note that by clicking on your (small) Twitter profile picture at the top right of the screen, you can access your account settings (or go here: https://twitter.com/settings/security when logged in).

Here's a screenshot:

Not much can be customized, but in this day of Internet hacking and piracy, I recommend that you turn on **login verification**, which will require a mobile phone code for any new login.

Following and Followers

Now that you've set up your account, you can "follow" people or brands on Twitter by finding their Twitter accounts and clicking on the "follow" link. Similarly, people can follow you on Twitter by doing the same.

This structure is the same as on Facebook: when people follow you on Twitter, they see your tweets in their news feed subject to the clutter of the rapidly-moving Twitter news feed and a secret algorithm in Twitter that attempts to prioritize interactive Tweets (e.g., similar to Facebook *Edgerank*). Similarly, you can share the tweets of others (called *retweeting* or *RT*) to your own followers and others can share your tweets to their followers. It's *social* media after all.

Understand a Tweet

Tweets are the heart and soul of Twitter, and correspond to posts on Facebook. A tweet is limited to 140 characters, and as you type your tweet into your Twitter account it will give you a convenient countdown of the remaining characters. If you use an app like Hootsuite, that app will also give you a character count. Or you can use a service like http://www.lettercount.com/ and pre-count your characters.

Think of a tweet as a news headline or very short micro blog post with just a little supporting information. If you tweet a link to a blog post or other Web page, use a URL shortener like http://bitly.com/, http://tinyurl.com/, or the "shortlink" feature in WordPress, so as not to waste characters. To read Twitter's own description of how to tweet visit http://jmlinks.com/1j. You can create a self-standing tweet, or you can tweet "outlinks" to blog posts, videos, or images.

Here's a screenshot of a tweet by Edwin Lee, Mayor of San Francisco:

Edwin Lee @mayoredlee · Jun 14
Testing out new #SFLIZ #SoundCommons to activate UN Plaza as part of Central Market revitalization

Notice that if your tweet references an external URL, and that URL has a featured image, Twitter will display that image. Here's a screenshot of a tweet by Trend Hunter that has a URL and Twitter "pulls" the image from the referenced website:

Trend Hunter @trendhunter · 11m
Compact Cubic Speakers - This Small Speaker Concept Features a Touch
Display trendhunter.com/trends/small-s... #ArtDesign

Understand Hashtags

A hashtag (#) in a tweet indicates a keyword or theme and is clickable in a tweet. Think of a hashtag as a keyword / subject / theme about which people are talking: *sports, the Oakland A's, global warming, the 2016 presidential campaign, the Academy awards.* Hashtags should be short, and can NOT include spaces. Anyone can create one, and the success, or failure, of a hashtag is a function of whether many, or just a few, people use them. And, yes because Twitter is totally open there is no control: anyone can use them for any purpose, and a hashtag can overlap two discussions.

> *Anyone can create a hashtag! Anyone can chime in on a hashtag! No one controls a hashtag!*

How it's used, however, is a function of the crowd: the crowd decides what the hashtag really means.

To find existing hashtags, use http://hashtagify.me or simply search Twitter using the # hashtag in front of a topic such as *#organicfood* or *#free*. Note that hashtags can NOT include spaces. So it's *#organicfood* not *#organic food*. Or just search Twitter by keyword and look for the # hashtag symbol. For example, here's a screenshot of a tweet with the hashtags highlighted in yellow:

Green Breeze Imports @GreenBreezeImpt · Jul 11
#Organic #Natural #Body #Lotion. Check it out!
Keep #skin #smooth and #soft.
amazon.com/dp/B010RFVQRI

I recommend that you research, identify, and maintain a running list of *hashtags* that are important to your company.

#HASHTAGS DESIGNATE

CONVERSATIONS ON TWITTER

In the tweet above, the hashtags *#organic* and *#natural* are "themes" around which people converse on Twitter. By including hashtags in your Tweets, you can be found by non-followers who are interested in, and following, that topic on Twitter. For example, if you are a seller of organic baby food and have a new flavor out, you might tweet with hashtags as follows:

> Hey followers! Our super baby plum recipe is out. **#babyfood #organic #natural #food**. http://bit.ly/1234

These hashtags become clickable in a tweet, and for people who are interested in that topic, your tweet becomes part of an enormous conversation around that theme. So, finding popular, relevant hashtags and tweeting on them is a good promotion strategy on Twitter. Remember, however, that you have to stand out and get attention amidst all the noise!

Understand the @ Sign or Handle

The @ sign designates a Twitter account, often called a "handle" on Twitter. When included in a tweet, it does two things:

- It becomes **clickable**. Anyone who sees this tweet can click on the @handle and go up to that account to view the account and possibly follow that person on Twitter; and
- It **shows up in the news feed of that person** and **sends an email alert** to him or her that they have been mentioned. This is called a *mention*. A *mention* means essentially that: someone has mentioned you (your Twitter account) in a Tweet.

Here's a screenshot:

KQED (@KQED) has tweeted to its followers that Barry Manilow (@barrymanilow) will be on its show July 4th, PBS. Anyone seeing this tweet can click "up" to Barry Manilow's account, and Barry Manilow would have received a "mention" notification in his account news feed.

Using the @ sign, you

can tweet to anyone

Importantly, this openness means that you can tweet "to" anyone on Twitter: it's completely open, and – unlike Facebook or LinkedIn – you do not need "pre-approval" to converse with someone via Twitter (more about this later, when we discuss promoting your Twitter account).

Again, when your Tweet contains the @handle of someone else, that generates an alert in their news feed and often via email. **Via Twitter, you can tweet to anyone!**

Understand Mentions and Retweets

We've already explained a **mention**. When someone includes your @handle in their Tweet, that's called a mention: clickable by anyone following them, to go "up" to your account and learn about you or your business.

A **retweet** is a special type of mention. In it, person *A* retweets the tweet of person *B*. Meaning, he takes your tweet and tweets it out to his followers. Imagine if Ellen DeGeneres recapped your joke on her TV show. That "retweet" of your joke would spur her followers to learn about you, and might result in a massive increase in your follower count.

Here's a screenshot:

Ellen DeGeneres ✓
@TheEllenShow

⚙ Following

Yeah I did. RT @justinbieber: I think today was our best hang out yet.
@TheEllenShow u got me. Lol

Ellen is "retweeting" Justin Bieber's tweet about how great their interaction was on her TV show. In this way, her fans see Justin Bieber's Twitter account @justinbieber and can learn about him, and possibly follow him, thereby increasing his follower count. Ellen and Justin are essentially having a public conversation via Twitter.

You don't have to be a Hollywood star to do this: identify important people in your industry and converse with them via the @sign (handles). Your followers can see this conversation, and their followers can see it too (if the person responds to you) – thereby cross-pollinating your accounts. (See technical details below).

Tweet (Privately) To Someone

Here's some esoterica about mentions or retweets. When you tweet directly at someone (by including their account (@sign) in your tweet), that tweet is visible to **only** those folks who follow **both** accounts. If you put a dot "." before the @ sign, your tweet shows up in the news feed (officially called your "timeline" on Twitter, but not to be confused with the "timeline" of Facebook) of all of your followers, even if they do not follow the mentioned account. For example, if I tweet:

> *@katyperry love your music, give me free concert tickets!*
>
>> (shows to ONLY those people who follow @jasoneg3 AND @katyperry) and it shows in Katy Perry's own timeline (if she actually checks it)).

vs.

> *.@katyperry loved your concert, give me free concert tickets!*
>
>> (shows to ALL people who follow @jasoneg3 AND it shows in Katy Perry's own timeline (if she actually checks it)).

To read more about the "dot" in front of the "@" sign in more detail, visit http://jmlinks.com/2k. For the official Twitter guide to Twitter for Business, visit https://business.twitter.com/ and for the official Twitter help files, visit https://support.twitter.com/.

▶▶ MAKE AN INVENTORY OF LIKES & DISLIKES ON TWITTER

Now that you understand the basics of how Twitter works, it's time to research whether your customers are on Twitter and identify competitors in your industry who are on Twitter and/or successful businesses on Twitter to make an inventory of your likes and dislikes.

Find Accounts on Twitter

Stay signed into your Twitter account. There are several ways to find accounts to follow on Twitter:

- **Visit their Websites**. Most big brands will have a prominent link to Twitter, right on their Website. For example, go to http://www.rei.com/ or http://www.wholefoods.com/, find the Twitter link, click on it, and hit follow. Go to your competitor websites and do the same.
- **Search on Twitter**. While logged in to your account, go to the top right of the screen and in the "Search Twitter" box, enter the names of competitors, businesses you like, or keywords. To find stuff on Twitter about organic food, just type in "organic food" into the search box. Then, when you find an account you like, just click "follow" and you are now following it.
- **Advanced Search on Twitter**. You can find Twitter Advanced Search by first doing a search, then in the results

Here's a screenshot:

You can also just visit this link: https://twitter.com/search-advanced.

Outside of Twitter, go to Google and type in *site:twitter.com* and your keywords. For example, on Google, *site:twitter.com "organic food"* will identify Twitter accounts with that keyword. Google is often a better way to find Twitter *accounts*, whereas Twitter search is a better way to browse individual *tweets*. Remember: there is no space between site: and twitter – it's *site:twitter.com* not *site: twitter.com*. To see this in action, go to http://jmlinks.com/2j.

Once you follow companies, you can browse their Twitter pages easily by clicking on the "following" link at the top left of the page while you are logged in to your Twitter account. Here's a screenshot –

Note that Twitter is completely open: anyone can see who you follow via your public Twitter account (unlike on, say, Facebook, where only you know whom you are following).

Your **TODO** here is to identify companies on Twitter, both in and outside of your industry, so that you can inventory what you like and dislike. Here are some inventory questions:

- **Username**. Usernames should be short yet convey the brand. Do you like / dislike the usernames of brands that you see?
- **Profile Picture**. As is true in all social media, the profile pictures shows when viewed on someone else's timeline. Do you like / dislike the profile pictures of various companies on Twitter? Why or why not?
- **Header Photo**. Similarly to the Facebook cover photo, this wide banner dominates that account visuals. How are competitors and other businesses using the header photo on Twitter?
- **Pinned Tweets**. Are any brands using the pinned tweet feature? If so, how?
- **Account Bio**. How are brands using their bio to market via Twitter? Do you see any opportunities or pitfalls here?

Posting or Tweeting Strategy

You'll quickly realize that Twitter offers little customization, and that most of the action on Twitter has to do with *posting strategy* or what would precisely be called *tweeting strategy*. What are businesses tweeting, and why? What is their *posting rhythm*? Similar to all social media, the idea is to spur interactivity, get shares (retweets), and drive traffic to desired actions.

Pay attention to companies in your industry as well as hashtags (see below) in your industry, all the while asking the question: are our customers on Twitter? If so, what are they tweeting about?

Let's review some accounts on Twitter and reverse-engineer their posting strategies. Do the same for businesses that you like and/or competitors in your industry.

Twitter Marketing: Common Uses

Here are common uses of Twitter and example accounts:

- **Celebrities**. Examples are Katy Perry (https://twitter.com/katyperry) , Justin Bieber (https://twitter.com/justinbieber), Ellen Degeneres (https://twitter.com/TheEllenShow).
    - **Marketing Goals**: stay top of mind, get social shares, use Twitter to cross-promote their concerts and TV shows, **posting rhythm** of *fun, fun, fun, fun, buy my concert tickets* etc.
- **Politicians**. Examples are Hillary Clinton (https://twitter.com/hillaryclinton), Barack Obama (https://twitter.com/potus), Bill de Blasio (https://twitter.com/billdeblasio).
    - **Marketing Goals**: stay top of mind, get social shares, use Twitter to motivate followers to take political action. **Posting rhythm** of newsworthy, newsworthy, newsworthy, take political action or donate...
- **Political Causes and Non-Profits.** Examples are Greenpeace (https://twitter.com/greenpeace), Red Cross (https://twitter.com/redcross), Catholic Charities (https://twitter.com/ccharitiesusa).
    - **Marketing Goals:** stay top of mind, get social shares, use Twitter followers to take political action or make donations. Posting rhythm is similar to politicians.
- **Brands.** Examples are REI (https://twitter.com/rei), Gucci (https://twitter.com/gucci), Marth Stewart Living (https://twitter.com/MS_Living).
    - **Marketing Goals:** stay top of mind, get social shares, use Twitter followers to connect to buy actions, also use Twitter as an "insider" or

"best customer" channel for secret coupons, inside deals and information. **Posting rhythm** is fun, fun, fun, fun, buy my stuff.

- **Restaurants and Food Trucks.** Examples are Kogi BBQ (https://twitter.com/kogibbq), Ricky's Fish Tacos (https://twitter.com/rickysfishtacos), Newark Natural Foods (https://twitter.com/newarkfoods).
  - o **Marketing Goals**. stay top of mind, get social shares, use Twitter to drive real-world traffic to a store or restaurant, usually looking for insider information or special deals / coupons.

For most for-profit businesses, common marketing goals for Twitter are:

- **Stay top of mind / one touch to many**. To the extent that your users are on Twitter (usually to follow up-to-the-minute news), you can use Twitter to continually remind users about your company, product, and/or service.
- **Insider / loyalty programs**. If you are a brand with a core group of loyal customers (e.g., REI's loyal group of outdoor fanatics, or Gucci's loyal group of fashion addicts), you can use Twitter to stay in touch with this elite group and reward them with insider information, tips, special deals, and even coupons.
- **Coupons / bargains**. If you use coupons or discounts, especially in retail, customers commonly scan Twitter for coupons and special deals.
- **Foodies / coupons / bargains / what's cookin'**. Especially in the food truck industry, but in any big downtown area with a lunch scene, foodies look to Twitter to identify special deals, coupons, and what's cookin'.
- **On-going Discussions**. By using #hashtags (e.g., #AIDS, #globalwarming, #obamacare), you can participate in an on-going global discussion and thereby market your products. A special case of this is trade shows, which often use a hashtag (#CES for Consumer Electronics Show, for example) to allow participants to converse via Twitter.
- **News Alerts**. To the extent that you generate and/or participate in news, Twitter is the go-to service for breaking news (especially vis hashtags and trending searches).
- **Political Action**. For non-profits and political groups, Twitter is the go-to place to organize politically and discuss politics.

IDENTIFY COMPANIES WHO DO TWITTER WELL, AND REVERSE ENGINEER THEM

For your first **TODO**, download the **Twitter Research Worksheet**. For the worksheet, go to https://www.jm-seo.org/workbooks (click on Social Media Workbook, enter the code 'smm2016' to register if you have not already done so), and click on the link to the "Twitter Research Worksheet." You'll answer questions as to whether your potential customers are on Twitter, identify brands to follow, and inventory what you like and dislike about their Twitter set up and marketing strategy.

≫ BRAINSTORM AND EXECUTE A TWEETING STRATEGY

Optimizing your account on Twitter is pretty straightforward. As indicated above, a good way to do this is to compare / contrast pages that you like and use your inventory list to identify ToDos. So, comparing Taco Bell (https://twitter.com/tacobell), the White House (https://twitter.com/whlive), and Kogi BBQ (https://twitter.com/kogibbq), let's go down the short list. As indicated above, the main elements are:

- **Your Account / Your Username / Twitter Handle**. A username such as **@jmgrp** becomes your Twitter URL (http://twitter.com/jmgrp) and shows up in your tweets. Choose a short user name that reflects your brand identity. **Shorter names are better** because tweets are limited to 140 characters and your username or "handle" counts as characters. As with most social media, you need an email address to sign up, or you can use a mobile phone number; unlike Facebook pages, you can only have one email address / password / user – or you can use third party apps like Hootsuite to control your account.
- **Profile Photo**. This is essentially the same as a profile photo on Facebook. The recommend images size is 400x400 pixels. It shows on your Tweets when viewed in a follower's news feed.
- **Bio**. You have 160 characters to explain your company brand, products, and/or services. Be sure to include a URL link to your company website.
- **Header Image**. Similar to the Facebook cover photo, you get 1500x500 pixels to run as a banner across your account page.
- **Pinned Tweet**. You can "pin" a tweet to the top of the page, so that it shows first when users click up to your Twitter account page. For example, compose a tweet

that promotes your email newsletter, and then "pin" this to the top of your Twitter account. Here's a screenshot:

If you haven't already signed up for Twitter, simply go to http://jmlinks.com/1h. For more complete information on setting up your business, go to http://jmlinks.com/1i.

Tweeting Strategy: Tweet Items That Your Customers Care About

That's all there is to Twitter at a structural level. The real work begins in identifying a tweeting strategy. What will you tweet? Who will care? Let's reverse engineer some companies and their tweeting strategies:

> **Kogi BBQ** (https://twitter.com/kogibbq). Their tweeting strategy is 90% about the location of the taco truck, with a few tweets about "what's cooking" or "insider specials," and the occasional back-and-forth with a hard-core Kogi fan about the joys of Korean BBQ. That's it.

> **REI** (https://twitter.com/rei). Their tweets are largely off-loads to blog posts, YouTube videos, and Instagram photos about the fun of outdoor activities, some participatory contests for hard-core REI fans, headline links to in-depth blog posts on outdoor fun, and about 10% shameless "buy our stuff isn't this a cool

product" tweets. Like many retailers, REI uses Twitter as a place to communicate deals, insider information, and special offers to its most devoted customers.

Woot (https://twitter.com/woot). Their tweets are 100% about discounts and bargains, as Woot (owned now by Amazon) is all about discounts and special deals. It's the home shopping network gone Twitter.

Greenpeace (https://twitter.com/greenpeace). This non-profit tweets photos that inspire about wildlife and nature, links to blog posts about environmental issues, and political calls to action.

Cato Institute (https://twitter.com/catoinstitute). This political action organization tweets about politics from a conservative perspective, with offlinks to its blog and videos plus the occasional call to action.

Zak George (https://twitter.com/zakgeorge). A dog trainer and huge YouTube success, Zak George tweets links to his YouTube videos, some links to his Facebook page, and the occasional tweet about a sponsored product.

Your job is to reverse engineer competitors or companies you admire in terms of their tweeting strategy. What are they tweeting (blog posts, pictures, infographics, videos), and why are they tweeting it (to stay top of mind, sell stuff, get viewers on YouTube). Who is following them and why? What's in it for the followers? How does all this tweeting activity lead ultimately to some sort of sale or business action?

For your second **TODO**, download the **Twitter Tweeting Strategy Worksheet**. For the worksheet, go to https://www.jm-seo.org/workbooks (click on Social Media Workbook, enter the code 'smm2016' to register if you have not already done so), and click on the link to the "Twitter Tweeting Strategy Worksheet." You'll answer questions to help you understand what other companies are doing on Twitter, and begin to outline your own tweeting strategy.

Content is King

As you work on a tweeting strategy, you'll quickly realize you need a lot of content! Remember: create a **content marketing system** of:

- **Other people's content**. Relevant content in your industry. By curating out the garbage and identifying the cool, fun, interesting stuff, you can use other people's content to help your tweets stay top of mind.
- **Your own content**. Twitter is all about off-loads to blog posts, infographics, images, photos, videos, Memes, and other types of your own content. Twitter and blogging go together like peas and carrots, while Twitter and video go together like scotch and soda.

To identify relevant content from other people, I recommend setting up a Feedly account (http://www.feedly.com/) and using tools like Buzzsumo (http://www.buzzsumo.com), and Google Alerts (https://www.google.com/alerts). Organize these tools into topic groups, and then as you find content useful to your target audience, "tweet out" that content. Use a tool like Hootsuite (http://www.hootsuite.com/) to schedule your tweets in advance.

As for your own content, Twitter is best used by staying on topic and sharing original useful content such as in-depth blog posts, free eBooks or webinars, infographics and instructographics, videos on YouTube. Twitter is a headline service pointing to the "rest of the story" on your blog, video, or infographic.

▶▶ PROMOTE YOUR TWITTER ACCOUNT AND TWEETS

Once you've set up your Twitter account, and begun to populate it with tweets on a regular basis, you've essentially "set up" your party on Twitter. Now it's time to send out the invitations.

In and of itself, a Twitter Page will not be self-promoting! You've got to promote it!

Assuming your Twitter account shares lots of yummy, useful, fun, provocative content that when seen by a user will entice him or her to "follow" you on Twitter, here are some common ways to promote your Twitter account and Tweets:

- **Real World to Social.** Don't forget the real world! If you are a museum store, for example, be sure that the cashiers recommend to people that they "follow" you on Twitter? *Why? Because they'll get insider tips, fun do-it-yourself posts,* *announcements on upcoming museum and museum store events, etc.* Get your staff to promote Twitter in that important face-to-face interaction. If you're a barbeque truck in Los Angeles, post signs to "follow us on Twitter" on the trucks, and have staff cajole customers to "follow you." *Why follow you on Twitter? To learn where the taco truck is, to get special deals, and to learn what's cooking.* Use the real world to promote your Twitter account, and be ready to explain "why" they should follow you on Twitter. What's in it for them?

- **Cross-Promotion**. Link your website to your Twitter Page, your blog posts to your Twitter Page, your YouTube to your Twitter Page, etc. Notice how big brands like REI do this: one digital property promotes another digital property.
- **Email**. Email your customer list and ask them to follow you on Twitter. Again, you must explain what's in it for them.
- **Twitter Internal**. Interact with other accounts via the @ sign, share their content, comment on timely topics using #hashtags, and reach out to complementary pages to work with you on co-promotion. (See below).
- **Use Twitter Plugins**. Twitter has numerous plugins that allow you to "embed" your Twitter Page on your website, and thereby nurture cross promotion. To learn more about plugins, visit https://dev.twitter.com/web/overview. Among the better ones –
  - **The Tweet Button**. Make it easy for people to tweet your content (e.g., blog posts).
  - **The Follow Button**. Make it easy for Web visitors to follow you on Twitter.
- **Leverage your Fans**. People who like your Twitter Page are your best promoters. Do everything you can to get them to retweet you to their own followers. Remember, it's *social* (!) media, and encouraging your customers to share your content is the name of the game. You want to leverage your fans as much as possible to share your content.

DON'T FORGET THE REAL WORLD AS A TWITTER PROMOTION STRATEGY

Three Special Ways to Promote via Twitter.

Twitter has three very special ways to promote yourself or your company that are much stronger than on other social media.

Use #Hashtags to Promote Your Company

The first is the **hashtag**. Because Twitter is all about news, the use of hashtags (designated on Twitter by the "#" or "hash" sign) on trending or controversial topics is bigger on Twitter than on any other social media. Identify trending or important hashtags and include them in your tweets. Use http://hashtagify.me to identify hashtags in your industry, and don't forget about major trade shows which often have (and promote) their own hashtags. Then include these hashtags in your tweets, and make sure that your tweets are not only on topic but also offlink to something useful, provocative or important. In that way, they'll discover you via a hashtag and then follow you permanently.

Industry Trade Shows and Hashtags

Here's a hashtag use you do not want to miss: industry trade shows. Nearly every industry has THE trade show, or a few KEY trade shows. Nowadays, these will have hashtags, such as *#CES2016* for the 2016 Consumer Electronics Show. To see the #CES2016 hashtag in action, visit http://jmlinks.com/12y.

Pre-identify the hashtags of your own industry trade show(s) as well as subordinate, session or topic hashtags, and start tweeting on those theme before, during and shortly after the show. Attendees know to look for the show hashtags to find out what's cool, exciting, and worth visiting.

For many businesses, simply knowing the hashtag of "the" industry conference and tweeting during the yearly, or twice yearly, trade conference in and of itself will justify using Twitter for marketing:

> *Hey #CES2016 attendees! Come by out booth by 2:30 pm for a free laser wand give-away.*

Identify the Twitter account of the industry trade show(s), and they'll easily show you the relevant hashtags. Make sure you have a robust Twitter account set up before the big show, and then during the show start tweeting on show-related hashtags. For many businesses, the trade show use of Twitter is the most important marketing use of Twitter.

Here's something devious. Identify the hashtags for all your industry shows, including the ones you do not attend, and insert them into your tweets during show time. In this way you can tweet "to" attendees of a show without actually being there!

@Someonefamous

The second promotion strategy is what I call **@someonefamous**. The idea here is to reach out and "have a conversation" with someone more famous (with more followers) than you. Think of it like Dr. Phil making it on the Oprah Winfrey show: her audience saw this new "doctor," and some of her fans became his fans. The trick is to find business partners, complementary companies, or other people / companies on Twitter who are influencers and who have more and/or different fan bases than you.

A useful tool to use is Buzzsumo (http://www.buzzsumo.com/). Search for your keywords and identify influencers tweeting about those topics. Identifying them is the easy part. The hard part is getting them to engage in a Twitter conversation with you. You have to convince them to have a conversation with you on Twitter, and then once you're talking to their fans… convince their fans to follow you, too.

Once you are lucky enough to start a conversation with someone more famous than you, remember to use the "dot" in front of the "@" sign to correctly broadcast your message. To learn more about this, visit http://jmlinks.com/2k.

Pitch Journalists via Twitter

Here's a key use of twitter you do not want to miss: pitching journalists via Twitter about your company, products, or services as "story ideas:"

@journalists. Identify journalists on Twitter, find their handles, and tweet "to" the journalists, pitching them on story ideas. Journalists love Twitter because it's where stories break first. They listen to their Twitter feeds as businesses, organizations, and individuals "pitch" them on story ideas via Twitter.

Indeed, you can even advertise to select lists of journalists by using username targeting on Twitter (see below).

Get Retweeted

The third Twitter promotion strategy is the **retweet**. By posting items that are funny, scandalous, interesting, shocking, outrageous or otherwise highly contagious, you get people to retweet your tweets, thereby (again) allowing their followers to see you, and hopefully begin to follow you as well. To research what is retweeted in your industry, simply do a Twitter search with the words RT in front of your keywords. For an example, visit http://jmlinks.com/2l.

Advertise

Besides these three promotion methods, there's (gasp!) paid advertising on Twitter. You can promote your tweets as well as create custom advertising campaigns to promote your account and/or clicks to your website. To learn more about advertising on Twitter visit https://biz.twitter.com/start-advertising or https://ads.twitter.com/. Because journalists and bloggers often follow Twitter intensely for breaking news, one strategy is to make an "influencer list" on influencers on Twitter, and then advertise your tweets directly to those high-impact Twitterers. To learn more about username targeting on Twitter, visit http://jmlinks.com/1k.

» MEASURE YOUR RESULTS

Measuring the success or failure of your Twitter marketing can be a challenge. Let's look at it from the "bottom up" in terms of items a marketer might want to know or measure vis-a-vis Twitter:

- **Sales or Sales Leads**. Have tweets or Twitter marketing resulted in actual sales leaders (completed feedback forms for a free offer, consultation, eBook, download, etc.) and/or eCommerce sales?
- **Branding / Awareness**. Has Twitter increased our brand awareness and/or improved our brand image?
- **Top of Mind / One Touch to Many**. Has Twitter helped us to stay "top of mind," by reminding potential customers of our company, products, and/or services?
- **Tweet Interactivity**. Have people read our tweets? Interacted with our tweets by favoriting them, and/or retweeted our tweets?
- **Twitter Account**. Is our follower count increasing, and if so, by how much and how fast? Where are our followers physically located, and what are their demographic characteristics?

The last of these is the easiest to measure: simply record your Twitter follower count each month, and keep a record of it month-to-month. I generally do this on my *Keyword Worksheet*, where I also track inbound links to my website, and my review count on review media such as Google+ and Yelp. (Watch a video on a Keyword Worksheet at http://jmlinks.com/1l).

Analytics Inside of Twitter

Inside of Twitter, click on your profile picture on the top right of the screen, and then in the pull-down menu, click on Analytics. Here's a screenshot:

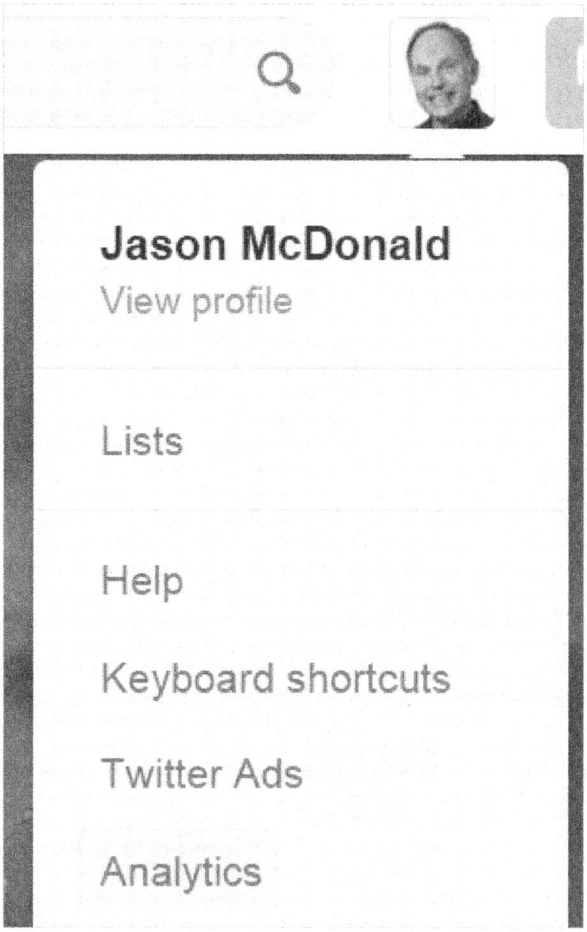

Jason McDonald
View profile

Lists

Help

Keyboard shortcuts

Twitter Ads

Analytics

There you can see which tweets gained the most impressions, as well as engagements by Tweet such as clicks, follows, and retweets. Twitter will also tell you whether links you are sharing are getting clicked on and so on and so forth. Twitter also has a feature called **Twitter cards** that bridges your website to/from Twitter activity According To Twitter:

> With Twitter Cards, you can attach rich photos, videos and media experience to Tweets that drive traffic to your website. Simply add a few lines of HTML to your webpage, and users who Tweet links to your content will have a "Card" added to the Tweet that's visible to all of their followers. (https://dev.twitter.com/cards/overview, browsed 7/8/2015).

If you enabled Twitter cards on your Website, you get attribution for your Web content plus more data on that inside of Twitter. Learn more at https://dev.twitter.com/cards/overview.

Google Analytics

Most of us want to drive traffic from Twitter to our website, or even better to our ecommerce store or to download a free eBook or software package to get a sales lead. Google Analytics will measure how traffic flows from Twitter to your website, and then what happens upon arrival.

Sign up for Google Analytics (https://www.google.com/analytics) and install the required tracking code. Inside of your Google Analytics account on the left column, drill down by clicking on Acquisition > Social > Overview. Then on the right hand side of the screen you'll see a list of Social Networks. Find Twitter on that list, and click on that. Google Analytics will tell you what URLs people clicked to from Twitter to your Website, giving you insights into what types of web content people find attractive.

You can also create a custom Advanced Segment to look at only Twitter traffic and its behavior. For information on how to create custom Advanced Segments in Google Analytics, go to http://jmlinks.com/1f. For the Google help files on Advanced Segments go to http://jmlinks.com/1g.

In sum, inside of Twitter you can see how people interact with your Twitter account and tweets. Inside of Google Analytics, you can see where they land on your website and what they do after they arrive.

▶▶ DELIVERABLE: A TWITTER MARKETING PLAN

Now that we've come to the end our chapter on Twitter, your **DELIVERABLE** has arrived. Go to https://www.jm-seo.org/workbooks (click on Social Media Workbook, enter the code 'smm2016' to register if you have not already done so), and click on the link to the "Twitter Marketing Plan." By filling out this plan, you and your team will establish a vision of what you want to achieve via Twitter.

▶ APPENDIX: TOP TWITTER MARKETING TOOLS AND RESOURCES

Here are the top tools and resources to help you with Twitter marketing. For an up-to-date list, go to https://www.jm-seo.org/workbooks (click on Social Media Workbook, enter the code 'smm2016' to register if you have not already done so). Click on the *Social Media Toolbook* link, and drill down to the Twitter chapter.

TWITTER ADVANCED SEARCH - https://twitter.com/search-advanced

> Search to see what others are saying about topics relevant and your organization's interests, before, during, after you use Twitter. Here's a nifty trick: Use the 'Near this place' field to find people in a city near you tweeting on a topic like 'pizza.' Great for local brands.
>
> **Rating:** 5 Stars | **Category:** tool

BUZZSUMO - http://buzzsumo.com/

> Buzzsumo is a 'buzz' monitoring tool for social media. Input a website (domain) and/or a topic and see what people are sharing across Facebook, Twitter, Google+ and other social media. Great for link-building (because what people link to is what they share), and also for social media.
>
> **Rating:** 5 Stars | **Category:** tool

HASHTAGIFY.ME - http://hashtagify.me

> Hashtagify.me allows you to search tens of millions of Twitter hashtags and quickly find the best ones for your needs based on popularity, relationships,

languages, influencers and other metrics. Also useful for SEO link building and keyword discovery.

Rating: 5 Stars | **Category:** tool

HootSuite - https://hootsuite.com/

Manage all of your social media accounts, including multiple Twitter profiles through HootSuite. HootSuite makes it easy to manage multiple users over various social media accounts and allows you to track statistics. LOVE THIS TOOL!

Rating: 5 Stars | **Category:** vendor

Hashtags.org - http://hashtags.org

Tool which attempts to organize the world's hashtags. Provides hashtag analytics for your brand, business, product, service, event or blog. Input words that matter to you, and Hashtags looks to see the trends on Twitter.

Rating: 4 Stars | **Category:** engine

Twitaholic - http://twitaholic.com

Tracks the most popular Twitter users based on followers. Use this to find top tweeters - sort of a top 100, 200, 300, etc list for the Twitterdom. Also just a great way to find out who's really famous on Twitter. Katy Perry, anyone?

Rating: 4 Stars | **Category:** service

Pay with a Tweet - http://www.paywithatweet.com/

Viral / share promotion tool focusing on referral marketing. Entice users to 'pay with a Tweet' in order to receive a discount or some wonderful freebie. Includes a limited functionality, limited usage free plan.

Rating: 4 Stars | **Category:** tool

SOCIALOOMPH - https://www.socialoomph.com/

SocialOomph is a powerful free (and paid) suite of tools to manage and schedule your Twitter and Facebook posts. Imagine going to the beach, forgetting about the office, yet having 67 different Tweets auto-posted...that's what SocialOomph is about. Use technology to appear busy and Facebooking / Tweeting all the time.

Rating: 4 Stars | **Category:** tool

TWITTER ANALYTICS - https://analytics.twitter.com

The official page for Twitter analytics and metrics. Sign up via Twitter, and learn how your tweets are doing!

Rating: 4 Stars | **Category:** tool

BITLY - https://bitly.com

Bitly is a URL shortening service that will track your click-throughs. Very useful for email marketing, blogging, and Twitter.

Rating: 4 Stars | **Category:** service

KEYHOLE - http://keyhole.co

This tool provides real-time social conversation tracking for Twitter, Facebook, and Instagram. Use this tool to measure conversations around your business, identify prospective clients and influencers talking about your services, and find relevant content. Enables tracking of hashtags, keywords, and URLs.

Rating: 4 Stars | **Category:** tool

TWITONOMY - http://twitonomy.com

Twitonomy is a free online Twitter analytics tool which provides a wealth of information about all aspects of Twitter, including in-depth stats on any Twitter user, insights on your followers, mentions, favorites & retweets, and analytics on hashtags. It also lets you monitor tweets, manage your lists, download tweets &

reports, and much more. Definitely worth checking out if Twitter is part of your social media strategy.

Rating: 4 Stars | **Category:** tool

TWITTER FOR BUSINESS - https://business.twitter.com

Straight from the bird's mouth...learn how to use Twitter for business.

Rating: 4 Stars | **Category:** overview

IFTTT - https://ifttt.com

This app, If Then Then That, is a great tool for linking multiple social media accounts. It allows you to create 'recipes' that link your tools exactly the way you like them! For example: make a recipe that adds to a Google Apps spreadsheet every time a particular user uploads to Instagram - a great way to keep up with your competitors SMM strategies! With over 120 supported applications, the 'recipes' are endless, making this a good tool for your SMM strategies.

Rating: 4 Stars | **Category:** tool

FOLLOWERWONK - https://moz.com/followerwonk/

Followerwonk helps you explore and grow your social graph. Dig deeper into Twitter analytics: Who are your followers? Where are they located? When do they tweet? Find and connect with new influencers in your niche. Use actionable visualizations to compare your social graph to others. Easily share your reports with the world. Brought to you by Moz.

Rating: 4 Stars | **Category:** tool

TWITTER HELP CENTER - https://support.twitter.com

Did you know Twitter has technical support? Yep, they do. It's relatively hidden, but here it is. It's more for users of Twitter, but it does have some juicy help for actual businesses on Twitter as well. Tweet, tweet, tweet.

Rating: 4 Stars | **Category:** resource

TAG BOARD - https://tagboard.com/

Hashtags have moved beyond Twitter. This amazing cool tool allows you to take a hashtag and browse Facebook and Twitter and Instagram, etc., so see posts that relate to that hashtag. Then you can find related tags. Oh, and you can use it as a content discovery tool, too.

Rating: 4 Stars | **Category:** tool

TAGDEF - https://tagdef.com

Looking to understand what a particular hashtag means? Use this nifty tool to define a hashtag and to research hashtags BEFORE you create or use them.

Rating: 4 Stars | **Category:** tool

TWEETDECK - https://tweetdeck.twitter.com

TweetDeck is your personal browser for staying in touch with what's happening now, connecting you with your contacts across Twitter, Facebook, MySpace, LinkedIn and more. Developed independently, now owned by Twitter.

Rating: 4 Stars | **Category:** service

BUFFER - https://buffer.com/

Schedule tweets and other social media activity in the future. Competitor to Hootsuite.

Rating: 4 Stars | **Category:** tool

5

YOUTUBE

YouTube (https://www.youtube.com/), in particular, and video in general, provide a two-for-one punch to your social media marketing. First, video itself can be the "there there," the content that you post to Twitter, Facebook, LinkedIn, etc. People love, watch, and share video as one of the most popular types of content across social media. Second, beyond being content itself, YouTube is in and of itself a social media platform. As on other platforms, people "like" (thumbs up in YouTube lingo), "comment on," and "share" your videos. They "subscribe" to your channel and get notifications when you release a new video. YouTube, in short, is both content itself and a social media platform in its own right.

In this chapter, we'll explore both aspects of YouTube. You'll see similarities to Facebook: setting up a channel ("Page") on YouTube, uploading a video ("post") to YouTube, and the fact that people subscribe to your channel ("like" your "Page"). All of these dynamics are similar to other social media platforms. But video also brings three very different marketing mechanisms to the social media party in its role as content. Video can be used as a **supportive medium**, it can be deployed via **SEO** (Search Engine Optimization) to show at the top of Google and/or YouTube searches, and it can be tweaked for **social sharing** or even **viral marketing**.

Let's get started!

To Do List:

» Explore how YouTube Works

» Inventory Companies on YouTube

» Set up Your Channel and Upload Videos

» Understand the Three Promotional Uses of Video

» Measure your Results

» EXPLORE HOW YOUTUBE WORKS

Video and YouTube are among the most dramatic, most viral components of the Internet. Who doesn't know the "Harlem Shake" (http://jmlinks.com/1m) or the "Ice Bucket Challenge" (http://jmlinks.com/1n)? Who hasn't watched "Will it blend" (http://jmlinks.com/1o) or "Dear 16 Year Old Me" (http://jmlinks.com/1p)? And who hasn't fallen into the trap of assuming all YouTube is are silly cat videos, Rihanna videos, and inappropriate High School humor? It is, but YouTube is much, much more than that as a marketing opportunity (and as a social phenomenon).

As we shall see, there are three basic ways that YouTube videos can help you with social media marketing:

1. **Video as a supporting medium**: acting as the "content" that you "share" via other social media, including your website.
2. **Video as a discovery mechanism via SEO** (Search Engine Optimization), helping you promote your company, products, or services via search.
3. **Video as a share / viral promotion tactic**, because people love and share provocative videos.

We'll dive into the details in a moment. But first, log on to YouTube and get your bearings. (For the official YouTube starter guide, go to http://jmlinks.com/1q). If you're familiar with Facebook and Twitter, you'll see many similarities right out of the gate:

- Individuals have an "account" or "**channel**" on YouTube, set up by registering with an email address and using Google+ to manage their account.
- Individuals can **upload videos** to their "channel," and when uploading give each video a TITLE, a DESCRIPTION, and KEYWORD TAGS as well as designate a VIDEO THUMBNAIL.
- Individuals "**subscribe**" to the channels of other individuals (or brands) on YouTube, and when someone you subscribe to uploads a new video, you get a notification on your YouTube logon as well as via email that a new video has been posted.

- Individuals can **thumbs up / thumbs down videos** (akin to "like" on Facebook of a post), comment (via Google+ comments), and share the videos via other social media as well as create playlists of videos on YouTube.
- Companies can create **brand channels** on YouTube. Like Twitter, YouTube is very easy and open: anyone can quickly create a channel, no serious user authentication is required.

For assistance on how to set up a company YouTube channel, visit http://jmlinks.com/1r. Like Twitter, YouTube is very open; anyone can set up a YouTube channel quickly, post a video, and the followers need not wait for approval to subscribe to a channel.

>> INVENTORY COMPANIES ON YOUTUBE

After you've signed up for YouTube at least as an individual, your mission is to identify competitors on YouTube as well as brands you like in order to make an inventory of your likes and dislikes when it comes to YouTube as a channel for marketing.

How to Browse YouTube for Videos and Channels

One obvious way to make your short list of companies to follow is to simply visit their websites, and look for a link from their website to their YouTube channel. A big brand like REI (http://www.rei.com/), for example, will usually have the YouTube icon somewhere on the page. Simply be signed into your personal YouTube account, click on their link to YouTube, and then once you land on their channel, click the red "subscribe" button.

A second way to find companies to subscribe to is to **browse YouTube**. When you are logged in to your YouTube account, simply click on the left hand side of the screen on "Browse channels."

There you'll see various subject-oriented groups of YouTube content, starting with *#PopularonYouTube*. On each category, you can click on the category name (e.g., *Film and Entertainment*), and drill down to channels in that category. Identify channels that interest you and hit the "subscribe" button. As you subscribe to channels, they will begin to appear on your home screen on the left column. To unsubscribe, just click on "Manage subscriptions" and/or go to the channel and hit the now-gray "Subscribed" button.

How to Search YouTube

Most of the action on YouTube really occurs at the level of the video, and not the channel. By this I mean that most of the high video counts, sharing, and even videos discovered via search occur via individual videos and not channels. You need to be a good searcher to understand YouTube!

To search YouTube directly, simply type keywords that matter to your company into the search bar at the top of the screen. For example type, *organic food*, to find YouTube videos on *organic food*. Here's a screenshot:

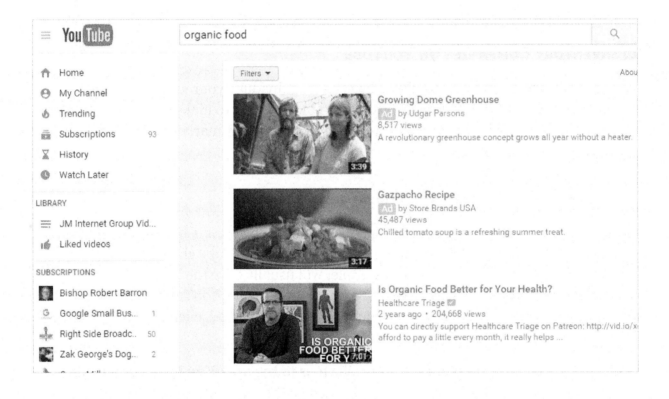

Like Google, YouTube will return a list of the most relevant videos. Simply click on a video to watch it, and then click "up" to the channel to learn more about the channel that produced it. Or you can just hit the red "Subscribe" button directly to subscribe to the channel. Here's a screenshot:

You can also thumb up / thumb down a video, comment on it (using your Google+ account), and share it. If you click on the share icon below a video, YouTube gives you all the social icons plus a link to "Embed," which provides the HTML code you need to embed a video on your own website or blog.

SEARCH YOUTUBE BY KEYWORDS TO FIND RELEVANT VIDEOS AND CHANNELS

Going back to search, type "organic food" into the search bar. Next, on the top left, click on "Filters," which opens up a set of parameters by which you can focus your search. Here's a screenshot:

Filters ▼				
Upload date	**Type**	**Duration**	**Features**	**Sort by**
Last hour	Video	Short (< 4 minutes)	4K	**Relevance**
Today	Channel	Long (> 20 minutes)	HD	Upload date
This week	Playlist		Subtitles/CC	View count
This month	Movie		Creative Commons	Rating
This year	Show		3D	
			Live	
			Purchased	
			360°	

Click *Upload date > This year*, which will turn on *filter #1* (videos of the last year), then reclick *filter*, and then click *Sort by > View Count*, which will turn on *filter #2* (most popular). In this way, you can find the most popular videos by view count vs. a time period (one year). You can also do this by week or month.

Remember: you are looking to understand what type of content is popular in your industry! Next click around at the various videos, and identify what sorts of topics you find people producing and watching in your industry. Pay attention to the thumbs up / thumbs down count, and comments per video. Like a good party planner, you are looking to identify the types of entertainment that attract and engage your guests.

With respect to an individual video, click on the "More" button underneath the video to see subscriptions driven and shares. By comparing one video to another, this data will help you understand not only what types of videos people like, but what types of videos cause them to take action: to subscribe to the channel and/or share the video with friends. Here's a screenshot of individual video data:

This means that this video had 5.6 million views, 14,234 thumbs ups, 927 thumbs down, drove 2,920 subscriptions to the channel, and had 4,351 shares via social media.

COMPETITOR VIDEO DATA IS HIDDEN UNDER THE "MORE" BUTTON

You can gather this data, first, for competitor videos or videos that intrigue you to reverse engineer what works in terms of marketing via YouTube. Then, on your own videos, you can use this feature to see how well an individual video is performing.

Search Google for Videos

Another way to find interesting videos by keywords is to search Google. First type your keywords into Google, and then click the more > videos button. Here's a screenshot:

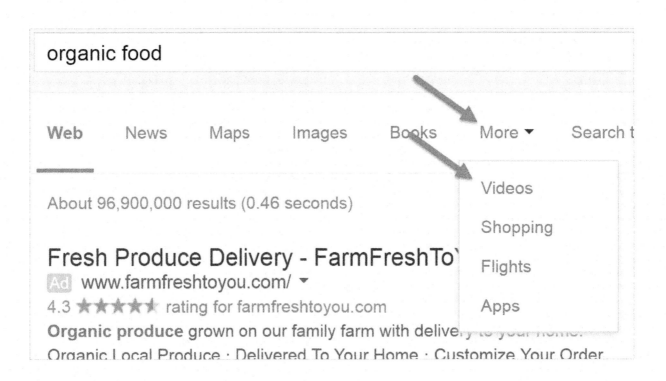

You can also use the button "Search Tools" to filter these results by videos of the last year, or by source (e.g., CNN.com or YouTube.com), but unlike on YouTube itself, you can't filter by view count.

By browsing, searching YouTube directly, or searching Google for videos, your objective is to identify videos that have high view counts as well as high thumbs up / thumbs down, comments, subscriptions driven, and share counts. What do people like? Why do they interact with it? How can this knowledge be applied to videos relevant to your company? Your goals or questions are:

- Are your potential **customers** on YouTube, and if so, what types of videos are they watching?
- Are **companies** similar to yours on YouTube, and if so, what kinds of videos are they producing?
- What types of videos are gaining the most **interactions** as measured by thumbs up / thumbs down, comments, shares, and subscriptions to the channel?

For your first **Todo**, download the **YouTube Research Worksheet**. For the worksheet, go to https://www.jm-seo.org/workbooks (click on Social Media Workbook, enter the code 'smm2016' to register if you have not already done so), and click on the link to the "YouTube Research Worksheet." You'll answer questions as to whether your potential customers are on YouTube, identify brands to follow, and inventory what you like and dislike about their YouTube channels and individual videos.

» SET UP YOUR CHANNEL AND UPLOAD VIDEOS

After you've made an inventory of YouTube channels and videos that interest you from a marketing perspective, you're ready to set up your own YouTube channel. Assuming you haven't done this already, the best way to do this is from your Google+ account. Here are the steps:

1. **Login to your Google account** (either via Gmail or an email address for which you have created a Google account).
2. **Go to YouTube** by typing https://www.youtube.com/ in the browser address bar, or using the Google pull down menu to go to YouTube.
3. Under your name / icon on the top right, use the **pull down menu** and you will see a list of your associated Google+ company pages. Those that do not have a YouTube channel will have a gray message that says "create channel."
4. Click the **blue OK button**.

(For the official YouTube help article on how to create a channel, visit http://jmlinks.com/12z). At that point, you will be "inside" your new YouTube channel. (If you already have a channel, simply login to YouTube.)

On the top right of the screen, click on your profile picture, and then **Creator Studio**. That gets you into the settings for your channel, as well as **video manager** (where you manage your videos). Click on "Community," where you can manage the ability of users to post comments to your video. Under "blacklist" you can also forbid the use of certain words, as well as ban users who have not behaved well from interacting with your channel.

To change your profile picture, click on your picture on the top right, hover over it, and click change. (Note that this will take you back to Google+; you'll have to return to YouTube to proceed.)

Click on *Channel,* on the left navigation. There are some basic set up and optimization tasks there, regarding how public your channel is, whether you allow advertising, etc. I do not recommend that you allow advertising or monetization on your channel, as your goal once you have a customer viewing your videos is for them to buy your product or service, not to go off and buy someone else's.

Furthermore, unless your view count is in the millions, you'll earn next to nothing via YouTube monetization. (The only practical reason to monetize a video is if you absolutely insist on using copyright-protected music; for that sort of music to be allowed, you must allow advertising on your video via monetization).

Next, click on the YouTube icon on the top left, and then My Channel. (*Confusingly, YouTube separates the Channel settings from the graphical look-and-feel of your channel*). As you hover over graphical elements, you'll see a tiny pencil. Click on the pencil and you can change and upload various elements.

- Hover and click the **pencil** to change your cover photo (called "Channel Art" in YouTube-speak).
- Click on the **About tab** to update information about your channel. At the bottom of this setting, you can create links to your other social media as well as your website.
- **Unsubscribed Trailer**. This is the YouTube name for the video that people see who are NOT subscribed to your channel. Think of it as a "Here's why you should subscribe video." It is often not enabled at first glance, so click on the pencil in the top right, then edit navigation, and then enable browse. (To watch a video explaining this visit http://jmlinks.com/1s).
  - Once this feature is enabled, you'll see a link "for new visitors" which sets the unsubscribed trailer and a link "for returning visitors" which sets what subscribers see.

Channel Optimization for SEO

YouTube is the No. 2 search engine, ahead of Bing (but behind its parent, Google). As I will discuss, you can optimize your YouTube videos for search by including relevant keywords. You should do the same with your channel. Place keywords in your channel keywords field. To enter your channel keywords, click on Creator Studio > Channel > Advanced > Channel keywords. Here's a screenshot:

CHANNEL	Channel keywords	SEO "Search Engine Optimization" "Social M
Status and features		
Monetization		
Upload defaults	**Advertisements**	
Featured content	☑ Allow advertisements to be displayed alongside my videos	
Branding	Does not apply to videos that you monetize and videos that are claimed by a third-party.	
Advanced		

On the Advanced tag, you can also link your YouTube account to your AdWords account, as well as to your Google Analytics account for metrics purposes. Don't forget to associate your YouTube account with your website as well.

Click up to the "about" tab, and then click on the little pencil icon. Be sure to include logical search keywords in your company description on the "about" tab as well as links to your website and other social properties such as Twitter or Facebook.

Upload Videos

To upload a video, click back to your profile picture, then select "Creator Studio." Then on the right hand side click "Upload." Select a video to upload, and start uploading. As we will discuss below, input:

- **Video Title**: Write a keyword-heavy but catchy video title.
- **Description**. Write a keyword-heavy but catchy video description. Include an *http://www.yourcompany.com* link to your website. Be sure to use the http:// prefix, as that makes it "clickable" to your website.
- **Tags**. Identify no more than five relevant keywords tags for your video.
- **Public**: set the video to *public* (anyone can see), *unlisted* (only people with the link can view), or *private* (restricted access).
- **Custom thumbnail**. Upload a custom video thumbnail, which will appear in YouTube search. Or, YouTube will automatically create three options for you.

For your second **TODO**, download the **YouTube Setup Worksheet**. For the worksheet, go to https://www.jm-seo.org/workbooks (click on Social Media Workbook, enter the code 'smm2016' to register if you have not already done so), and click on the link to the "YouTube Setup Worksheet." You'll answer and outline the basic setup issues for your YouTube channel.

» UNDERSTAND THE THREE PROMOTIONAL USES OF VIDEO

While other social media have a posting strategy and posting rhythm, videos on YouTube are best understood by their three promotional strategies. While YouTube does have channels, subscriptions, and social spread just as other social media, the lion's share of activity comes directly from the videos themselves. Thus, it is very important to understand the three promotional uses of video.

YouTube Noise: Pop Culture

Before we turn to those uses of video, however, let's pause for a moment and consider the tremendous noise caused on YouTube by pop culture. When you innocently login to your YouTube account, you will be bombarded by a) music videos, b) ridiculous college humor / professional / silly videos, c) movie trailers, d) crazy trending news and so on and so forth. This is the dominant use of YouTube in terms of views, but just as cable TV has hundreds of channels and you can drill down to very specific, and very useful channels and programs (think, for example, about cooking or fishing shows on cable TV, that are not high volume but are very high value to people who really care about cooking or fishing). So, before your boss freaks about and dismisses YouTube because of the crazy videos on cats and the video by pop culture media icons, remember that for most of us marketers the value of YouTube is in the niches that matter to us: the niches that create and contain content that our customers care about. They exist: you just have to find them.

YouTube's riches are in the niches

Let's investigate the three basic uses of YouTube.

#1: Supportive Use of Video

If a picture is worth a thousand words, a video is worth ten thousand. If you are selling a complex product or service, creating and hosting explanatory videos can really help your sales process. Let's face it. Today's busy consumer doesn't really want to read a lot of text! They like videos because videos convey a lot of information quickly and easily, and videos convey emotional content.

Let's assume, for example, that you are a personal injury attorney in San Francisco. People are going to search for you via Google with keyword searches like "Personal Injury Attorneys SF," or "Auto Accident Attorney Bay Area." Then, they're going to land on your website, see a lot of intimidating text, and want to learn more about you as an attorney. Are you smart? Are you nice? Are you someone that they can trust?

In the old, pre-video days, they'd have to call you on the phone and come in for a quick interview. Then, they'd get in the car with their spouse, and have a little chat: *did you like her? Did she seem smart? Could we trust her with our case?* It would be all about "emotional intelligence," and "gut feeling."

Video allows you to post a quick introduction to you and/or your firm on your website, and start that process of "emotional intelligence" in just a few clicks of the mouse. In a very non-threatening way, videos give you the opportunity to pitch to a potential customer.

Here are some examples of this "supportive" use of video: videos that are not meant to "go viral," but rather to "support" the content of a website:

> **Mary Alexander Law** (http://www.maryalexanderlaw.com/). Notice the video right on the home page.
>
> **Sally Morin** (https://www.sallymorinlaw.com/). Ms. Morin produces a series of videos, again right on her home page.
>
> **Walkup Law** (http://www.walkuplawoffice.com/). Click on "watch our firm's approach."

Now, these videos may or may not be hosted on YouTube. That's not the point. The hosting location is not important: what's important is that in a complex industry such as legal services, these companies are using video to "support" the content of their website, and provide potential customers and "easy" way to acquire some "emotional intelligence" about the law firm.

Another area that uses videos in a supportive way is the technology industry. Take a look at the Analog Devices channel (http://jmlinks.com/13b). Watch a playlist of their videos from the Embedded World Trade Show at http://jmlinks.com/1t. Essentially, they are taking a video recorder to the trade show, and recording the "dog and pony show" that each product marketing engineer gives to a prospect who walks up to the trade show booth. The dance goes like this:

- *Hi, what does Analog Devices have new and exciting for engineers that you're exhibiting at the Embedded World Trade show?*
- *Oh, hi there, my name is John Doe, Product Marketing Manager at Analog Devices of the super widget. Let me walk you through what we're exhibiting.*
- *Thank you. (Mentally: oh that's interesting, that fits what I need, he seems like a nice guy, and they seem like a great company... I'll follow up on doing business together after the show).*

By posting these videos to YouTube, Analog Devices creates linkable, sharable **content**, that it can post to its Facebook, Twitter, LinkedIn, and even website pages. It can also email these videos out to prospective clients who inquire but were unable to attend the industry trade show. They are using video to **support** their marketing efforts, and none of these videos are designed to "go viral" like a cat video or Rihanna's latest over-the-top music video. That's not their purpose.

A third way to see the supportive use of video is to go to Facebook, and look at brands you admire. You'll often see them sharing video content. Use a tool like Buzzsumo (http://www.buzzsumo.com/), enter your keywords, and look for videos that are being shared on social media. In most cases, these videos are functioning to "support" the social media marketing: like blog posts, videos can be simply content that you share.

If you sell something complex, something that people use "emotional intelligence" to evaluate, video allows you the opportunity to share that information quickly and easily. If you have "how to" content that is best explained visually, videos can be fantastic for your social media marketing. Any type of content that is better explained by "showing" than by "writing" is an excellent candidate for video. You can also, of course, use video for "after the sale" events such explanations to commonly asked technical support questions.

The supportive use of video, with free hosting of those videos on YouTube and a universal player, is not an opportunity to be missed!

#2: Search Discovery or SEO Use of Video

YouTube is the No. two search engine, behind Google and far ahead of Bing. One of the heaviest uses of YouTube is for "how to" searches. Simply go to YouTube and start typing "how to" and you'll see a list of common YouTube searches.

Here's a screenshot:

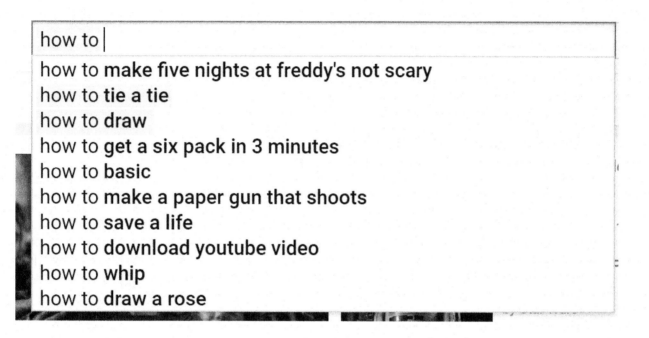

If you're company has any type of "how to" content, especially "how to" content that is best explained in a visual way, you can SEO-optimize YouTube videos to show up for search.

Let's say, for example, that you sell pet food. People who have new puppies are often curious about how best to feed their new puppy. So they'll Google or search via YouTube "How to feed a puppy." Presto! You know have an idea for an informative video, and in that video you can embed mentions, and links to your website for more information and products to buy. Or let's say that you sell makeup. People are dying to know the best way to put on mascara. So they search "How to put on Mascara." Here's a screenshot of common "how to" searches with makeup:

```
how to put on

how to put on fake eyelashes
how to put on eyeliner
how to put on makeup for beginners
how to put on makeup
how to put on eyeshadow
how to put on a tampon
how to put on a tie
how to put on lipstick
how to put on a wig
how to put on mascara
```

So your first step is to do some keyword research. What types of searches are people making on YouTube that are relevant to your product or service? Use "YouTube suggest" by simply typing keywords into YouTube and paying attention to what people enter (this is driven, largely, by keyword search volume). Use a tool like Ubersuggest (https://ubersuggest.io/) which will pull all the "suggestions" from Google. And use the Google keyword planner tool (http://jmlinks.com/1u) to identify high volume, high value keyword searches on Google (which generally also translate to YouTube). For a video on how to use the Google Keyword Planner, visit http://jmlinks.com/1v.

A video channel that is 100% built around "how to" searches is Zak George's Dog Training rEvolution at http://jmlinks.com/13c. Notice how each of his videos is optimized for searches that puppy and dog owners do to learn "how to" train their dogs. In a similar way, if your company, service, or product touches on something that customers are eager to learn "how to" do, then create videos on these topics and optimize them for relevant keywords.

Branded Keywords: Your Competitor Names

As for keywords, also pay attention to very specific branded searches. If a competitor has a hard-to-use product, and you know that people search YouTube for that product, you can include that product name in your video headline, to snag viewers who are searching for the product. Identify adjacent, branded search terms and snag that traffic to your own videos. For example, a YouTube search such as "Netgear router set up" or "How to use a Black and Decker drill" are ripe for this type of adjacent keyword optimization.

Optimize Your Video via SEO for YouTube

Once you've identified keywords that people search on Google and/or YouTube, looking for video content, it's time to optimize your video using that tactics of Search Engine Optimization or SEO. Here's what to do:

1. **Create Your Video**. Obviously, you have to create a short, informative video that explains "how to" do what people are looking to understand. It should be primarily informative, but showcase your product or service nonetheless.
2. **Optimize the Video Title**. Write a keyword-heavy video title.
3. **Optimize the Video Description**. Write a keyword-heavy video description and include a link in http:// format to your website for more information.
4. **Optimize the Video Transcript**. YouTube pays attention to what you "say" in the video via voice recognition software, so be sure to "say" the keywords when you are presenting. For example, "In this video, I am going to explain how to tie a tie."
5. **Optimize the Video Tags**. When you upload the video, be sure to use no more than five keyword-relevant tags.

Important. It's a best practice to have your keyword-heavy content ready to go upon upload, as the first indexing by YouTube is the strongest. Don't upload first in a temporary version, and come back later to optimize.

Take a look at some of these "how to" searches, and browse the top-ranked videos to confirm how they optimize their video titles and descriptions:

- How to Put on Eyeliner at http://jmlinks.com/1w
- How to stop a puppy from chewing on a leash at http://jmlinks.com/1x
- Living wills and advanced directives at http://jmlinks.com/1y.

It's easy to optimize the video headline, description, and tags (not visible to the user). That's your first step.

Next, you need to think about **interactivity**. In rewarding videos with top search positions, YouTube pays a lot of attention to how many views a video has and how interactive a video is, similar to the way that Facebook rewards posts that have high Edgerank. You want users to "interact" with your video: thumbs up / thumbs down, comment, share, and embed. How do you get that?

- **Ask.** In your video, ask users to "subscribe to your channel," or "thumbs up" if you like the video, or "enter questions in the comments below." You can drive interactivity simply by asking for it.
- **Annotations.** Use annotations (text messages) on the top of the video to promote interactivity. In YouTube's Video Manager, click on a video, and then click on "Annotations" in the top row.

Here's a screenshot of annotations:

You can create clickable links to other videos as well as to the subscribe feature, and you can create messages to users that ask for interactivity. For the official YouTube help article on annotations, visit http://jmlinks.com/13a.

Advertising and Overlays on YouTube

YouTube advertising, especially on search keywords, can be very cost effective. YouTube rewards videos with high view counts in its organic search, so by first advertising a new video you can drive up the view count, thereby helping it show for free in the organic results.

Also, by advertising on YouTube (with a minimum budget of just a dollar or less per day), you can put clickable *YouTube overlays* on your videos. *These overlays show on the video on all times, including when it is being viewed or found organically.* To set up an overlay, first turn "on" advertising of the video in AdWords. Then create a "video ad" for your video. Next, fill in the overlay information. Finally, set a very low budget such as $1.00 per day per 10 videos. Presto! All of your video views, including those that originate from organic (non-advertising) searches, will have overlays. In short, once a video is being advertised via Google AdWords, the overlay function is turned on, *regardless of how small the budget being spent.*

Once you are advertising a video via AdWords, this "call to action" overlay feature is turned on (though it can be a little hard to find). Here's a screenshot of it in AdWords:

And here's a screenshot of the "call to action" inside of YouTube's Video Manager:

Third, you'll need to think about external **promotion**. Since YouTube pays attention to the **view count** (*higher is better*) as well as interactivity, use your other social networks to promote your video. Post your video to Facebook, Twitter, LinkedIn, etc., email your video link out to your email link. Even consider advertising the video upon launch on YouTube (http://jmlinks.com/13d), to drive the view count up as well as the interactions. "Embeds" of your video (when your video is embedded or linked to from an external website) are also important to drive a video to the top of search. The more views of your video, the more embeds of your video across the Web, the higher it will rank in relevant YouTube and Google searches.

CREATE A VIRTUOUS CIRCLE:

THE MORE A VIDEO IS VIEWED, THE MORE IT SHOWS IN SEARCH

The on page text optimization of the video, interactivity, and external promotion all drive a video to the top of YouTube. Once on the top of YouTube search, a **virtuous circle** can kick in: the more it shows at the top of YouTube search, the more people watch it, the more they watch it, the higher the view count and interactivity, which drives it higher on search and so on and so forth.

#2: Sharing and Viral Videos

Videos are one of the most shared content across social media. We've all seen compelling videos, and shared them across Facebook, Twitter, or LinkedIn. Videos are highly shareable! Why? Largely because video can convey emotional content in a much easier way than can text or images. And emotion drives sharing: funny, shocking, provocative, outrageous – any of the big human emotions are the ultimate driver of sharing across social media.

VIDEOS GET SHARED BECAUSE

OF EMOTIONAL CONTENT

If you have a product or service that people do not heavily search for, then you can attempt to leverage the share path via YouTube. How? First and foremost, identify a logical **emotion** to drive the shares. Utility is one emotion, in the sense that people will share a video that is useful with friends of family. For example, a video on "how to make your Facebook completely private" (http://jmlinks.com/1z) has over 1.6 million views. So creating something so useful that people share it with friends and family is one way to leverage YouTube sharing to promote your product.

But utility is the weakest of human emotions. **Fear, anger, outrage, humor** – all of these emotions are much, much stronger than mere utility!

For most businesses, the best emotion to tap is **humor**, because humor can encourage sharing without having negative side effects on your brand image. One business that has really leveraged YouTube sharing is Blendtec Blenders (http://www.blendtec.com/). Their YouTube channel, entitled, "Will it blend" (https://www.youtube.com/user/Blendtec) is all about taking crazy items and blending them in their powerful blenders: being humorous and yet showcasing their product. One of my favorite viral videos produced by Blendtec concerns Justin Bieber, with over 3.4 million views. Watch it at http://jmlinks.com/2a.

If you can connect your product to something insanely funny, then you can use humor as the "fuel" to drive social sharing of your product or service. Just remember it has to be insanely funny. Other examples are "Girls don't poop" (http://jmlinks.com/2b) or "The man your man could smell like" (http://jmlinks.com/2c). For the latter, I recommend you read the Wikipedia discussion at http://jmlinks.com/2d, where you'll learn that "behind the scenes" an immense amount of work and promotion went on to make the video "go viral."

Going Viral

To "go viral," a video must be so highly shared that one person shares it with two, and the two share it with four and so on and so forth. For a video to go viral, it must have strong emotional pull, and to get started, must usually have strong external promotion including advertising.

It takes a match to ignite a forest fire, after all.

Humor is one emotion that can start viral sharing. Another is **sentimentality**. Especially for non-profits, videos that tug on the emotions can be used to encourage social sharing. Examples of this strategy are "Dear 16 Year Old Me" (http://jmlinks.com/1p) and "Dear Future Mom" (http://jmlinks.com/2e). These videos feature real people, sharing authentic emotional stories about a social cause or problem. People share them to "support" the cause. The "Ice bucket challenge" and "It gets better" are other example of this use of "showing support" to promote a cause.

Finally, I want to draw your attention to Mike Tompkins (http://jmlinks.com/13e) as an example of a marketer who leverages viral sharing via YouTube. Tompkins produces "covers" of pop songs on YouTube, such as his first on Miley Cyrus "Party in the USA" (http://jmlinks.com/2f). The strategy is to "piggy back" on popular YouTube searches for "branded content" (e.g., "Party in the USA" or "Party in the USA cover") and then "hijack" users to his own wonderful videos. Then, users "subscribe" to his channel, and he has a promotional vehicle combining YouTube search and viral sharing, because his videos are strong and innovative enough to be shareable in their own right.

It's not search OR share on YouTube: it's search AND share.

Indeed a video such as Tompkins' "Starships" (http://jmlinks.com/2g) is leveraging search, share, and the use of influencers (the cast of Pitch Perfect) to promote it and get it to "go viral"). Similarly, the "It gets better project" (http://www.itgetsbetter.org/) is leveraging influencers, sentimentality, user generated content, and a "cause" that many people agree with to get its videos to "go viral" and spread its message.

As a marketer, the task is to "reverse engineer" these efforts at sharing and virality and determine if there is a path to viral marketing that fits your company. Again, for most for-profit companies, the best emotion is humor, while for many non-profits, sentimentality and causes that people actively support are good mechanisms to spur social sharing.

To summarize, brainstorm which of the following uses of YouTube are most relevant for your company:

Supportive. Create and upload videos that support your website and other social media. This is largely using YouTube as a hosting platform as opposed to a promotional system.

Search / SEO. To the extent that people search for keywords near your product or service, you can optimize your videos for discovery by search.

Share / Viral. To the extent that your videos have an emotional content, you can encourage discovery by social sharing and even virality.

Remember that in all cases you usually need to use external promotion tactics such as sharing your videos on Facebook, Twitter, and LinkedIn, reaching out to influencers who will help promote your videos, and even advertising on YouTube to extend the reach of your videos.

» MEASURE YOUR RESULTS

Owned by Google, YouTube provides very good metrics on both your channel and your videos. From insider your YouTube account, click on *Creator Studio > Analytics*. Next, you can drill down to any video, and investigate:

Views. Total views and views over time.

Estimated Minutes Watched. Total minutes watched.

Engagement. Variables such as likes, dislikes, comments, shares, videos in playlists, and subscribers generated by the video.

Demographics. Your top countries and gender distribution.

Discovery. How people found your video. Click into "top traffic sources" to view the actual search keywords, "external" to view referrer websites, "suggested videos" to view related videos that generated traffic

You can also manage your user comments from insider Creator Studio. Click on Community > Comments to view, respond, and even delete comments from users.

Google Analytics

For many of us, we want to drive traffic from YouTube to our website, even to our ecommerce store or to download a free eBook or software package to get a sales lead. Sign up for Google Analytics (https://www.google.com/analytics) and install the required tracking code. Inside of your Google Analytics account on the left column, drill down by clicking on *Acquisition > Social > Overview*. Then on the right hand side of the screen you'll see the word "Social." Click on that, and then find YouTube on the list, and YouTube to your Website, giving you insights into what types of video people find attractive.

You can also create a custom Advanced Segment to look at only YouTube traffic and its behavior. For information on how to create custom Advanced Segments in Google Analytics, go to http://jmlinks.com/1f. For the Google help files on Advanced Segments go to http://jmlinks.com/1g.

In sum, inside of YouTube you can see how people interact with your channel and videos. Inside of Google Analytics, you can see where they land on your website and what they do after they arrive.

▶▶ DELIVERABLE: A YOUTUBE MARKETING PLAN

Now that we've come to the end of our chapter on YouTube, your **DELIVERABLE** has arrived. Go to https://www.jm-seo.org/workbooks (click on Social Media Workbook, enter the code 'smm2016' to register if you have not already done so), and click on the link to the "YouTube Marketing Plan." By filling out this plan, you and your team will establish a vision of what you want to achieve via YouTube.

>> Appendix: Top YouTube Marketing Tools and Resources

Here are the top tools and resources to help you with YouTube marketing. For an up-to-date list, go to https://www.jm-seo.org/workbooks (click on Social Media Workbook, enter the code 'smm2016' to register if you have not already done so). Click on the *Social Media Toolbook* link, and drill down to the YouTube chapter.

YouTube Tools - http://bitly.com/ytcreatecorner

YouTube has done more and more to make it easier to publish and promote videos. This page lists six tools: YouTube Capture, YouTube Editor, Captions, Audio Library, Slideshow and YouTube Analytics. All of them are fantastic, free tools about YouTube by YouTube.

Rating: 5 Stars | **Category:** resource

YouTube Creator Hub - http://youtube.com/yt/creators

Help center for those creating YouTube content. Learn how to better edit your videos, get them up on YouTube, etc. Has lessons on growing your audience, boot camp, and how to get viewers and even how to earn money via YouTube.

Rating: 5 Stars | **Category:** resource

iMovie for Mac - https://apple.com/mac/imovie

Apple's free, downloadable movie / video editor. Great for making YouTube videos!

Rating: 4 Stars | **Category:** tool

YouTube Capture - https://youtube.com/capture

YouTube Capture is an app for your mobile phone, which makes it easy to capture and edit videos right on your phone. Imagine you are a marketer / retailer and you want to use your phone to easily capture customer interactions, and upload (quickly / easily) to YouTube. Get the picture?

Rating: 4 Stars | **Category:** tool

YOUTUBE ADVERTISING RESOURCES - https://www.youtube.com/yt/advertise/

YouTube wants you to advertise! But, it also hides some good free SEO-oriented resources here for how to use YouTube effectively. Worth a look, and a bookmark.

Rating: 4 Stars | **Category:** resource

YOUTUBE SPOTLIGHT - https://www.youtube.com/user/YouTube

Trying to understand YouTube? This is the official YouTube Channel by YouTube on YouTube. Use to to discover what's new and trending around the world from music to culture to Internet phenomena, must-watch videos from across YouTube, all in one place.

Rating: 4 Stars | **Category:** video

POPULAR ON YOUTUBE - https://www.youtube.com/channel/UCF0pVplsI8R5kcAqgtoRqoA

An auto-generated collection of what's popular on YouTube, and - shall we say - 'going viral.' As a marketer, seek to observe and understand why things go viral and how to leverage the video popularity wave.

Rating: 4 Stars | **Category:** service

SMALL BUSINESS GUIDE TO YOUTUBE - http://simplybusiness.co.uk/microsites/youtube-for-small-business

Interactive step-by-step flowchart to YouTube marketing. Comprised of key questions and linked resources with more information. Excellent resource. Worth a look.

Rating: 4 Stars | **Category:** resource

YOUTUBE HELP CENTER - http://support.google.com/youtube

The official help site for YouTube, conveniently located on Google. Google owns YouTube, but you already knew that.

Rating: 4 Stars | **Category:** overview

WINDOWS MOVIE MAKER - http://bitly.com/windowsmov

For those on the Windows platform, Movie Maker is the goto free program to edit videos for YouTube and other platforms.

Rating: 3 Stars | **Category:** tool

6
PINTEREST

Some social media like Facebook, YouTube, and LinkedIn are broad, reaching many people with many diverse interests. Others are narrow, reaching only specific people (demographic groups like *young people* or *women*, for example) or specific usages (e.g., *plumbing, restaurants, dentistry*, etc., for example). Yelp, Tumblr, Instagram, Twitter, and Pinterest fall into this latter category. They are very strong in the niches, but not so strong in the generalities. If your specific customer segment or usage is active on the particular social media, it works wonders. If not, not.

Pinterest is such a platform: incredibly strong in **online shopping** and the **female demographic**, and all but absent from nearly everything else.

Pinterest focuses its marketing strengths on three intertwined segments: **consumer retail**, **do-it-yourself**, and **women**. Shoppers use Pinterest to browse the Internet and "pin" items they might want to buy to "boards." Do-it-yourselfers use Pinterest to share ideas on how to build this or that, knit this or that, or construct this or that. Women, always a heavy shopping demographic, have been the early adopters of Pinterest both as a "buying / idea platform" and as a great platform for do-it-yourself crafting and recipe-sharing.

Pinterest, in short, is *the* network for consumer retail, *the* network for craftsy do-it-yourself, and *the* network for women (especially in shopping mode).

Why consider Pinterest? Here's a recap.

First and foremost, Pinterest is about shopping. Consumers use it as an "idea board" for their college dorm room, their wedding, the doggie toys they want to make or buy, their house redecorating project, their recipe ideas for their next family reunion. The site makes it easy to "pin" ideas to a "board," and each pin can be instantly clickable to a blog post or online store where a person can learn more, or (*gasp!*) buy the item. The ROI from Pinterest can be very high because consumers are often in a buying mindset then they use the platform! Do-it-yourself is also very big on Pinterest; because, let's face it, people often see "do-it-yourself" and then "buy" related products. Second, the unique "idea board" system makes Pinterest a wonderful mechanism for collaboration among customers, and between you and your customers. If an idea has a visual component, Pinterest may prove to be a wonderful way to share and brainstorm that idea. Third, Pinterest is highly visual and can act as a bookmarking system, whether social or not. Once you get the hang of it, you may fall in love with Pinterest just for its bookmarking capabilities alone.

Let's get started!

To Do List:

» Explore How Pinterest Works

» Inventory Companies on Pinterest

» Set up and Optimize Your Account

» Brainstorm and Execute a Pinning Strategy

» Promote Your Pinterest Account, Boards, and Pins

» Measure Your Results

»» Deliverable: A Pinterest Marketing Plan

» Appendix: Top Pinterest Marketing Tools and Resources

» Explore How Pinterest Works

The best way to understand Pinterest and social bookmarking is to grasp the concept of an "idea board."

Let's use the example of someone planning out her ideal dorm room for freshman year at college. First, she signs up for Pinterest and creates a profile. Compared with Facebook, Pinterest is very basic: not a lot of information is displayed in a Pinterest profile, pretty much just a profile picture and a very brief description. Next, she should download and install the Pinterest button (see http://jmlinks.com/2m) or Chrome Pinterest extension (see http://jmlinks.com/2n). Once installed, she can now surf the Web (or use the Pinterest app for iPhone or Android) and "pin" interesting items to "boards" that she sets up.

For example, she'd set up a board "my dream college room" or even more specific boards like "my dream bathroom supplies," or "my dream desk." Let's say she goes to Amazon and finds an amazing desk light. She can "pin" this desk light to her "dream desk" board. People who follow her (or this board) on Pinterest, thus see this desk light in their Pinterest news feed, whereupon they can comment on it and (*gasp!*) and even buy it for her. And of course, she would pin not just one desk light, but several possible desk lights, several pencil holders, several ink pads, a few art posters for above her desk, and on and on. It's as if she's building a collage of desk possibilities, from which she can select the perfect accessories. As she creates idea boards for her dream desk, dream closet, dream door room, and dream bathroom supplies, she can invite her friends, her Mom, her sorority sisters to collaborate by commenting and pinning to the boards as well. Pinterest, in short, is a visual bookmarking and idea board system, one that can be social as well, and one that makes online shopping as easy as discover, click, buy. People also use it before purchase in the real world, as a social scrapbook to group together products and services they might want to buy at a brick and mortar store. And do-it-yourselfers use it to share ideas about how to build this or that, how to cook this or that.

THE ESSENCE OF PINTEREST IS THE IDEA BOARD

The structure of Pinterest in a nutshell is:

Individual profile: me, Jason as a person.

A board: collections of items from the Web on topics like my "dream dorm room," "dog toys to possibly buy," "do-it-yourself Christmas decorations," or "recipes for summer parties."

Pins: I can "pin" things I find on the Web such as blog posts, videos, images, or products to buy to my "boards" as a collection of ideas, things to buy. I can also upload items directly.

Search. I can browse Pinterest, search Pinterest, or search the Web for interesting things to "pin" to my boards.

Collaboration: I can invite others to comment on my board or pins, and to pin items to my boards directly. I can also pin things to their boards.

Social: I have a news feed, wherein Pinterest shows me the pins of people, brands, and boards I follow as well as suggestions based on my (revealed) interests. People can also follow me and my boards, and like, comment, and reshare items that I am pinning. Through collaborative boards, we can pin and share ideas together.

To get the hang of Pinterest, create your personal profile, create some boards, download the "Pin it" button, and start playing with the site. Using Pinterest is the best way to begin to understand how to market on Pinterest. For example, to view a Pinterest search for "dream college dorm rooms," visit http://jmlinks.com/2o. To visit some sample idea boards, visit http://jmlinks.com/2p or http://jmlinks.com/13f. Here's a screenshot:

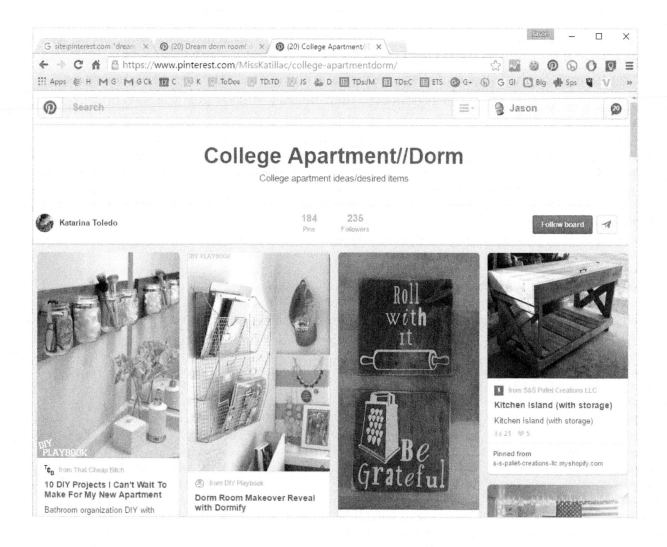

Notice how people use Pinterest as a **visual bookmarking system** of ideas (largely, but not exclusively, of stuff to buy or make), and how others can comment on, and even contribute to these boards in a collaborative fashion.

Pay attention to marketing opportunities on Pinterest! Realize that when a consumer creates a board on her "dream wedding," you as a maker of wedding dresses, supplier of wedding flowers, or owner of a wedding venue, would love to get your product or service "pinned" to her board as a possible option. Realize that if you, as a knick knack store, create a board called "gift ideas for moms," you can do the hard work of collecting great gift ideas, so that last minute Mother's Day shoppers will use your board to select the gifts that they want, and these items can "live" on your own eCommerce online store.

Once you understand the idea of visual bookmarking or "idea boards," then you've "got" Pinterest. One you grasp the idea of being a "helpful vendor" with "helpful boards" that identify fun, lively things to do, buy, or make, and you grasp the idea of encouraging your customers to "pin" your products to their boards, you've "got" the idea of marketing via Pinterest.

As on other social media, people can "follow" other people or brands (or just their boards) and when that person, brand, or board has a new pin, that new pin shows in their news feed. In addition, notifications are generated when someone likes, comments, or repins one of your pin (or boards, or account).

Search or Browse Pinterest

People can search Pinterest directly, or by clicking on the categories button, one can browse Pinterest by categories. To do that, simply click on the categories button at the top right of the search screen. Here's a screenshot:

Home feed	History
Popular	Holidays and events
Everything	Home decor
Gifts	Humor
Videos	Illustrations and posters
Animals and pets	Kids and parenting
Architecture	Men's fashion
Art	Outdoors
Cars and motorcycles	Photography
Celebrities	Products
Design	Quotes
DIY and crafts	Science and nature
Education	Sports
Film, music and books	Tattoos
Food and drink	Technology
Gardening	Travel
Geek	Weddings
Hair and beauty	Women's fashion
Health and fitness	

The "home feed," of course, is your news feed on Pinterest: pins selected for you by the Pinterest algorithm based on your previous interests and engagements. The other categories are a way to browse Pinterest by topic, just as you might browse Amazon.

While most of Pinterest is retail-oriented and most of that female-oriented, if you sell to men, do not despair. There are men to be found on Pinterest and topics of interest to men. For example, check out Men's fashion at http://jmlinks.com/2q or pet accessories at http://jmlinks.com/2r. Classic cars, sporting goods, and other shopping and/or do-it-yourself activities are popular with the male demographic and can be found on Pinterest. Anything connecting to do-it-yourself or recipes / cooking / home decor is also a good bet as a marketing opportunity.

Pinterest has an excellent guide on how to use the platform at http://jmlinks.com/2s, an in-depth help center at http://jmlinks.com/2t, and a *Pinterest for business center* at http://jmlinks.com/2u. Between using these official guides, and systematically researching what's happening on Pinterest, you'll easily see marketing opportunities for your product, service, or company. (*Or, you'll quickly realize that Pinterest is not for you, and you can move on to a more promising social media.*)

>> INVENTORY COMPANIES ON PINTEREST

The best way to research whether Pinterest has any value to your marketing is to research other companies on Pinterest and observe how their fans interact with them on the platform. First, you need to understand how to find companies on Pinterest. Second, you should make a list of companies (and boards) to follow on Pinterest (and follow them with your personal profile). Note: it's important to realize that you can and should follow BOTH companies AND boards, as one company (e.g., Whole Foods) can have multiple boards (best soups, ideas for grilling, salad concepts, etc.). Third, you need to know how to determine what customers are doing on Pinterest, and fourth, you must assess whether any of this has potential value for our company's marketing strategy.

Ways to Search Pinterest

First identify the keyword themes that matter to you and your potential customers. For example, if you are a maker of dog toys, then your targets are people who have dogs and are using Pinterest as a way to brainstorm toys for dogs and interact with other Pinterest users about the pros and cons of specific dog toys. In some cases these will be items to buy, in other cases items to make, and in still others blog posts, infographics, pictures or videos that relate to the theme of "dog toys."

Type the words "dog toys": into the search box while you are logged into Pinterest. Here's a screenshot:

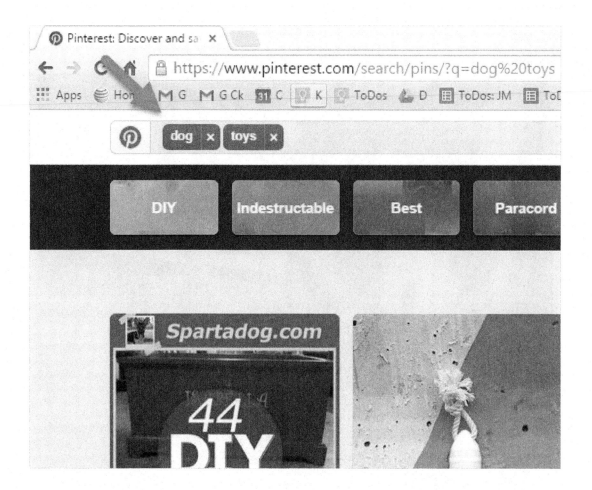

Pinterest, like any search engine, displays results below that have the words "dog toys" in them. If you click on a pin, then you can go down to view that pin and also see the board and/or account associated with that pin. For example, here's a pin that came up when I searched for "dog toys" at http://jmlinks.com/2v.

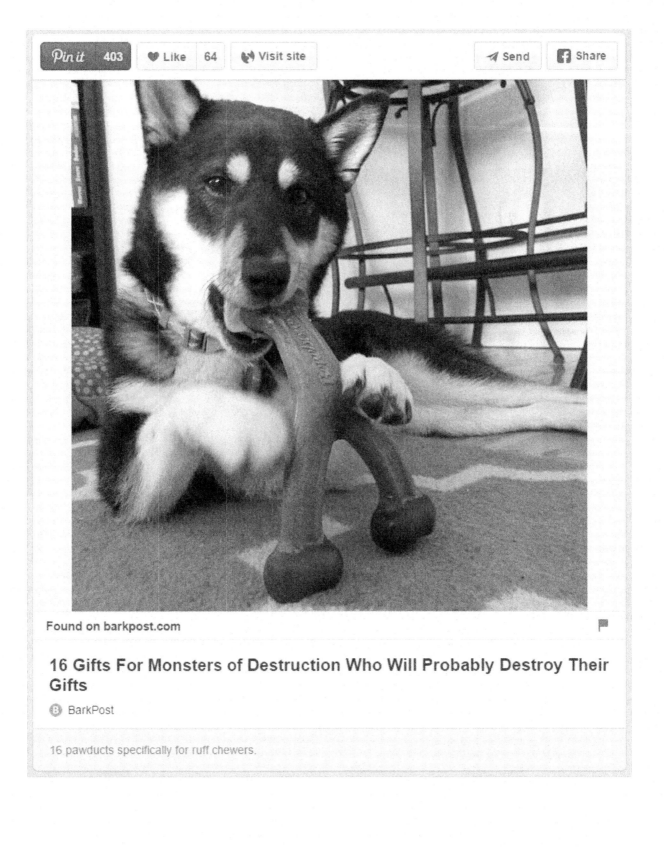

Found on barkpost.com

16 Gifts For Monsters of Destruction Who Will Probably Destroy Their Gifts

Ⓑ BarkPost

16 pawducts specifically for ruff chewers.

If you click on the Pin, you go their website at http://jmlinks.com/2w, where (guess what) you can not only **read** about the products, but you can also **buy** them! Back to the pin on Pinterest, on the right hand side you can see the "account" and "board" to which this item has been pinned. Here's a screenshot:

If you click on *Liz Schloegel*, you go up to her account at http://jmlinks.com/2x or the board itself by clicking on *Follow board* at http://jmlinks.com/2y. Users can like, comment on, or repin pins by clicking into them and then selecting the appropriate button.

Now, Ms. Schloegel, of course, is just an average person, simply pinning and sharing items of interest to her because of her passion for dogs. You are more interested in how competitors and other companies use Pinterest as a marketing vehicle. To find companies, look at the pins returned for your search and at the bottom look for URL's that sound corporate or pins that indicate "promoted pins." For instance, you might end up at any of these companies' Pinterest pages:

> **Waggo Pet** (https://www.pinterest.com/WaggoPet/) - Lifestyle brand and purveyor of design-driven, happy-centric goodies for home and pet. You'll see that they have a board called "ETC" focused on dogs at https://www.pinterest.com/WaggoPet/etc/.

> **Ruff Guides** (https://www.pinterest.com/source/ruffguides.com/) – a purveyor of dog-friendly guides to the United States.

> **Collar Planet Online** (https://www.pinterest.com/collarplanet/) - specializes in unique Martingale Collars, Pet Jewelry, Jeweled and Leather Dog Collars and Leashes. Large assortment of dog costumes, dog clothes and more!

> **Swanky Pet** (https://www.pinterest.com/swankypet/) - Stylish dog collars and more! All items are made-to-order --- let them know what to make for you!

A quick way to find companies after a search is to hit CTRL+F on your keyboard (COMMAND F on Mac) and type in "promoted." That will highlight the promoted (company) pins. These are pins that are being advertised, and consequently will originate from companies as opposed to individuals. As you research companies via your keywords, look for companies with many followers and whose boards / pins show a great deal of interaction: many pins, likes, repins, and comments. Pinterest, after all, is a *social* medium, and your goal is to identify companies that "get" Pinterest well enough to build large, engaged follower communities.

You can also browse Pinterest by category at https://www.pinterest.com/categories/. Again, within relevant categories, try to identify companies as opposed to individuals so you can "reverse engineer" their marketing efforts.

Use Google to Search Pinterest

A second way to search Pinterest to find companies of interest is to use Google. Simply go to Google and type in *site:pinterest.com* plus your keywords, as for example:

site:pinterest.com dog toys at http://jmlinks.com/2z. Remember there is *no space* between the colon and *pinterest.com*! Note that at the top of the search results, Google will usually find the Pinterest category page, in this case at https://www.pinterest.com/explore/dog-toys/. There, you can drill down to pins, boards, and pages of interest.

A third way is to simply go to competitor websites, or websites of companies you like, and look for the Pinterest icon. Then just click over to Pinterest and follow their company or specific boards of that company. For example, from http://www.rei.com/, you'll see the link to their Pinterest page at https://www.pinterest.com/reicoop/.

Not surprisingly, since Pinterest is so successful in consumer retail, many of your large retailers have the most sophisticated marketing efforts on Pinterest. Identify a few consumer retailers you like, follow them on Pinterest, and "reverse engineer" their marketing strategies. Here are some of my favorites:

Target at https://www.pinterest.com/target/.

Martha Stewart Living at https://www.pinterest.com/marthastewart/

Chobani at https://www.pinterest.com/chobani/.

Birchbox at https://www.pinterest.com/birchbox/.

Everyday Health at https://www.pinterest.com/everydayhealth/.

Free People at https://www.pinterest.com/freepeople/.

Intel at https://www.pinterest.com/intel/.

A Pinterest Trick

It's a little geeky, but you can create a very special type of URL, type this into your browser, and see what pins are being pinned for any given website. For example,

https://www.pinterest.com/source/nytimes.com/ = pins from the New York Times

https://www.pinterest.com/source/rei.com = pins from REI.com

You can do this for your own website, as in

https://www.pinterest.com/source/jm-seo.org/ = pins from JM-seo.org.

Simply replace *jm-seo.org* in the string above with your own domain, and then copy/paste the complete URL into the address bar of your browser. Do this for your company on a regular basis (bookmark the URL), and you can see what customers and potential customers are pinning from your website; within Pinterest analytics, you can verify ownership of your website and get even more details on your own site.

This is important because you want to see what types of pins are getting customer interaction on Pinterest. Another method to see what's being shared on Pinterest about a specific domain is to use a tool like Buzzsumo (http://www.buzzsumo.com/). Simply type in the domain of interest into Buzzsumo, sort the Pinterest column on the right, and you can see the most popular content on Pinterest for a particular domain.

IDENTIFY COMPANIES WHO DO PINTEREST MARKETING WELL,

AND REVERSE ENGINEER THEM

Don't be afraid to "follow" companies via Pinterest (even your competitors). In fact, I strongly encourage it: by "following" companies you actually "like," you'll experience them marketing to you, and you can then reverse engineer this for your own company.

For your first **TODO**, download the **Pinterest Research Worksheet**. For the worksheet, go to https://www.jm-seo.org/workbooks (click on Social Media Workbook, enter the code 'smm2016' to register if you have not already done so), and click on the link to the "Pinterest Research Worksheet." You'll answer questions as to whether your potential customers are on Pinterest, identify brands to follow, and inventory what you like and dislike about their Pinterest set up and marketing strategy.

Now that you've got the basics of Pinterest down, it's time to set up or optimize your Pinterest page. Remember, people have "profiles" and businesses have "accounts" on Pinterest, often also called "Pages." You'll generally want a business account, or Page, on Pinterest. To set one up for the first time, go to *Pinterest for Business* at https://business.pinterest.com/. You can also convert a "profile" to a business "account" if you mistakenly joined as an individual at https://business.pinterest.com/ and click on the "Convert now" text in white.

Once you've joined, you have only a very basic set up – your profile picture, username (URL), "about you," location, and website. That's it. Once you've filled out this information, you're set up on Pinterest as a business.

Next, set up some boards by clicking on the "Create a Board" on the left of the screen. Here's a screenshot:

When you create a board, give it a name, a description, a category, a map or location (useful if you are a local business). If you're just building out the board, you can also temporarily make it *secret* and then change it to *public* at a later date.

If you want to make a board collaborative, you identify "collaborators" by typing in their names or email addresses. Pinterest will then invite them to start pinning items to your board. The easiest way to start pinning items to your board is to download the "Pinterest button" onto your browser at http://jmlinks.com/2m. You can also manually copy URL's over to pin an item. With the concept that a board is an "idea board," start identifying and pinning items from the Web such as blog posts, images or photos, and yes, even products from your eCommerce store to your new board.

Board Strategy

Social media is a *party*, not a *prison*, and so it goes with your Pinterest boards. Your boards should attract people to follow them by providing something useful, something visual, something fun. Ask these questions. What is the board "about"? Who will want to "follow" it, Pin stuff from it (or to it), comment, share, and click from the board to your products. Take a board like "Gifts for Dog Lovers" at http://jmlinks.com/3a vs. the board "Dog Gifs" at http://jmlinks.com/3b. The purpose of the former is to identify fun dog gifts to BUY, while the purpose of the latter is to share funny pictures of dogs and build the brand image of *BarkPost* (http://barkpost.com/), a New York-based blog on dogs that also sells dog-related products. Both are legitimate social media marketing users of Pinterest – the former is just a more direct plea to "buy our stuff," whereas the latter is more a "look at this cool stuff" (and by the way check out all the cool stuff we sell).

Hard sell or *soft sell*: both work on Pinterest.

In sum, it is incredibly important to brainstorm your boards! The questions are:

- **What is this board about?** What ideas does it collect, how does it function as a useful "idea-generator" on a particular topic?
- **Who will be interested in this board?** What value are you providing as the board-creator and board-curator by having this board? A board on dog toy ideas "saves time" for people who a) love dogs and want toys and/or b) need to buy a gift for a person who loves dogs and wants toys. Your value is curating "in" the cool stuff, and curating "out" the dumb stuff. A board that collects funny pictures of dogs is meant to give viewers a quick and easy way to get a few laughs during their busy day, and a board that collects do-it-yourself ideas for cheap dog toys

helps dog lovers save money, and have fun, by building their own dog toys. Who will be interested is a function of what the board is about.

- **What will you pin to this board, and where does that content live?** Is it stuff from your eCommerce store? Stuff on Amazon? Blog posts, or how to articles? Items from your own blog? YouTube video? Content is king, on Pinterest, as on all social media.

For your second **TODO**, download the **Pinterest Setup Worksheet**. For the worksheet, go to https://www.jm-seo.org/workbooks (click on Social Media Workbook, enter the code 'smm2016' to register if you have not already done so), and click on the link to the "Pinterest Setup Worksheet." You'll answer and outline the basic setup issues for your Pinterest business account (page) and boards.

» BRAINSTORM AND EXECUTE A PINNING STRATEGY

Content is king, and queen, and jack. Now that you've set up your Pinterest Page, you need to think about posting (or rather pinning). Turn back to your Content Marketing plan, and remember you'll need both other people's content and your own content to pin:

- **Photographs and Images**. Pinterest is very visual, and you'll need to systematically identify photographs and images that fit with your brand message and ideally encourage likes, comments, and repins (shares).
- **Blog Post and Content Summaries**. To the extent that you have an active blog and are posting items that fit with the common uses of Pinterest, pin your blog posts to Pinterest.
  - Note that the first or "featured" image will become the shareable image. Choose striking, fun images for your pins, even if what you are pinning is just a blog post!
- **Quotes**. People love quotes, and taking memorable quotes and pasting them on graphics is a win/win.
- **Infographics and Instructographics**. Factoids, how to articles, especially ones that are fun, do-it-yourself articles, lists or collections of tips or products, are excellent for Pinterest. Anything that helps a person organize ideas about products or services to buy or make will work well on Pinterest.
- **Items to Buy**. Yes! You can (and should) pin items to buy on your Pinterest boards. Unlike most other social media users, Pinterest users are "in" the shopping mode in many ways, so tastefully pinning cool items that can be bought is not just expected but encouraged.

Indeed, Pinterest realizes that buying is a logical way to monetize the site, and so they have announced "Buy it on Pinterest" at https://about.pinterest.com/en/buy-it. You can also read about *buyable pins* at http://jmlinks.com/3d. Another option here is so-called *rich pins*, which are dynamically updated pins from your eCommerce store. Learn about them at http://jmlinks.com/3e.

Clearly, Pinterest will help you shamelessly promote, link to, and sell your stuff via Pinterest! In this sense it is unique among social media in being so unabashedly pro-ecommerce.

» PROMOTE YOUR PINTEREST PAGE, BOARD, AND PINS

Once you've set up your Pinterest business account, and begun to populate it with boards and pins on a regular basis, you've essentially "set up" the party. Now it's time to send out the invitations. In and of itself, neither a Pinterest Page nor a Pinterest board will be self-promoting!

MAKE YOUR BOARDS USEFUL, FUN, AND MESMERIZING FOR YOUR USERS

Remember: social media is a **party**. You must have yummy yummy food and entertainment for people to show up, and stick around. So as you promote your Pinterest Page, always keep front and center "what's in it for them" – what will they get by "following" your Pinterest page and/or Pinterest boards, and checking them out on a regular basis?

Assuming your Page and/or boards have lots of useful, provocative content, here are some common ways to promote your Pinterest account and boards:

- **Real World to Social.** Don't forget the real world! If you are a museum store, for example, be sure that the cashiers recommend to people that they "follow" your Pinterest Page and/or boards? *Why? Because they'll get insider tips, fun do-it-yourself posts, announcements on upcoming museum and museum store events, selected items from your online museum store, etc. Oh, and we'll share collections of do-it-yourself tips as well as gift ideas for that hard-to-buy-for someone in your life.*

- **Cross-Promotion**. Link your website to your Pinterest Page, your blog posts to your Pinterest Page, your Twitter to your Pinterest Page, etc. Notice how big brands like REI do this: one digital property promotes another digital property.

- **Email**. Email your customer list and ask them to "follow" your Page or boards. Be specific: you can drill down to specific **subgroups** and match their interests with **specific boards**. Again, you must have a reason why they'll follow it: what's in it for them? Have a contest, give away something for free, or otherwise motivate them to click from the email to your Page, and then "follow" your page or board.

- **Pinterest Internal**. Interact with other Pages, Pins, and Boards, repin their content, comment on timely topics using #hashtags, and reach out to complementary Pages to work with you on co-promotion.

- **Pinterest SEO / Search**. People use Pinterest to generate ideas, especially before shopping for something big like a wedding or a dorm room, and therefore search is very big on Pinterest. Research your keywords and name your boards and pins after those keywords, and include keywords in your description. As you get likes, pins, and repins, the Pinterest algorithm will rewards your pins with higher placement in Pinterest search results.

- **Use Pinterest Plugins**. Pinterest has numerous plugins that allow you to "embed" your Pinterest items on your website, and allow users to easily "pin" your eCommerce or blog posts to their own boards. Get it at http://jmlinks.com/13g. In this way, your blog can promote your Pinterest Page, your eCommerce site can promote your Pinterest Page, and your Pinterest Page can promote your eCommerce store and/or blog. Similarly, your YouTube videos can promote your Pinterest Page, and your Pinterest Page can promote your YouTube Videos. And the same goes, of course, for your Pinterest boards.

- **Leverage your Fans**. People who like your Page are your best promoters. Remember, it's *social* (!) media, and encouraging your customers to share your content is the name of the game. You want to leverage your fans as much as possible to share your content. Asking key influencers to participate in a board is a great way to both build content and encourage publicity.

ENCOURAGE YOUR FANS TO CONTRIBUTE TO YOUR BOARDS, AND SHARE YOUR CONTENT

Here are some specific items worth mentioning:

Group boards. Group boards allow you to collaborate with your employees and customers on Pinterest. Check them out at http://jmlinks.com/3c. Brainstorm a collaborative project between you and your customers, and use Pinterest as a means to cooperate online.

Rich Pins and "Buy it" Pins. These two mechanisms link your eCommerce store to/from Pinterest. They are not promotion mechanisms per se, but they make the buying process as easy as possible. Check out the links at http://jmlinks.com/3d and http://jmlinks.com/3e to learn more about these cross-linking strategies.

Hashtags. Like Twitter, Pinterest has hashtags which are ways that people can communicate on a theme. Anything marked with a #hashtag is clickable in a pin. Here's a screenshot of a pin with the hashtag #weddingdresses highlighted:

W from Wedding Inspirasi

Anna Campbell Wedding Dresses — Spirit Bridal Collection

Wedding Dress by Anna Campbell — Spirit Bridal Collection For wedding dress inspiration visit: www.boutiquebrida... #annacampbell #weddingdresses #wedding

623   114   2

And here's what happens if you click on that link: http://jmlinks.com/13h. It generates a search on Pinterest for wedding dress with a little ambiguity about the space. So the long and short of it is that by including hashtags in your pins, you become more findable in Pinterest search whether directly or by the search engine function. Identify relevant hashtags and include them in your best pins.

Search. Throughout, remember that search is very important on Pinterest. Make sure that you know your keywords, and that you weave these keywords into the titles and descriptions of your pins and boards. People use Pinterest as a "search engine" to find interesting products and ideas, similar to how people use Yelp to identify fun restaurants and great plumbers.

> *Search, and therefore search optimization, should be a major part of your Pinterest promotion strategy.*

Advertise. Advertising is increasingly important to success on Pinterest. I've mentioned rich pins and "buy it" pins, which are integrations between your online store and Pinterest. "Promoted pins" function much the same way as "promoted posts" on Facebook: you identify a pin to promote, and by advertising, Pinterest pushes these pins to the top of the news feed and search functions on the site. Learn more at https://ads.pinterest.com/.

» MEASURE YOUR RESULTS

Once you set up a business account and boards on Pinterest, Pinterest gives you decent metrics on how popular they are. To find them, click on the gear icon beneath your profile picture at the right. Here's a screenshot:

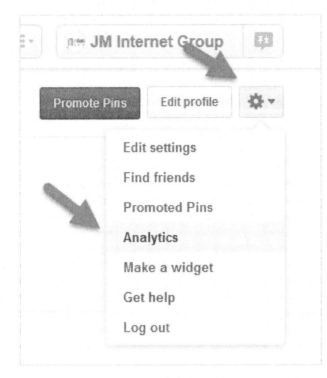

That will transport you to https://analytics.pinterest.com/. You can also confirm your website and Pinterest will show you what people are pinning from your website or blog. (Note: analytics are only available for corporate accounts, not personal profiles).

Google Analytics

For many of us, we want to drive traffic from Pinterest to our website, even to our ecommerce store or to download a free eBook or software package to get a sales lead. Sign up for Google Analytics (https://www.google.com/analytics) and install the required tracking code. Inside of your Google Analytics account on the left column, drill down by clicking on Acquisition > Social > Overview. Then on the right hand side of the screen you'll see a list of Social Networks. Find Pinterest on that list, and click on that. Google Analytics will tell you what URLs people clicked to from Pinterest to your Website, giving you insights into what types of web content people find attractive.

You can also create a custom Advanced Segment to look at only Pinterest traffic and its behavior. For information on how to create custom Advanced Segments in Google Analytics, go to http://jmlinks.com/1f. For the Google help files on Advanced Segments go to http://jmlinks.com/1g.

In sum, inside of Pinterest you can see how people interact with your Page and posts. Inside of Google Analytics, you can see where they land on your website and what they do after they arrive. This includes eCommerce, as Google Analytics is very well integrated with eCommerce. You can learn not only if Pinterest is sending traffic to your website but also whether that traffic is converting to inquiries, downloads, and eCommerce sales.

»»» DELIVERABLE: A PINTEREST MARKETING PLAN

Now that we've come to the end of our chapter on Pinterest, your **DELIVERABLE** has arrived. For the worksheet, go to https://www.jm-seo.org/workbooks (click on Social Media Workbook, enter the code 'smm2016' to register if you have not already done so), and click on the link to the "Pinterest Marketing Plan." By filling out this plan, you and your team will establish a vision of what you want to achieve via Pinterest.

» TOP PINTEREST MARKETING TOOLS AND RESOURCES

Here are the top tools and resources to help you with Pinterest marketing. For an up-to-date list, go to https://www.jm-seo.org/workbooks (click on Social Media Workbook, enter the code 'smm2016' to register if you have not already done so), and click on the link to the *Social Media Toolbook* link, and drill down to the Pinterest chapter.

PINTEREST PIN IT BUTTON - https://business.pinterest.com/en/pin-it-button

> Want your business to be discovered on Pinterest? The Pin It button allows your customers to save what they like to Pinterest and shows their followers what they're interested in. An easy way to get referral traffic and what Pinterest calls, 'a button that works for you'.
>
> **Rating:** 4 Stars | **Category:** tool

PINTEREST GOODIES - https://about.pinterest.com/en/browser-button

> Made more for the end user than the business user, this is a resource by Pinterest about Pinterest. For example, both the iOS and Android apps are available here. Don't miss the 'Pin It' button which makes it easy to pin content from your browser, as well as widgets for your website to encourage Pinterest.

Rating: 4 Stars | **Category:** tool

PINTEREST RICH PINS - https://business.pinterest.com/rich-pins

Rich Pins are pins that include extra information on the pin itself. The six types of rich pins are: app, movie, recipe, article, product, and place. Use these six rich pins in addition to your 'pin it' link to further enhance your post for your viewers.

Rating: 4 Stars | **Category:** tool

PINTEREST TOOLS FOR BUSINESS - https://business.pinterest.com/en/tools

Yes, you wanted it. Yes, they created it: a one-stop resource of tools to help your business succeed on Pinterest. Has not only official Pinterest tools, but also a compilation of third party business-friendly tools to help you pin it, to win it.

Rating: 4 Stars | **Category:** tool

PINTEREST ANALYTICS - https://business.pinterest.com/en/pinterest-analytics

Use this tool to easily see what people like from your Pinterest profile and what they pin from your website. Learn about your audience by viewing metrics and common interests. Great tool to analyze your Pinterest marketing strategy.

Rating: 4 Stars | **Category:** tool

IFTTT - https://ifttt.com

This app, If Then Then That, is a great tool for linking multiple social media accounts. It allows you to create 'recipes' that link your tools exactly the way you like them! For example: make a recipe that adds to a Google Apps spreadsheet every time a particular user uploads to Instagram - a great way to keep up with your competitors SMM strategies! With over 120 supported applications, the 'recipes' are endless, making this a good tool for your SMM strategies.

Rating: 4 Stars | **Category:** tool

REBATE OFFER

CLAIM YOUR $39.99 REBATE! HERE'S HOW -

7. Go to Amazon.com and search for **'Social Media Marketing Workbook'** or click http://jmlinks.com/smm.
8. Write a short, honest **review of the book** and indicate you've been gifted a 'review copy'.
9. Click https://jm-seo.org/rebate/ and fill out the **REBATE FORM.**

WE WILL THEN -

- **Refund** you the full price of the print edition (**$39.99**), so that you will have received a **FREE** review copy

~ $39.99 REBATE OFFER ~

~ LIMITED TO ONE PER CUSTOMER ~

EXPIRES: 10/1/2016

SUBJECT TO CHANGE WITHOUT NOTICE

GOT QUESTIONS? CALL 800-298-4065

7

LOCAL

Let's suppose you have a restaurant, or you're a local plumber, dentist, CPA, or divorce attorney or any of the thousands of local businesses that service customers in their day-to-day life. Before the advent of social media sites like Yelp, Google+, YP.com, TripAdvisor and their kind, consumers might have gone to the physical yellow pages or perhaps visited your website after a Google search. You were in charge of your marketing message: *customers couldn't really "talk back."*

The "Review Revolution" led by Yelp and since followed by Google+, YP.com, TripAdvisor, Angie's list, Amazon, and other sites has dramatically changed the local landscape. Yelp made it possible for customers to "talk back," sharing their positive and negative reviews about local business across social media.

Reviews, in short, allow consumers to talk back: the good, the bad, and the ugly.

A happy customer can leave a **positive** review about your business, and a not-so-happy customer can leave a scathing **negative** review. Moreover, it's a fact that many (if not most) potential customers go online and check reviews before engaging with a local business. If they see five star or four star reviews on Google or Yelp, they may reach out to your business with a phone call or email inquiry, or visit your restaurant, bar, or coffee shop. If they see two star or many negative reviews (perhaps even just one) on Yelp, Google+ or another local review site, they may skip over you and go to competitors who have better online reviews.

Online reviews, in short can make, or break, your business.

Using Yelp and Google+ as models, this chapter explores the "Review Revolution." First, we'll explore why and how customer reviews have dramatically changed the local business landscape. Second, we'll explore how to claim and optimize your listings on Yelp, Google+, and other review sites. Third, we'll investigate how reviews work and how you can nurture positive reviews about your business without getting into trouble. Finally, we'll finish up with a discussion of online reputation management.

Let's get started!

TODO LIST:

>> Explore How Review Sites Work

>> Inventory Companies on Yelp, Google+ or Other Relevant Sites

>> Claim and Optimize Your Listings

>> Cultivate Positive Reviews

>> Monitor and Improve Your Online Reputation

>> Measure your Results

>> >> Deliverable: A Yelp / Local Marketing Plan

>> Appendix: Top Local Review Marketing Tools and Resources

>> EXPLORE HOW REVIEW SITES WORK

The first big thing to grasp as a local business is the **Review Revolution** brought to us by Yelp in 2004. Imagine it's 1994, ten years prior to Yelp's founding, and you have a local Italian restaurant in Los Angeles, California. One day you are lucky enough to be visited by the review critic for the *Los Angeles Times*. You recognize her from her picture in the *LA Times*, and you realize that she can make – or break – your new Italian eatery. You do your best to not let her know you recognize who she is, and you do your utmost to ensure that she has a positive experience at your restaurant. One week later your hopes and prayers are answered: a positive restaurant review in the local newspaper. Business booms.

Alternatively, if she had written a critical review of your restaurant, business would not have *boomed*. It would have *busted*. **The review critic, in short, had an immense amount of power over local restaurants.** However, if a) you were a small restaurant you had minimal chance of ever getting reviewed, and b) if you were a divorce attorney, plumber, massage therapist, CPA or many other types of local businesses, there were essentially no reviewers available. Your main marketing channel was not reviews but customer word of mouth.

Enter the **Review Revolution**. In October, 2004, Yelp (http:www.yelp.com) was founded. Consumers of all types could now review not just local restaurants but local plumbers, dentists, massage therapists and thousands of other types of local businesses. The Review Revolution was like any other mass revolution: the masses burst open the doors of the castle, executed the ruling class, and turned over the table and chairs. *It was a bit bloody. It was a bit noisy. And it was a bit unpleasant.* If, for example, you were the *Los Angeles Times* restaurant critic, your absolute power over restaurants was broken. Professional critics, from restaurant reviewers to product reviewers to book reviewers, look on the review revolution with disgust.

The Review Revolution brought democracy to local reviews. Now anyone could review anything. No control: democracy arrived to reviews.

But here's the rub. Like the French Revolution, the Review Revolution brought the masses into the ecosystem. It has not been very organized or coherent; online reviews run the gamut from informative to ridiculous. Whereas the big reviewers of the *Los Angeles Times, San Francisco Chronicle*, and *New York Times* were educated and civilized (though they could be brutal in their reviews), the new review class can be rough and tumble. Anyone – and I do mean anyone – can write a review: good, bad, or ugly. To be frank, we are still living in this unsettled Review Revolution, and like the French Revolution, there is no going back: the old system is dead.

UNDERSTAND THE

REVIEW REVOLUTION

If you're reading this chapter, you've probably already grasped that online reviews can make or break your local reviews. Many, if not all, potential customers consult online review sites like TripAdvisor, Yelp, or Google+ before engaging with local businesses. If they see *positive* reviews, they are primed for a *positive* experience. If they see *negative* reviews, they are so *negatively* primed that they may avoid any contact whatsoever with your business. Reviews now impact all types of local businesses; nearly every local business is being reviewed online 24/7 365.

Let's step back for a moment and understand the **review ecosystem**. With Yelp as the most important local review site, we will use Yelp as our model, and recognize that what's true for Yelp is generally true for all review sites because the all follow the same social media rules of engagement.

Here's how review sites work:

1. **Local businesses have profiles**. Business profiles are created *without the permission or participation of the business owner*, and exist whether or not the business owner has claimed, optimized, and participated in the review ecosystem. *You as the business owner do not have the right to "delete" your listing on Yelp!* It's like a business Page on Facebook, to the extent that your business has an online "Page" on Yelp. But unlike on Facebook, you are not in control!

2. **Customers write reviews**. Registered Yelp users are able to write reviews about any local business they choose. *If your business is not listed, Yelp users can even create a listing for your business and then review it*. These reviews may be good or bad, extremely positive or so negatively scathing as to infuriate you as the business owner. The Yelpers are basically in control.

3. **Customer reviewers also establish a reputation**. The more reviews a customer writes, the older his or her profile as a reviewer on Yelp, the more friends on Yelp, the more thumbs up or thumbs down to their reviews, the stronger their profile gets. Yelp has filters to filter out "fake" or "weak" reviews from showing entirely. The stronger the customer profile, the higher their reviews rise on the pages of those businesses that they have reviewed. Your business and the Yelpers are both simultaneously establishing a reputation, and that reputation impacts whether your information (your listing, their review) shows prominently on Yelp. (Remember: the same is true for Google+, TripAdvisor, Airbnb, and even Amazon).

4. **Business establish a reputation**. As your business is reviewed on Yelp, the more positive reviews it has, the more customers come to visit it (especially first time customers). But the more negative reviews you have, the fewer customers you get. This is called a "virtuous circle" and a "vicious circle."

5. **Prospective customers read reviews**. Potential customers visit sites like Yelp, CitySearch, TripAdvisor, Google+, and search for businesses via keywords. They find businesses of interest and read the reviews. Generally speaking, if they find positive reviews, they are primed to engage with that business. If they find negative reviews, they may not so much as even call or visit the business.

6. **Businesses claim their local listings**. Businesses have the right to claim, and optimize, their listings. By claiming their listing on a site like Yelp, the business

can "optimize" it by improving the business description with accurate keywords, uploading photos, responding to reviews, and in some cases like Google+ post updates. While businesses cannot delete their listings nor their negative reviews, they can participate in the new social media ecosystem of reviews.

For an overview to Yelp by Yelp, visit http://www.yelp-support.com/. For your first **TODO**, sign up for a Yelp account (as a consumer not a business) if you do not already have one. Next, go to Yelp (http://www.yelp.com/) to explore some of the following categories in your local city by typing these keywords into the Yelp search box:

Sushi Restaurants

Jazz

Plumbers

Divorce Attorneys

DUI Attorneys

Bail Bonds

Let's take Bail Bonds, for example. Here's a screenshot of how to search for "bail bonds" near San Francisco, CA:

Use the clickable links below to do the search:

- Here's a search for "Bail Bonds" near San Francisco, CA at http://jmlinks.com/4i.
- And here's one of the top search results: *New Century Bail Bonds* http://jmlinks.com/4j

Here are some things to notice about the *New Century Bail Bonds* listing.

First, scroll down about half way and look for "From the business" in red. It starts with "JAIL SUCKS." This is the **business listing**, as edited and submitted by the business. This indicates that this business has claimed their listing. Note the inclusion of relevant keywords, the types of search queries users might type into Yelp.

Second, notice the **photos** at the top of the listing (http:jmlinks.com/4k). These can be submitted either by the business, or by users. So, if you don't submit some, your users might (and they might be favorable, or unfavorable, to your business).

Third, read some of the **reviews**. Notice that for any individual reviewer, Yelp indicates how many friends they have on Yelp and how many reviews they have written. For example, here is a screenshot of one of the reviews, showing two friends and two reviews:

Tonya T.
San Leandro, CA
2 friends
2 reviews

★★★★★ 12/23/2013

Would like to take a moment to send a HUGE THANK YOU to Tiki Maxwell and her team at Bail Now Bail Bonds for doing an excellent job with my brother's bond.

Tiki did a fantastic job of being very clear and precise with regards to the details of my brothers charges as well as keeping us up to date regarding the status of his case, as well as upcoming court dates. She remained professional, however was extremely compassionate and sympathetic regarding my family's situation.

Fourth, click on a **reviewer photo**, and you'll go up to their **Yelp profile**. For example, click on Tonya T (http://jmlinks.com/4l) and you'll go up to her profile. Read her reviews and make a guess as to how "real" and how "unsolicited" her reviews are. Some reviewers will look very legitimate, and others might look solicited, paid, or even faked. You'll soon realize that Yelp, like all the review-based sites, is a hodgepodge of unsolicited and solicited reviews, real and fake reviews, and so on and so forth.

For example, here's a screen shot of a suspicious review:

Chloe D.
Midtown West, Manhattan, NY
0 friends
1 review

★★★★☆ 9/11/2013

First to Review

My first time being arrested and I was terrified. Got in touch with my mom and a friend, and they got in touch with bail now. So beyond helpful!!! They went above and beyond letting us know step by step what's happening.

Was this review ...?

Useful 3   Funny   Cool

Notice how Chloe D, has *zero* friends, has written only *one* review, lives in *Manhattan* and yet reviewed a *San Francisco* Bail Bonds. Is this a real review? A solicited review? Or a faked review?

Fifth, scroll to the very bottom and click on "review that are not currently recommended." Yelp has a filter that attempts to filter out "fake" reviews and filter in "real reviews." Here's a screenshot:

5 other reviews that are not currently recommended ▾

Read some of these "non-recommended" reviews and attempt to guess which ones are truly real and which ones might be fake. Do you think Yelp is doing a good, or bad job, with its filter? How do the reviews shown prominently compare or contrast with the reviews at the bottom, or the reviews that are hidden?

Compare Yelp to Amazon

Reviews do not exist only on Yelp, however. Take any review site and do the same exercise.

For instance, check out some reviews on Amazon, as a contrast to Yelp, by clicking on http://jmlinks.com/4m and http://jmlinks.com/4n. Notice how many reviews these people are writing; read their reviews. Do they look fake to you? Perhaps paid or solicited? Realize that all the review sites – Yelp, CitySearch, Google+, Amazon – have essentially the same structure: profiles of businesses, reviewers with profiles, reviews by reviewers rated by stars, a filtering system, and a search process generated by user search queries and showing the "best" results based on keywords in their description and in their reviews, geographic proximity to the searcher, and number or quality of reviews.

Is this fair? Is it a better opportunity for your business than in 1994 when there were no online reviews? Whether it's fair or not, good or not, is a different issue than how you as a local business can (and should) play the game of local reviews to win. You do not make the review world: you simply live in it.

LIFE IS NOT FAIR.

NEITHER ARE REVIEWS.

GET OVER IT.

None of this is perfect, and I am not singling out Yelp. I am drawing your attention to the Review Revolution and the fact that it is not just real people spontaneously reviewing businesses but rather a mix of people writing spontaneous real reviews, people writing solicited (yet real) reviews, and even fake people writing fake reviews.

Users Believe Reviews

Users believe online reviews! According to a BrightLocal study, fully 92% of consumers now read online reviews (vs. 88% in 2014), and 68% say positive reviews make them trust a local business more (vs. 72% in 2014). You can read the full study at http://jmlinks.com/5b. Another excellent book on the social aspects of the Review Revolution is Bill Tancer's, *Everyone's a Critic*, at http://www.billtancer.com/.

The reality is the users believe reviews, both good and bad, and both real and faked. The review ecosystem is a mess, yet as a business owner you have to realize (and accept) that reviews of all types impact your business. You can't change this fact; you can only work within the new "rules of the game."

That's the reality of the Review Revolution.

Is it fair that many consumers are not sufficiently skeptical about the reviews they read? No.

Is it fair that Yelp, Amazon, Google+, TripAdvisor and other vendors are not doing as much as they could to filter out fake reviews as well as address the lopsided problem that the most likely unsolicited review is often a negative one? No.

Do any of these companies care about your business or the fact that you now live within the Review Revolution? No.

Is life fair? No. Is the Review Revolution fair? No.

Do both life and the review revolution offers fabulous opportunities despite their flaws? Yes, yes, yes!

Unhappy Small Business Owners

In my face-to-face classes on social media, review sites are among the most controversial. Yelp, in particular, is literally hated by many small businesspeople because a) they have received what they think are unfair negative reviews on Yelp, and b) Yelp has a reputation for strong-arming businesses into paid advertising. (Yelp disputes this charge, though rumors have dogged the company for years).

Here's why local businesses often get quite emotional about sites like Yelp:

1. Often times, the only reviews they have about their business are negative reviews, which they feel are inaccurate or unfair.
2. They do not understand how to claim or optimize their listings, nor how to respond to reviews.

3. They do not understand how reviews work, and how to influence reviews in their favor.

Moreover, many small business owners do not step back and compare 2016 with 1994. Then, only the rich, famous, connected, or lucky got reviews in the local papers. Getting reviewed was like winning the lottery: great if it happened in a positive way, but not something upon which you could build a marketing strategy. Today, however, any business can get reviews, and consumers can read those reviews online. The reality is that the Review Revolution created an enormous **positive marketing opportunity** for your business.

Let me repeat that:

> *The Review Revolution created an enormous positive marketing opportunity for your business!*

If you know how to optimize your business listing and get reviews (more on this later).

Who Writes Reviews?

Let's talk about who writes reviews. Let's get real. Let's assume you are a local plumber. I have a clogged toilet. I go online and find your business. You come out, you fix my toilet, and you give me a bill for $300. You did a good job, and I am happy about the service.

Will I go online to Yelp and write a review? It's doubtful. Unlike my relationship with a local French restaurant, I am not "proud" that I have a leaky toilet and I got it fixed. While I will likely go on Facebook and share a selfie of me and my wife at the local French restaurant, and likely go on Yelp and write a positive review to "showcase" how wealthy I am, and what a great husband I am, I am not "excited" that you provided me with excellent service with respect to my waste removal system in my bathroom, otherwise known as my toilet. No selfies to Facebook, no positive review to Yelp.

As a happy customer, I am unlikely to leave a positive review.

My toilet has been fixed. I'm happy. Done. Over. End. Writing a review is the last thing on my mind.

Now, let's say you come out for my toilet repair, and you do NOT do what I consider a good job. Perhaps you crack my tile floor, or perhaps you get dirty water on my rug, or perhaps I just don't like you, or perhaps I find your fee of $300 unreasonable.

I'm mad. I hate you. I pay the bill. I'm angry and I want revenge.

I think to myself, "I'll show you." I go online, and vent my anger in a Yelp review. I explain to fellow Yelpers (and the world) how terrible you are, how they should never use your business, etc. etc. I do this to "let off steam" as well as to "feel good about myself" that I am "doing the world a favor" by righting the wrong of your terrible business. I want you to go out of business. I want you to fail. That's justice to me, the unhappy customer.

(Don't believe this happens? To read reviews of the "worst food of my life" on Yelp, visit http://jmlinks.com/4z; to read reviews of the "best food of my life" on Yelp, visit http://jmlinks.com/5a.) You'll see both good, and bad, reviews on Yelp.

Two scenarios: a positive experience, and a negative experience.

Here's the **dirty little secret** of the review ecosystem (with the possible exception of entertainment venues like restaurants, bars, museums, etc.):

- The **most likely customer to leave an unsolicited review is the unhappy customer.** The very unhappy customer is very likely to spontaneously write a nasty review about your business.
- **Happy customers are NOT likely to write reviews**. They are not pre-motivated to share their experience with your plumbing company, your CPA firm, your DUI attorney services on Yelp without a nudge from you. (For restaurants, bars, and entertainment-type businesses, happy customers are much more likely to leave reviews.)

Two other customer segments are likely to leave reviews.

- **Review geeks / Extreme Yelpers** – which would be people like myself, digitally connected and participatory in the Yelp (or Google+, TripAdvisor) ecosystems. Review geeks are not necessarily primed to leave positive, or negative reviews. They just tend to review frequently. As Yelp has evolved, more and more people ARE leaving reviews spontaneously about local services, which is a good thing.
- The **hostile minority** - these are unhappy campers who, because of sites like Yelp, now have a way to vent their rage at nearly everything. These "unhappy campers" tend to leave unhappy review after unhappy review: bitter and negative, they tend to hate everything and leave a destructive trail of negative reviews in their wake. Unfortunately without any fault on its part, Yelp enabled the very unhappy, bitter people of the world to spread their negativity by venting against businesses. Don't believe me? Try some Yelp searches, look for negative reviews, and click "up" to the profiles of the reviewers. In just a few minutes, I guarantee that you will find some very negative, pathetic sad little people.

UNHAPPY CUSTOMERS OFTEN WRITE REVIEWS

Yelp was built around restaurants, the one case in which satisfied customers are likely to leave reviews. Why? To show "to the world" that they have the disposable income and prestige to dine out. Similar to what you see on Facebook, people like to "showcase" their positive achievements. *Look at me! I went to Disneyland, I went out to dinner, I went to this amazing museum, ate at this exclusive restaurant.*

Still, even in the entertainment sectors, unhappy customers are very likely to leave reviews.

The takeway here is to realize the following:

If you do nothing, the most likely reviews you will get will be negative reviews.

Let me repeat that because it is incredibly important to understand the dirty little secret of the Review Revolution:

If you do nothing, the most likely reviews you will get will be negative reviews.

Official Policy

It gets worse. The official policies of Yelp, Google+, TripAdvisor and the like is that you – as the business owner – are not allowed to solicit reviews in any way shape or fashion. Yelp, for example, advises business owners:

Don't ask your customers to review your business on Yelp. Over time, solicited reviews create bias in your business listing — a bias that savvy consumers can smell from a mile away. (Source: http://jmlinks.com/4g).

TripAdvisor states as follows:

The following actions may be considered fraudulent:

– Attempts by an owner to boost his/her own property's reputation by:

- *Writing a review for his/her own property*
- *Asking friends or relatives to write positive reviews*
- *Submitting a review on behalf of a guest*
- *Copying comment cards and submitting them as reviews*
- *Pressuring a TripAdvisor member to remove a negative review*
- *Offering incentives such as discounts, upgrades, or any special treatment in exchange for reviews*
- *Hiring an optimization company, third party marketing organization, or anyone to submit false reviews*
- *Impersonating a competitor or a guest in any way*

– Attempts by an owner to damage his/her competitors by submitting a negative review.

Bottom line: Any attempt to mislead, influence or impersonate a traveler is considered fraudulent and will be subject to penalty. (Source: http://jmlinks.com/4h).

The Review Dilemma

So here's the **review dilemma**:

- *On the one hand*, if you do nothing, you are very likely to receive negative reviews from unhappy customers and not so likely to receive positive reviews from happy customers (true in all cases, except perhaps entertainment-type industries), but
- *On the other hand*, the official terms of service forbid you from soliciting reviews from customers.

Damned if you do, damned if you don't.

The reality of the Review Revolution is that in most cases and certainly in competitive industries like divorce law, DUI cases, plumbers, roofers, etc., most successful companies are pro-actively soliciting reviews. This does not mean that they are faking or buying reviews; it only means that they are nudging, cajoling, begging, emotionally incentivizing, and otherwise motivating happy customers to go online and take the time to write positive reviews around their business.

Is this fair? No.

Is this in accord with the terms of service? No.

Is it the reality? Yes.

Is it the public reality? No. Yelp, Google+, TripAdvisor, Amazon, and all the other companies do their best to police reviews, but the reality is that the fact that reviews are heavily manipulated by vendors is an open secret.

But wait a second.

Is life fair? No.

Was it likely that your plumbing company would have been reviewed in the paper in 1995? No. Your small restaurant? No.

Even though the posted speed limit on the highway is 60 mph, do most cars actually go 60 mph? No.

The Review Revolution has given you an enormous, positive opportunity to reach new customers, just like the Interstate Highway System gives you the opportunity to travel cross-country at 65 to 80 mph even though the posted speed limit may by 75 mph (in the West) and 60 mph (in the East).

Don't be the fastest car on the road. Don't be the red Mazda Miata going 95 mph in front of the cop. Just be in the fast car group, just not the fastest, most egregious car.

For now, just understand that positive reviews are the key to success, that soliciting reviews is technically against the terms of service, and begin to realize that you are going to have to create a strategy to solicit positive reviews, despite the posted terms of service.

Let's turn, first, to identifying companies to emulate on the various review sites.

» INVENTORY COMPANIES ON YELP, GOOGLE+ OR OTHER RELEVANT SITES

If you are a local business, it will be pretty obvious that reviews matter. Even if you are a national business, you may realize that reviews matter. Your first step therefore is to identify the review sites that matter to your business. Your second step is to then browse similar businesses on those sites and conduct an inventory of what you like and dislike about their listings, realizing that unlike on Facebook, listings on review sites generally occur with or without the permission of the business. Actual control is much more limited.

Among the most important review sites are:

Yelp (http://www.yelp.com/) – the largest local review site with great strength in restaurants, more popular in "Blue" states like New York or California than in "Red" states like Florida or Texas.

Google+ (http://www.google.com/). Accessibly by doing Google searches on relevant keywords. In some cases, you'll need to first find a company, and then Google its name to find its Google+ page (more below).

TripAdvisor (http://www.tripadvisor.com/). The leading travel review site.

YP (http://www.yp.com/). The traditional yellow pages gone digital.

VRBO (http://www.vrbo.com/) – a site for identifying short term vacation rentals.

Airbnb (http://www.airbnb.com/) – the leading site for vacation rentals.

Amazon (http://www.amazon.com/) – earth's largest retailer, with reviews on billions of products.

GlassDoor (http://www.glassdoor.com/) – reviews about businesses from the perspective of employees.

IDENTIFY COMPANIES WHO DO REVIEW MARKETING WELL, AND REVERSE ENGINEER THEM

The easiest way to find logical review sites for your company is as follows:

1. Identify the **keywords** by which prospective customers might search for you. For example, if you are a Sushi restaurant in San Francisco, those keywords might be words such as "Sushi," "Sushi Bar," "Japanese Restaurant," "Japanese Caterers," etc.
2. **Google** those keywords and note which review sites come up.
3. Click over to the listing sites, and **make a list** of them.
4. Go over to each review site, re-input your search query keywords, and begin to browse company listings on the review site(s) you have identified.

For example, take "vacation rentals Lake Tahoe" and search it on Google (http://jmlinks.com/4p). Then, browse the search results and you'll see:

https://www.flipkey.com/

http://www.homeaway.com/

http://www.vrbo.com/

http://www.tripadvisor.com/

https://www.tahoeaccomodations.com/

http://www.vacationrentals.com/

https://www.airbnb.com/

Obviously the sites returned will vary with your keywords. By using this technique, however, you can use Google to identify the most important review sites and directories in your industry. Your **TODOS** here are

1. Take out a piece of paper, or set up a Word or Google document. Title this "keyword list."
2. Using tools like the Google *keyword planner*, Google *suggest* (the terms suggested by Google when you type), or Google *related searches* (the terms that appear at the very bottom of the page) as well as just brainstorming "how customers might search for you," create a keyword list of relevant terms. (To watch a video on how to use the Keyword Planner, visit http://jmlinks.com/5c, and to watch a video on how to build a Keyword Worksheet, visit http://jmlinks.com/5d).

3. Conduct these searches on Google, and create an organize list of relevant search queries customers might use on Google, Yelp, etc.
4. As you search, write down the top review / directory sites that come up. Build a list of relevant review sites in your industry.

You now have an organized list of which reviews sites matter to you and your business. This list will, of course, be different for a *Bed and Breakfast* vs. a *CPA* vs. a *divorce attorney* vs. a *sushi restaurant*, but the review marketing game has the same rules across all review sites.

Google+ is Special

Among listing and review sites, Google+ / Google is special. First and foremost, it's owned and operated by Google and has clear priority on Google search. Having a strong Google+ local presence is the No. 1 way for your business to show on local-related Google searches. It doesn't take much to look forward and realize that if local matters to you, and your customers use Google, you'll need to optimize your Google+ local listing!

However, Google has done a **terrible** job of managing Google+ local (now renamed to Google My Business (https://www.google.com/business)). They are constantly changing the format, rules, structure, setup – enough to drive a social media marketer insane!

As of July, 2016, here's the current set up:

> **Consumers simply browse Google**. Consumers simply go to Google, type in keywords such as "Pizza," "Italian restaurants," or "Family Law Attorneys" and see companies show up in the "snack pack," which is the three listings showing (usually but not always with stars). Here's a screenshot:

Rating ▾   Price ▾   Hours ▾

Strizzi's Restaurant - Fremont
4.0 ★★★★☆ (34) · $$ · Italian
Buzzy Italian option for eclectic meals
2740 Mowry Ave

Ristorante Il Porcino
4.4 ★★★★⯪ (20) · $$ · Italian
Casual hangout spot for Italian eats
3339 Walnut Ave

Olive Garden
3.8 ★★★★☆ (96) · $$ · Italian
Family-friendly Italian restaurant chain
39145 Farwell Dr

≡ More places

Consumers need a Google account to post reviews. Consumers can post reviews to Google / Google+ with either a Google+ account or just a Google account. But, they must have one type of Google account to be able to post a review. Anyone, however, can read a review.

Consumers rate businesses. Consumers rate businesses on a five star system, and can leave detailed reviews (good, bad, ugly) on the system, whether or not the business likes it.

Businesses can "claim" their Google+ listings at Google My Businesses. To "claim" their listings, businesses go to Google My Business at https://www.google.com/business which is the moribund Google+ system, and they can add a description (now invisible to consumers), photos (visible on Google), and respond to reviews. If so desired, businesses can post to Google+ as a social network (like Facebook) via this system, but the reality is that Google+ is essentially dead as a social network (but very alive as a review system). Its only real value is in the review ecosystem.

However it evolves, if local matters to you, you must master Google+ / Google reviews. Here's why:

1. **Reviews drive your company to the top of Google**. The *more* reviews you have on the Google system, the *higher* you show on Google searches for local keywords.
2. **Consumers read and rely on Google reviews**, even if they don't understand where they came from or how to write them. The reality is that while *few* consumers *write* reviews, *many* if not most people *believe* them.

Inventory Companies and Their Local Listings

As you browse local review sites, identify relevant companies and make a list of their listings on Yelp, Google+ local, or other sites that are relevant. Make note of:

- Does their **listing** appear **claimed**?
- **Photos**: cover photos and profile pictures. Do you like what you see? Why or why not?
- **Reviews**. How many reviews do they have? Are the mostly positive or mostly negative? Click on the reviewers. Do they seem "real"? Unsolicited? Solicited? Faked? Try to reverse engineer how they might be soliciting or encouraging reviews.
- **About Tab**. Check out their about tab, or listing. Read it. Do you like how it's written? Does it include relevant keywords?

For your second **TODO**, download the **Review Research Worksheet**. For the worksheet, go to https://www.jm-seo.org/workbooks (click on Social Media Workbook, enter the code 'smm2016' to register if you have not already done so), and click on the link to the "Reviews Research Worksheet." You'll answer questions as to whether your potential customers are using reviews, which review sites are important, and inventory what you like and dislike about their review marketing set up and marketing strategy.

» CLAIM AND OPTIMIZE YOUR LISTINGS

Now that you've identified which local review sites matter, it's time to claim and optimize your listings. All of the sites work in essentially the same way, although there are differences in the details. The basic steps are:

1. Identify the local review site for which you want to "claim" your company listing.
2. Find your listing on the site.
3. Follow the instructions to "claim" it, usually by phone or postcard verification.
4. Optimize your listing description by writing keyword-heavy text, uploading photographs, and populating your listing with your hours of operation and other details.
5. Make sure that your website links back to your listing, and your listing links to your website.
6. Make sure that the business name, address, and phone number are the same on both the listing site and your website (be consistent).

To do this for Yelp:

1. Go to http://biz.yelp.com/
2. Enter your business name, and address and hit **Get Started** in red.
3. Follow the instructions to claim your business, usually by phone verification.
4. Once you have claimed your listing:
   a. Click on Business Information on the left; re-write your description to contain logical keywords that potential customers might search for, including synonyms (*pizza, Italian restaurant, catering*, for example).
   b. Choose relevant categories from the list provided.
   c. Enter your basic information, hours, specialties (business information), history, and "meet the business owner" with an eye to logical keywords.
   d. Click on photos on the left, and upload nice photos.
5. Make sure that the address and phone on Yelp are the SAME as the address and phone on your website.
6. Make sure that your website links to your Yelp listing (usually in the footer), and that your Yelp listing links to your website.

To do this for Google+:

1. Sign in to your Google account or Gmail (if you use Gmail).

2. Go to https://www.google.com/business
3. Click on the green "Start Now" link on the top right.
4. Be sure to select "Add a location" or "Local Business"
5. Enter your business name and address.
6. Follow the instructions to claim your business, usually by postcard verification.
7. When you get the postcard, enter the PIN as indicated in the instructions.
8. Optimize your business description by clicking on the red "edit" button.'
9. Choose relevant categories.
10. Click on "manage photos" to change your profile picture, and cover photos, as well as add interior and/or exterior photos.
11. Make sure that the address and phone on Google+ are the SAME as the address and phone on your website.
12. Make sure that your website links to your Google+ listing (usually in the footer), and that your Yelp listing links to your website.

Other local listings like YP.com or Citysearch follow similar procedures. To find all of your "second tier" listings, you can go to Yext (http://www.yext.com/) and enter your business name and phone number in the box on the right. Here's a screenshot:

For free, Yext will identify all your local listings. You can then click over to each and claim and optimize each. Or, if you have budget, you can subscribe to Yext and they will do this for all local listings including Yelp but EXCLUDING Google+. A competitive service to Yext is MOZ Local at https://moz.com/local.

Citation Consistency and Google Local Searches

To show up on Google search, it is important that ALL review sites and your website have the SAME company name, the SAME phone number, and SAME physical address. Make sure that your company name, phone number, and physical address appear on your website, usually in the footer. (This is called your NAP (Name, Address, Phone)).

"Citation" refers to the external listings on review websites that confirm (to Google and Bing) that your business has a certain phone number and physical address. This is used by the search engines to filter local search results by their proximity to the searcher or the geographic terms used in the search query.

Using a service like Yext allows you to claim, optimize, and make consistent this information across hundreds of review sites. This consistency is a big help to showing at the top of local searches on Google or Bing / Yahoo.

Todo

For your third **TODO**, make a spreadsheet of ALL relevant local review sites. Go to each, and claim / optimize your local listings. Be sure to note your login and password!

- CLAIM YOUR GOOGLE+ AND YELP WITH A PERMANENT CORPORATE EMAIL (NOT AN EMPLOYEE EMAIL)
- **DO NOT LOSE YOUR GOOGLE+ AND YELP LOGIN AND PASSWORDS!**

Lost password retrieval on Yelp and Google+ is a **disaster**! Neither system has a good password retrieval function; on Yelp in particular, if your password is lost, God help you. Do not lose your passwords.

▶▶ CULTIVATE POSITIVE REVIEWS

We'll assume you've claimed and optimized the relevant listing services for your local business. Most often this will be at least Google+ and Yelp, and in specific industries it might include TripAdvisor, VRBO, or Airbnb. If you sell products, it might be your product listings and uploads on Amazon. Or it might be on Glassdoor.com.

At this point, you have two options:

1. Wait **passively** for positive customer reviews, and hope that the positive reviews will outpace the negative reviews (according to the official policy of Yelp, Google+, etc.).
2. Be **pro-active** and try to encourage your happy customers to post reviews.

Which do you think the winners in local search and social media are doing?

Legal Disclaimer

You are responsible for everything you do in terms of your Internet marketing. Nothing I am writing here should be construed as required or recommended advice. Legally, I am recommending that you do nothing (option #1).

Take responsibility for your own actions as a marketer, and act on your own risk!

Soliciting Reviews

That said, here is the reality. If you wait passively for reviews (unless you are in the entertainment industry like a restaurant or bar), the most likely scenarios will be a) no reviews, or b) bad reviews, or at least a preponderance of bad reviews. The reason for this is if a customer's plumbing experience is good, she's happy and she goes on with her life. If her plumbing experience is bad, however, she might get angry and be motivated to go on Yelp, Google+, CitySearch, etc., and "tell the world" about how much she hates the company that did her wrong.

> *This dynamic is the dirty little secret of review marketing: unhappy customers are the ones most likely to leave unsolicited reviews.*

You the business owner or marketer can, however, fight back against this dynamic. Here are some strategies to solicit positive reviews about your business:

Face to Face. This is the most powerful way to get positive reviews. The employee who is "face to face" with the customer builds rapport with customer. A scenario might be:

> *Technician: "OK, I've fixed your toilet. Let's run through it together, and verify it's in working order.*
>
> *Client: Yes, it's great. Thank you so much!*
>
> *Technician: You're welcome. Hey, if you have a moment, could you do us a HUGE FAVOR and write a review on Google+ or Yelp about your experience?*
>
> *Client: Yes.*

- If client knows how to do this, just give him or her a card with a direct link to the review site location.
- If client does not know how to do this, give him or her a card with step-by-step instructions.

Phone Reminders. Either at the time of service, or shortly thereafter, call the customer to see "how it went," and if they're happy, ask them to write a review online.

Paper Reminders. Either at the time of service, or shortly thereafter, mail a physical postcard thanking the client for their business, and asking them to write a review on Yelp, Google+, etc.

Email Reminders. Either at the time of service, or shortly thereafter, send an email thanking the client for their business, and asking them to write a review online.

The reality is that face-to-face is, by far, the strongest way to motivate customers to write reviews, phone contact the next strongest, and so on and so forth.

Help Customers Write Reviews

Many customers may not understand how to write a review, so a step-by-step instruction sheet would be helpful. Use a URL shortener like http://bit.ly, or http://tinyurl.com to shorten the link to your local review listing page.

Google+: Generate a REVIEW US URL on Google

Google+, as I have explained earlier, is really a mess. To find a short, easy link to your customer reviews on Google follow these steps.

1. Go to the GradeUS Google review generator tool at http://jmlinks.com/13j.
2. Enter your business name and city or postal code, and press the blue "Get Google Review Links."
3. Select your company from the list it provides, and hit "Continue."
4. Click on the link for "Open in Search Results" and highlight the huge URL string it gives you from Google.
5. Copy this URL string.
6. Go to http://tinyurl.com/ and past this URL into the box "Enter a long URL to make it tiny."
   a. If you like "customize" your URL to make it easy to remember / or just cool.
   b. Here's an example: http://tinyurl.com/revjasonseo.

Alternatively –

1. Go to Google at https://www.google.com/ and enter your company name plus a keyword and/or your city.
2. Click on the "blue" Google reviews link (you MUST have at least ONE Google Review to use this method!).
3. Highlight the huge URL Google gives you in the top of the browser.
4. Copy this URL string.
5. Go to http://tinyurl.com/ and past this URL into the box "Enter a long URL to make it tiny."
   a. If you like "customize" your URL to make it easy to remember / or just cool.
   b. Here's an example: http://tinyurl.com/revjasonseo.

You can write this in an email or on a printed sheet of paper. Here's an example of an email I might send to my clients:

Greetings!

Thank you so much for the opportunity to serve your Internet marketing and consulting needs. As the owner of the *Jason McDonald SEO Consulting Agency*, I truly appreciate your business!

If you have a moment, I would REALLY appreciate an honest review on one of the local listing sites. Here are the instructions:

Google+.

1. Sign in to your Google and/or Gmail account at https://www.google.com/.
2. Go to http://tinyurl.com/revjasonseo.
3. Click on the white "Write a review"
4. Write your review

Yelp:

1. Sign into your Yelp account at http://www.yelp.com/.
2. Go to http://bit.ly/jason-yelp.
3. Click on the red "write a review" button
4. Write your review

Thank you,

Jason McDonald

TO GET POSITIVE REVIEWS, ASK HAPPY CUSTOMERS TO REVIEW YOU.

A few free services have tools to help you create nice-looking Web pages and handouts to encourage reviews:

Bright Local at http://jmlinks.com/4s.

WhiteSpark at http://jmlinks.com/4t.

A few paid services are emerging that "pre-survey" your customers. Essentially, they ask your customer if they liked your company and its product or service. If yes, then that customer is prompted to write a review. If no, then the customer is given a longer detailed survey and that that survey is sent to you the business owner; the customer is NOT prompted to write a review. One such service is ReviewBuzz (http://www.reviewbuzz.com). Others are ReviewInc (http://www.reviewinc.com) and YotPo (https://www.yotpo.com/).

Be Judicious. Understand "Plausible Deniability"

Understand that according to the official policy, even a mild handout asking for an "honest review" is a violation of the terms of service of most of the review providers! Therefore, I do NOT recommend that you post these publically on your website. Be judicious: give them out in printed or email format, and only to those happy customers who have been pre-selected by your staff.

Obviously, if a client is unhappy and you cannot fix it to make them happy: DO NOT ASK THEM FOR A REVIEW.

In fact, a really smart strategy is as follows:

- **Conduct a survey** of customers after they use your service asking them a) if they are happy, b) if they would write a review, and c) if they know how. This could be done formally (an email survey on a site like Surveymonkey (http://www.surveymonkey.com)) or informally just be pre-asking the customer face-to-face, over the phone, or via email.
- **If they ARE happy**, then ask them nicely to **write a review**.

- **If they are NOT happy**, either a) make them happy, or b) do **NOT** ask them for a review.

In this way, you avoid motivating unhappy customers to review you online. Indeed, if you are in a sensitive industry (e.g., Bail Bonds, apartment rentals) in which many customers are not happy, I do not recommend you even publicize to your clients face-to-face or in the real world that you are on the review sites. If many of your customers will be negative, then do not make it "easy" for them to give you a negative review!

Paying for Reviews

Let's face it. Review marketing is the "contact sport" of social media marketing. In certain industries (e.g., DUI attorneys, private detectives, breast augmentation services), many reviews are solicited if not faked, and sometimes incentivized with monetary incentives.

Should you pay for reviews? Generally speaking, I would not pay for reviews. (I am talking about real clients not completely faked reviews). Some companies do incentivize by giving $25 Starbucks or Amazon gift cards once a review is published; however, if this becomes known to a Yelp or a Google+ you wrong a very strong risk of being severely penalized.

> *Offering monetary incentives to get reviews is a dangerous strategy, so be forewarned.*

Yelp will even mark your listing with an aggressive naughty notice if you are busted paying for reviews. You can browse real examples of this on Yelp at http://jmlinks.com/4u. First and foremost, therefore, if you choose to "go to the dark side" and offer payments, I would not publicize it! And I AM NOT RECOMMENDING THAT YOU DO THIS. I am just pointing out that it is done.

Also, note that not only is "paying for reviews" likely to bring down the wrath of Yelp, you can also bring down the wrath of Yelp by offering to pay a negative reviewer to take down their review. Anytime you are offering money in exchange for a Yelp behavior then you run that risk – so be forewarned about just how uptight Yelp is about reviews and payments! (Google and other sites have similar policies).

Incentivize Employees

A better way to incentivize is to offer your employees an incentive, rather than the customer, for reviews published online. Assume for example you are a local pizza joint. Offer your employees a $25.00 bonus EACH after each positive review on Yelp. Or if you are a roofing company, give the technician a handout explaining how to write a review online, and give him a $25.00 bonus EACH TIME a customer posts a review. In that way, you motivate your front-line employees to be customer-friendly, and when there is a positive customer experience, to politely ask the customer to write an honest review on Yelp, Google+, etc.

Motivate your employees to ask for reviews!

I would not put any pro-active review solicitation strategy in writing on the Internet, just as I would not call the California Highway Patrol and inform them that, in general, I go five miles faster than the posted speed limit while driving the highways and byways of the Golden State.

Let sleeping dogs lie.

But just as going 65 mph in a 60 mph zone is unlikely to cause a police action, polite nudges to encourage real reviews from real customers are unlikely to be a big problem. If you do it, just keep it private.

Don't Overthink It. Just Ask for Reviews from Real Customers

In my experience, if most businesses would simply *ask* a few clients for reviews, they would get them. Yes, you'll ask ten clients to get one review. But you'll get that one review. The real problem is to motivate employees to ask and ask and ask and ask to get that one review to go live on Yelp, Google+, or other review sites.

Recognize, understand, and accept that you will ask ten people to get just one review. That's just how it is: customers are self-centered and lazy (but we love them).

Why Reviews Matter (a Lot)

Getting positive reviews is hard work. It's not done in a day. Slow and steady will win the race. Just create a culture at your business of great customer service and an awareness of that "special moment" when a customer is happy to ask for a positive honest review.

Reviews, however, are worth their weight in **gold**. No, in **platinum**. Here's why:

1. **Reviews are a "trust indicator."** For better or worse, consumers tend to believe reviews and use them as trust indicators about your business. A company that has many positive reviews will crush a company that has negative reviews, and outperform a company that has just a few or zero reviews.
2. **Reviews help you in search.** The MORE reviews you have the HIGHER you will show at the top of Google, Yelp, CitySearch, TripAdvisor, Amazon, and even iTunes!

REVIEWS ARE WORTH THEIR WEIGHT IN PLATINUM

Do anything and everything honestly and ethically possible to encourage your best customers to "spread the word" by writing reviews about your business online. After just a few positive reviews, you will be amazed at what they do for your business.

Responding to Negative Reviews

Negative reviews will happen. As the business owner, you may feel as if someone walked up to your newborn baby sleeping calmly in her stroller and said to you:

Your baby is ugly. Your baby stinks. I hate your baby. I had a bad experience with your baby, and I am going to tell the world how much the baby that you are working for blood, sweat, and tears is terrible.

Here's an example:

You're human. You're close to your business. It is like your baby. Your first reaction will be **ANGER**.

Resist the temptation to respond in kind. Do not go online and argue with the negative consumer. Do not insult them. Do not use unprofessional language. *When you wrestle with a pig, the pig gets dirty and the pig likes it.*

Instead:

- **Calm down**. Wait at least 24 hours before doing anything. Sleep on it.
- **Have someone else deal with negative reviews**: an outside consultant or employee who is not emotionally involved. Let a calm head prevail, and it probably will not be the head of the business owner.
- **Try to fix the problem**. If at all possible, reason with the person (you can usually contact them via Yelp, Google+, etc.), and see if you can fix the problem. In some cases, you can, and then you can politely ask them to change the review.
- **Respond**. State your side of the situation in a positive, professional manner while acknowledging the right of the reviewer to her own opinion.

To **respond to a negative review**, do as follows. First and foremost, take the high ground. You can log into your business account / profile and respond to negative reviews. This is one of the benefits of "claiming" your business profile. But be positive and professional: acknowledge their right to their opinion, but be firm as to your right to state your opinion as well. Second, state your side of the situation but realize you are NOT talking to the unhappy customer. You are talking to the person reading your reviews and deciding whether to reach out to you for a possible business engagement. Explain your side of the story. Often times, the negative reviews come from nasty, unhappy people (which you can politely point out as for example, asking the reader to click on the reviewer's name and see all their other negative reviews to realize that this is just a negative person). Or, the person wasn't a good fit for your business (so explain why). Or the person is being plain crazy. For example, I have had plastic surgeons condemned on Yelp because their waiting room was too hot, or other clients condemned because they didn't respond to an email. Finally, if the review is fake (i.e., by a competitor) or obscene or racist, you can complain to Yelp, Google+, etc., and in some cases they will remove the reviews. (To do this, log in to a personal account on Yelp, and right click on the offensive review. You can then flag it and complain).

To read Yelp's official guide to responding to reviews, visit http://jmlinks.com/5e. To read Google's, visit http://jmlinks.com/5f. To read TripAdvisor's, visit http://jmlinks.com/5g. For whatever review site matters to your business, you can usually search their help files for advice on how to respond to reviews. However, remember that the official policies are often very naive about how the game is truly played.

SWAMP NEGATIVE REVIEWS WITH POSITIVE REVIEWS

Again, in no way shape or form, am I advising you to be dishonest or solicit fake reviews. I am simply advising you to ask happy customers to just take a few minutes and tell their happy stories. If you pro-actively solicit positive, real reviews you can drown out or swamp the negative reviews with a preponderance of positive reviews. In short, getting positive real reviews is the best way to respond to negative reviews.

You don't ask, you don't get.

For your fourth **TODO**, download the **Review Solicitation Worksheet**. For the worksheet, go to https://www.jm-seo.org/workbooks (click on Social Media Workbook, enter the code 'smm2016' to register if you have not already done so), and click on the link to the "Reviews Solicitation Worksheet." You'll create a strategy to encourage positive reviews about your company.

≫ MONITOR AND IMPROVE YOUR ONLINE REPUTATION

Reputation management is a new buzzword about protecting one's online reputation, whether for an individual or a business. To understand reputation management, first back up and consider the sales funnel, often explained as *AIDA: Awareness, Interest, Desire and Action*. Prospective customers go through distinct phases as they consider solutions for their problems, needs, or desires:

Awareness. An **awareness** of the problem and the beginning of Internet searches and social media outreach to friends, family, and colleagues about the problem, need, or desire and possible solutions. In this phases, searches are often "educational" in nature as in "how to cater a wedding" or "wedding ideas."

Interest. As a customer becomes aware of available market solutions, they develop an **interest** in vendor offerings, and even may make a shortlist. At this stage, and the next, they move closer to an "action," i.e. a purchase or engagement with a vendor solution. Searches at this point become "best wedding caterers" or "Boston catering companies," etc.

Desire. Interest shifts towards **desire**, and the customer begins to narrow down his or her shortlist. At this point, searches become *reputational* in nature. They may search a business name PLUS words like *reviews* or *complaints*. If your business were named Gina's Italian Kitchen, for example. They might search Google for "Gina's Italian Kitchen Reviews" or "Complaints against Gina's Italian Kitchen," or "Gina's Italian Kitchen Wedding Catering Reviews." **Reviews** is the operative word; if he or she finds *positive* reviews, that confirms your business is a good choice, whereas if he or she finds *negative* reviews, they may take you out of the consideration set entirely.

Action. A choice is made to purchase the service or engage with your business. Upon completion, the customer may decide to leave her own review about your business for others.

Reputation management, in short, is monitoring and protecting your online **branded** and **reputational** searches. To be frank, it is also about attempting to upgrade positive reviews and positive brand mentions so that your online brand image shines.

To understand the search patterns, you can use the example of my company, The JM Internet Group. For example –

a "branded" search is: "JM Internet Group"

a "reputational" search is "JM Internet Group Reviews"

Review sites such as Yelp, CitySearch, Google+, etc., as well as ones specific to your industry can have an extremely positive – or extremely negative – impact on your online reputation. Indeed, branded searches on Google (searches for your company name, or your company name plus 'reviews') often return Google+ profiles and reviews directly on the right side of the page. For example, here's a screenshot for the search "JM Internet Group" on Google:

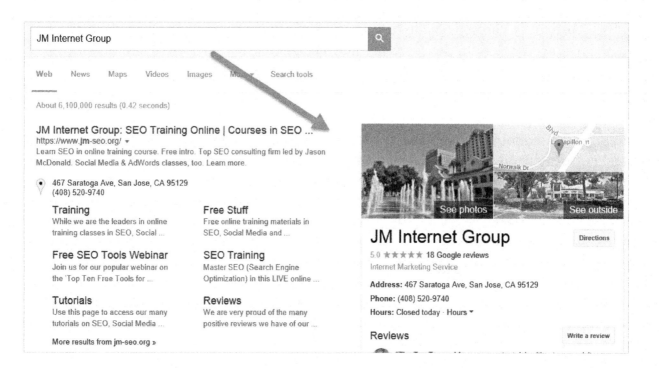

You can try the search at http://jmlinks.com/4v/. Notice the primacy of reviews and the highlighted Google+ listing information plus review count on the far right. If the search is for "JM Internet Group Reviews" at http://jmlinks.com/4w, notice that the No. 2 search result is Yelp, with the Better Business Bureau also on the page.

For a truly local business like a Pizza restaurant, even more local sites will be returned. For example, a search with respect to the very popular "Joe Momma" pizza restaurant in Tulsa at http://jmlinks.com/4w as "Joe Mommas reviews" has Yelp in positions No. 1, and 2, followed by zomato.com, and tripadvisor.com, both review sites.

Local review sites, in other words, are critical components of your online reputation management strategy. Google+ in particular can give you the marketer control of the branded search and the impressive right-hand side of the page, including photos. Check out a search for Joe Mommas Tulsa at http://jmlinks.com/4y.

In addition to identifying, claiming, and optimizing your business listings on relevant review sites, you should also monitor your business on these sites. Usually the act of claiming your listing in and of itself will generate an email any time someone reviews your company. Paid services such as ReviewPush (https://www.reviewpush.com/), Free Review Monitoring (https://freereviewmonitoring.com/), and ReviewTrackers (http://www.reviewtrackers.com/) are sophisticated alert systems so that you always know whenever a new review is published about your business.

For your fifth **TODO**, at a minimum set up a monthly checkup of your listings on the major review sites you have identified. Note in a spreadsheet how many reviews you have, how many are 5, 4, 3, 2, or 1 stars. If you have budget, consider using a paid monitoring service.

» MEASURE YOUR RESULTS

Reviews impact your business in two important ways:

- as a positive (or negative) "trust indicator" that you are a trustworthy business partner; and
- as a signal to search engines and review sites that you should rank high on searches for relevant keywords.

Reviews, in short, communicate that you are a "smart choice" and they propel you to the "top of search" whether that search is on Google, on Yelp, on TripAdvisor or on any other relevant review site.

MONITOR YOUR REVIEWS

Measurement of reviews, therefore, is focused on these two variables. On your keyword worksheet, I recommend that you create a tab called "local." Then every month, create a line item (for example, February 2016), note down for your business:

The review site, number of reviews you have, and cumulative star rating.

Secondly, try searches for your strategic keywords on Yelp, Google and/or on other relevant review sites (e.g., Airbnb, TripAdvisor, etc.), create a line item for each month, and indicate your position on those searches. For example, Andolino's Pizzeria was measured as No. 2 for the Google Search "pizza Tulsa" as seen in this screenshot on September 12, 2015.

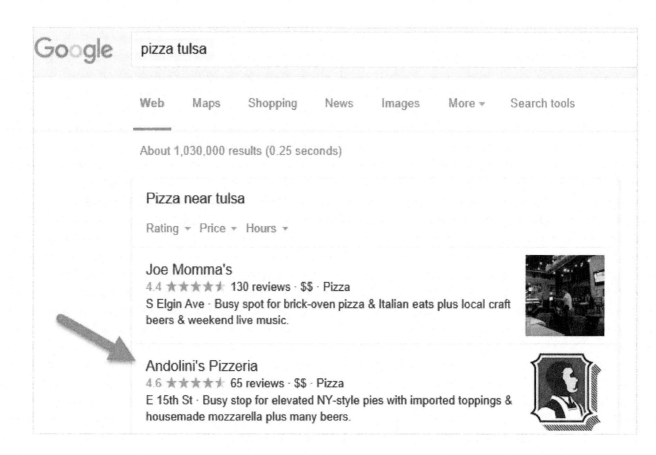

On Yelp, Andolini's is listed as No. 1. In other words, the restaurant is in good shape on both review sites. If it had dipped to a lower position on Yelp, for instance, then a Todo would be to encourage more Yelp reviews.

The two major aspects of monitoring your reviews, therefore are 1) your review count on each review site, and 2) your position on keyword searches on those sites. To the extent possible, you can then accelerate your efforts for a lagging site and relax a bit for a site for which you rank well and have positive reviews.

▶▶▶ DELIVERABLE: A YELP / LOCAL MARKETING PLAN

Now that we've come to the end our chapter on local reviews, your **DELIVERABLE** has arrived. For your final **TODO**, download the **Yelp / Local Marketing Plan Worksheet**. For the worksheet, go to https://www.jm-seo.org/workbooks (click on Social Media Workbook, enter the code 'smm2016' to register if you have not already done so), and click on the link to the "Yelp / Local Review Marketing Worksheet." By filling out this plan, you and your team will establish a vision of what you want to achieve via local reviews.

>> TOP LOCAL YELP / LOCAL MARKETING TOOLS AND RESOURCES

Here are the top tools and resources to help you with local review marketing. For an up-to-date list, go to https://www.jm-seo.org/workbooks (click on Social Media Workbook, enter the code 'smm2016' to register if you have not already done so), and click on the link to the *Social Media Toolbook* link, and drill down to the local reviews chapter.

GOOGLE MY BUSINESS (GOOGLE LOCAL / GOOGLE PLACES) - https://business.google.com/

Google My Business is the new official name, but behind-the-scenes they still call it Google Places or Google Local or Google+ Local. Or whatchamacallit. This is the official entry point to find and claim your small business listing on Google's local service.

Rating: 5 Stars | **Category:** resource

GOOGLE+ REVIEW LINK GENERATOR - https://www.grade.us/home/labs/google-review-link-generator

Lost as to how to find your company's Google+ reviews? Use this nifty tool to find the exact URL for your reviews. You can also use this to give to clients, directly.

Rating: 5 Stars | **Category:** tool

YELP - http://biz.yelp.com

Yelp is a local reviews service. Businesses can have (and claim) a FREE listing on Yelp, which can be helpful for local listings and local link building. This link is to the 'business' portal at Yelp - how to find, and list your business.

Rating: 5 Stars | **Category:** service

BING PLACES FOR BUSINESS (BING LOCAL) - https://www.bingplaces.com/

Bing is a distant #2 to Google, behind probably Yahoo...but nonetheless, for local search purposes, it's still valuable to find (and claim) your local listing on Bing Local. So go for it, be a Binger!

Rating: 5 Stars | **Category:** service

GOOGLE MY BUSINESS (GOOGLE+ LOCAL / GOOGLE PLACES) HELP CENTER - https://support.google.com/business#topic=4539639

A wonderful and rather hidden microsite in the Googleplex with many help topics to learn about, modify, and update your Google+ Local listings. Google Local begot Google Places begot Google+ Local begot Google My Business. You and I both wish Google would settle on a name for its local service!

Rating: 5 Stars | **Category:** resource

MOZ LOCAL - https://moz.com/local

If local matters to you, you need to see where you're listed (Google+, Yelp, etc.), and how you're listed. You also want consistent address, phone number, and other data across local sites (called 'citations'). Moz has a new paid service for this, but this free tool will analyze (and find) your listings pretty easily.

Rating: 5 Stars | **Category:** tool

GOOGLE+ PAGE SEARCH - http://www.gpluspagesearch.com/

Use this nifty site to find competitor Google+ pages easily. Just enter a competitor name (or your own business name), and this search engine will identify the relevant Google+ page.

Rating: 5 Stars | **Category:** tool

REVIEWBUZZ - http://www.reviewbuzz.com/

This is the new (PAID) thing in local review marketing. Services like this, ask customers to first rate you, and then if, and ONLY IF, they like you, the customer is prompted to leave a review on Google / Yelp, etc. Probably a violation of the official terms of service, but this is probably the future of the thin gray line between what's allowed and what's not. USE AT YOUR OWN RISK.

Rating: 4 Stars | **Category:** service

SMALL BUSINESS GUIDE TO GOOGLE MY BUSINESS - http://www.simplybusiness.co.uk/microsites/google-my-business-guide/

Interactive step-by-step flowchart to using Google My Business. Comprised of key questions and linked resources with more information. Chart is divided into different areas including setup, page management and optimization, engagement and reviews, and citations.

Rating: 4 Stars | **Category:** resource

YELP HELP CENTER - http://www.yelp-support.com/

Here is the official Yelp help center, for both consumer and businesses. If you are new to local marketing, this is a great place to understand how it works from an official Yelp perspective. Remember, however, that what is officially presented as 'how Yelp works' isn't 100% accurate.

Rating: 4 Stars | **Category:** resource

YELP SUPPORT CENTER (FOR BUSINESS OWNERS) - http://www.yelp-support.com/Yelp_for_Business_Owners?l=en_US

Yelp's site to support both users and businesses. As a business owner, click on the links to the left, or on 'Yelp for Business Owners' card. It's better than nothing, but Yelp still has a long way to go to be easy-to-use for business owners. Easy password reset?

Rating: 4 Stars | **Category:** resource

YEXT - http://www.yext.com/

Follow the instructions to 'scan your business.' This nifty tool allows you to input your business name and phone number and it will go out and find all the relevant listings across many, many different local listings services. Then you can (pay) to have it fix many of them. Not perfect, but a good start on identifying logical local listing opportunities for your business.

Rating: 4 Stars | **Category:** tool

GOOGLE PLACES CATEGORIES - http://blumenthals.com/google-lbc-categories/

When setting up your free listing on Google Places, be sure to choose categories that are already existing. Use this to tool help you identify extant categories as you work on your five free categories for Google Places. Perform a search by entering a term or click the search button.

Rating: 4 Stars | **Category:** tool

CITATION BUILDING STRATEGIES - THE COMPLETE LIST FOR LOCAL BUSINESSES - http://www.localstampede.com/citation-building-strategies-list/

It's always great when someone has done the brainstorming for you. If you are a local business, local 'citations' or links are incredibly helpful.

Rating: 4 Stars | **Category:** article

BEST LOCAL CITATIONS BY CATEGORY - https://moz.com/learn/local/citations-by-category

If you're 'into local,' then you gotta know your citation sources. Obviously, Google+ is the most important for Google, and in many markets Yelp is #2. But for a plumber vs. a chiropractor, where to get citations (listings on local sites) can be different. Moz breaks out the 'best' citation sources by common category.

Rating: 4 Stars | **Category:** article

LOCAL RANK CHECKING VIA ADWORDS - https://adwords.google.com/apt/AdPreview

This is the OFFICIAL Google AdWords preview tool. But, guess what. You can use this to vary your city location, and check your rank against various cities. If, for example, you are a pizza restaurant serving San Jose, Milpitas, and Santa Clara, you can type in 'Pizza' and see your rank in different cities. You can login to your AdWord account and click Tools - Preview Tool or use this direct link.

Rating: 4 Stars | **Category:** tool

GOOGLE MY BUSINESS (GOOGLE PLACES / GOOGLE LOCAL) HELP CENTER -
https://support.google.com/business

Help with Google Places, conveniently hidden by Google..but here is where you can browse helpful articles on setting up and managing your free advertising and promotion efforts via Google Places.

Rating: 4 Stars | **Category:** resource

GOOGLE AND YOUR BUSINESS HELP FORUM -
https://www.en.advertisercommunity.com/t5/Google-My-Business/ct-p/GMB#

Forums by people using Google Places, er Google and Your Business. You can get help from the community here, which is often more effective than those annoying canned emails you get from Google itself!

Rating: 4 Stars | **Category:** resource

GET FIVE STARS - https://www.getfivestars.com/

This is the new (PAID) thing in local review marketing. Services like this, ask customers to first rate you, and then if, and ONLY IF, they like you, the customer is prompted to leave a review on Google / Yelp, etc. Probably a violation of the official terms of service, but this is probably the future of the thin gray line between what's allowed and what's not. USE AT YOUR OWN RISK.

Rating: 4 Stars | **Category:** service

SEO LOCAL RANKING FACTORS 2015 - https://moz.com/blog/local-search-ranking-factors-2015

Moz.com does a great job of first surveying SEO's and then compiling its best guestimate on the factors (in order) that propel a company to the top of local searches on Google.

Rating: 4 Stars | **Category:** resource

REBATE OFFER

CLAIM YOUR $39.99 REBATE! HERE'S HOW -

10. Go to Amazon.com and search for **'Social Media Marketing Workbook'** or click http://jmlinks.com/smm.
11. Write a short, honest **review of the book** and indicate you've been gifted a 'review copy'.
12. Click https://jm-seo.org/rebate/ and fill out the **REBATE FORM**.

WE WILL THEN -

- **Refund** you the full price of the print edition (**$39.99**), so that you will have received a **FREE** review copy

~ $39.99 REBATE OFFER ~

~ LIMITED TO ONE PER CUSTOMER ~

EXPIRES: 10/1/2016

SUBJECT TO CHANGE WITHOUT NOTICE

GOT QUESTIONS? CALL 800-298-4065

8

EPILOGUE

There's always something new! That's what makes social media fun, isn't it? Come on, admit it: you can't wait for the next new thing. (*Just kidding, you probably can wait but it won't wait for you*). I guarantee there will be a next new thing, and I guarantee that they will hype it in such a way that you just "gotta" be doing it.

As we end our journey through the world of social media marketing, I want to point out some of the newer media (ones which do not yet have substantial traction for small businesses), and give you a conceptual framework to think about and evaluate them.

Finally, I want to motivate you to "just do it" and "never stop learning."

Let's get started!

TODO LIST:

>> New Kids on the Block

>> Just Do It

>> Never Stop Learning

>> >> Deliverable: a Social Media Marketing Plan

>> NEW KIDS ON THE BLOCK

There seems to always be a "new" new thing in Social Media. At the time of this writing, I'd award the "new kid on the block" award to Snapchat (https://www.snapchat.com/). Another important "new kid" is Instagram (https://instagram.com/), which while not as new as snapchat, is just beginning to come into its own as a social media *marketing* venue. For most small to medium businesses, I do not yet see either of these as full of opportunities, but if you do – then by all means, use them!

Here are my recommendations:

- **Identify** a new social media that might be relevant to your business like Snapchat or Instagram.
- **Sign up for a user account**, and find the "business" help files or "how to advertise" information. Begin your research.
- **Research** whether your potential customers are "on" this social media and – if so – figure out what they are doing.
- Keep an eye out for **competitors** or **big brands**. "**Reverse engineer**" what they are doing in terms of marketing, and translate their actions into doable items for your own company.
- **Brainstorm** how you and your company can participate in an authentic way and yet still have a marketing objective. Is it possible to use Snapchat or Instagram to interact with potential customers? How or how not?
- Start slowly, **learn by doing**, and don't be too heavy-handed.

In most cases, you'll see many similarities between the "new" social media like Snapchat or Instagram and the "old" social media like Facebook or Twitter. Snapchat, for example, is beginning to overtake Twitter as a place for real-time or instantaneous communication, as well as a way for brands to offer exclusive information, coupons, or deals to their most avid fans. The fact that a snapchat disappears over time, isn't really that different from a tweet. Instagram, in turn, isn't that different from photo-sharing on Facebook (it's really just the photo element of Facebook), plus some similarities to Twitter. Remember Flickr? It was really just Instagram before it's time.

Indeed, once you see how Snapchat and Instagram are "going after" Twitter, it makes a lot of sense why Twitter has earned the dubious title of the "troubled" social media.

But beyond Snapchat and Instagram, you may find social media like Tumblr or even ones overseas. New ones will no doubt pop up, but the structural realities of social media make them all the members of the same genus if not the same species.

There is, my friend, nothing really new under the sun.

≫ JUST DO IT

Voltaire said, "The perfect is the enemy of the good," and today's Nike corporation said, "Just do it!" In both cases, the thought is to "learn by doing" and to just "get started."

- Don't be intimidated!
- Do some research, make a plan, and get started!
- Just do it!

Many companies get stuck in "analysis paralysis," always researching and never doing. Don't be one of them! Others get stuck in "doing with no strategy," as in tweeting 24/7 when none of their customers are on Twitter.

Do it! But keep your eyes and ears open to strategy, tactics, and results. If it isn't working, try something else. Don't be afraid to try, and fail.

Everyone – including myself- is just learning how to "do" social media marketing. Don't be intimidated. There are no real experts. Just fools like me who pretend to know what we're doing.

So just do it, please. *(And email me your ideas, thoughts, suggestions, and questions. I learn more from my students than from anyone else).*

» NEVER STOP LEARNING

If you haven't already, download my *Social Media Toolbook*, and turn to the chapter on publications and conferences. Read the social media blogs (I'm partial to the Social Media Examiner (http://www.socialmediaexaminer.com/)) and their yearly trade show in San Diego.

Never stop learning!

»» DELIVERABLE: OUTLINE A SOCIAL MEDIA MARKETING PLAN

Now that we've come to the end of the book, go back to the "Party On" chapter. If you haven't already completed it, your **DELIVERABLE** has arrived. For the worksheet, go to https://www.jm-seo.org/workbooks (click on Social Media Marketing, enter the code 'smm2016' to register if you have not already done so), and click on the link to the "Social Media Marketing Plan Big Picture Worksheet." By filling out this plan, you and your team will establish a vision of what you want to achieve via social media marketing.

Party On!